C000257496

SMOKING IN BED

SMOKING IN BED

CONVERSATIONS WITH

BRUCE ROBINSON

EDITED BY ALISTAIR OWEN

BLOOMSBURY

First published in Great Britain 2000
This paperback edition published 2001

Copyright © 2000 by Bruce Robinson and Alistair Owen

Extract from the introduction by Dylan Thomas to the 1952
edition of his Collected Poems, published by J. M. Dent, reprinted
by permission of David Higham Associates.

The moral right of the authors has been asserted

Bloomsbury Publishing Plc, 38 Soho Square, London W1D 3HB

A CIP catalogue record for this book is available
from the British Library

ISBN 0 7475 5259 2

10 9 8 7 6 5 4 3 2 1

Typeset by Hewer Text Ltd, Edinburgh
Printed in Great Britain by Clays Ltd, St Ives plc

I read somewhere of a shepherd who, when asked why he made, from within fairy rings, ritual observances to the moon to protect his flocks, replied: 'I'd be a damn' fool if I didn't!' These poems, with all their crudities, doubts, and confusions, are written for the love of Man and in praise of God, and I'd be a damn' fool if they weren't.

Dylan Thomas, *Collected Poems 1934–1952*

Contents

Introduction

'Would you mind signing my copy of *Withnail & I*?' I ask, picking up the screenplay from the coffee table and holding it out to its author, Bruce Robinson. 'Did you buy this?' he responds, taking a pen and inscribing the book. 'No,' I reply sheepishly, 'I got it free with *Sight and Sound*.' 'Oh', he says flatly, probably thinking, 'Well, that's another chunk of royalties I won't be getting.' I didn't buy the video, either, I recorded the film off the TV, and taking into account review copies of his fiction and preview tapes of his other films, I'm now the proud owner of all his published and produced work, none of which I've had to pay for. The least I can do, then, is listen to his comments on this introduction. 'It reads like a press-release, doesn't it?' I suggest, looking critically at the first draft. 'I wasn't going to say that,' he smiles, leaning back in his deckchair beside the pool, 'but yes.' So for the second time I find myself, in effect, inscribing *his* book, and it's still hard to know what to say. It's equally hard to convey what *he* says without resorting to pages of brackets, footnotes and similar editorial interruptions, since he dramatises his past using a variety of accents, gestures and expressions, with a swig of wine here, a drag on a cigarette there, and every now and again a wry laugh.

Four years after our first interview for a student newspaper, and two years since we talked again, for the *Observer*, the cosy lounge which provided the venue has become an echoing dining room, and the new lounge fills an extension straight out of *Country Life*. There's a grand piano, a fairly grand fireplace, and a very grand view: sheep on the hills and horses in the paddock. Turn the page, and you'll find one of those big farmhouse kitchens with an Aga and a long wooden table where family, friends and others invariably congregate. Completing the picture are a wire-haired fox-terrier named Harry, a stray cat and an orphan duck. 'I always end up feeding them,' complains Bruce, who looks more like the rock star he played in the comedy feature *Still Crazy* than he does the local squire and master of almost all he surveys. The clues to his real day job lie on the table: a flyer, boasting the distinctive writing of Ralph Steadman, for last year's Channel Four film about Robinson's career, and beside it a pile of scripts bound in the bold red covers of the powerful Hollywood talent agency CAA. An inevitable hiatus in the development of existing projects means his agent has sent him some new ones to think about, but right now Bruce has got other things on his mind.

'I've become obsessed with old books on alcoholism,' he says, buffing up the dull leather of a slim hardback with casual skill. The remark is classic Robinson, in the same league as 'Cooking and masturbation are the only things I'm really good at', a quote I noted when we met for a third time to discuss the book. It's lines like these, delivered off-the-cuff in conversation or hammered out to order on his ageing IBM, which have won him an army of fans, and when I tell him that anything he does is fair game for the introduction he insists I take a look at the bizarre titles arranged neatly in front of him: *Stammering and its Permanent Cure* jostles for space alongside *A Guide to the Examination of the Nose*, and a few more bodily orifices are explored in *The Essentials of Anatomy, Sanitary Science and Embalming*. Just down the hall, his modest study is lined floor to ceiling with thousands more, the rewards of trawling regularly through second-hand shops for every subject from political history to true crime, and when he's not working he sometimes likes to pull one from a shelf or out of a box and flick through it. *Diseases of the Male Generative Organs*, for example.

'Are there any dicks in it?' asks his thirteen-year-old daughter, Lily, sitting with her mother on the sofa after fighting a successful rearguard action against going to bed. 'I'll find you some, darling,' promises Bruce, and he does, studying the illustrations with the indulgent smile of a doting father and a devoted collector: in the barn is a vintage Aston Martin which he likes to drive fast with the top down, in his study is an antique Martini Henry rifle as used to shoot Zulu warriors at the Battle of Rorke's Drift, and in his workshop is another workshop – a miniature one – with a toy steam engine which he plans to restore for his six-year-old son, Willoughby. 'He's a fabulous little bloke,' he tells me proudly when his wife, Sophie, brings the children back from school. 'But he can be very rude,' he adds, demonstrating the point with one of his entertaining solo conversations. [*Aggressive voice*] 'I'd like to put their bollocks on an anvil and whack them with a hammer.' 'Whose bollocks, Willy?' 'Anyone's. A giant's. Get hold of a giant and whack his bollocks on an anvil.'

The kids make no mention of the stranger in their midst, but then I'm not the first scribbler to pass through this corner of Herefordshire, and I probably won't be the last. 'There's a guy who wants to do a biography of me,' Bruce told me when we started, 'and I can't think of anything worse than raking through all those miserable years and having them in print, even if it's done right.' This is not a biography. It is an edited transcript of roughly thirty hours of interviews, complete with the inevitable omissions, repetitions, contradictions and highly subjective opinions which come with more than ten days of questions and answers. At this point, my thanks must go to Bruce and Sophie for putting me up and putting up with me for those ten days; to my friend and agent Justin Robinson for his advice and encouragement; to the lovely Rosie for all her support; to Adrian Sibley for letting me pick his brains and nearly pilfer the title of his documentary *The Peculiar Memories of Bruce Robinson*; to Julian Sheldon for his help on the photograph front; to the folks at Bloomsbury, particularly Matthew Hamilton, Mike Jones, Helena Drakakis and Jocasta Brownlee, for their endless patience; and to *my* folks for just about everything else. I hope it *has* been done right.

Alistair Owen, August 2000

Chapter One

'An unknown, untried writer'

From Camden to Cambodia

You're now known as a writer and director, but you began your career as an actor, training at the Central School of Speech and Drama. Why the change?

I auditioned for Central in the spring of 1964 and I went there for the autumn term, but being at drama school never really worked very well for me; I couldn't relate to what was going on there. Retrospectively I realise I didn't want to be an actor, but at the time I didn't realise I wanted to be a writer – even though I wrote my first play when I was fifteen. In my twenties I wanted to be a film star; I had a nonsense ambition to be rich and famous. From writing I knew there was no question of either; it didn't cross my mind. Writing hit my life like a meteor, and whether I was successful or not was of no interest whatsoever. I just had to be a writer.

Were your problems at Central related to the strictures of the course?

I think it was more the strictures of the life I'd come out of. I went to Central with such a paucity of confidence because of my father. If my son grew up and wanted to go to drama school and got accepted at Central, we'd open the champagne. When I told my father I'd been accepted – which was no mean feat; three thousand applicants and they take thirty – he looked at me, then walked away. Didn't say anything. It's devastating when you're a kid, that kind of stuff. No congratulation, enthusiasm or support because he wanted me to stay in that crummy business of his, drive the van and deliver newspapers. He was extremely upset that I'd been successful. So I was taking all that heavyweight luggage into my new life in London and giving myself problems that didn't exist. Anyone in authority – because *he* was an authority in my life – was *de facto* an enemy, and if you think, 'This person isn't going to like me,' you invite them not to like you.

They were going to throw me out of Central because it wasn't working, and then I ran into Eric Thompson who saved my bacon. Had it not been for Eric I would never have survived three years there. He was an actor at the Bristol Old Vic with George Hall, who was subsequently the head of Central, so consequently Eric came in to teach and direct the students. His claim to fame was *The Magic Roundabout*, which he used to write and do the voice-over for on television. I didn't know until later, but he personally went to see George Hall and said, 'I know this bloke's got some talent. We've got to get it out of him somehow because he's so inhibited.' Which I was. I wrote an introduction to his script for *Dougal and the Blue Cat* that Bloomsbury published and in there I describe my first meeting with Eric: 'Get a bit of *back-tension* and *sit the fuck up*' was an incredibly important statement in my life. Sometimes when I can't write I still hear Eric in my head. 'Sit the fuck up' is a code for myself, rather like the James Joyce quote fixed to my typewriter: 'Write it, damn you, what else are you good for?'

How old were you when you went to Central?

I was eighteen. I left school at about fifteen with no qualifications whatsoever. But you don't need any qualifications to be an actor, and in three years at Central we were required to read but not to write anything. I was a pretty little bastard. I looked like a girl, actually, when I was around that age, and I got parts predicated on the fact that I was good-looking; always the bum-boy round the back.

Benvolio in Zeffirelli's film *Romeo and Juliet*, for example.

Benvolio is a lousy part. Even if Laurence Olivier was playing it, it's got nothing much going for it. There isn't anything of substance in Benvolio. In my case, 'Bendovrio' would be a better name for that character. From night one, Zeffirelli was interested in more than my acting abilities. I arrived in Rome – I'd never been on a jet aircraft before; I'd barely been abroad before – I'm in his apartment, in the shower, and he says [*Italian accent*], 'Let me dry your hair.' Next thing I'm in a kaftan in a room full of queens, they gradually disappear and suddenly the tongue's down my throat. And worse. It was a monstrous shock to me, and a very bad start to our relationship, because I'm not gay. Plus here comes another father figure, another figure of authority, and I immediately react in the way I've been taught to react all through my childhood: you're going to hate me and manipulate me, which was what I felt.

Next morning the producer of the film, Dyson Lovell, is in the apartment – he's got white shoes on, pink hipsters with a white belt, and a gold bauble hanging off his chest – and I went up to him and said, 'Dyson, you're not going to believe what happened last night.' I told him, and he said [*camp voice*], 'Really?' He was a raver too, and I was so naïve I didn't know. I didn't know anything. I don't condemn gays; one of my closest friends is homosexual, and he's a guy I could sleep in the same bed with and feel safe because it's just not on the agenda. But Zeffirelli likes pretty young blokes, that's his gig, and it freaked me out. You have a lot of power as a director, especially as a famous director, and because I didn't want to go to bed with him he did everything he could to harm me both physically and emotionally – and succeeded in both. I was levitating with terror all the time because he was so cruel.

But out of that experience came Uncle Monty in Withnail & I.

To an extent, yeah. [*Italian accent*] 'Are you a sponge or a stone?' That was a direct quote, night one, from Zeffirelli. I think that's the only line in the film that is taken from somebody else. When I was young I did have a lot of problems with queens. Rome crawls with faggots, and the first time I tasted really good wine was in Italy when some old fruit took me to dinner. This wine was like nectar, and it was a wine that I still buy when I'm drinking now. It's an Antiniori from Tuscany, and it's heavenly. I remember drinking it and thinking, 'I've been missing this all my life!' From that first glass I was instantly hooked, and the only lucky side of my drinking is I've never been into booze – Scotch and gin and stuff – because I think I'd be dead with the capacity I have. A bottle of vodka or more a day and you'd kill yourself, but two bottles of wine a day I don't think is excessive. It's never bothered me.

I take it that you didn't learn much about directing from Zeffirelli?

I tell you what I learned from Zeffirelli: to do the opposite of what he did, which was yell at kids and technicians. My philosophy as a director, I think, was influenced by Eric and by François Truffaut. The only acting I've ever enjoyed was doing *Journey's End* for Eric several years later at the Mermaid Theatre, and being in *Still Crazy*. I remember struggling with a scene with Eric, and I had this line, 'Let me get by, Stanhope,' and out of the gloom comes [*snaps it out*], 'Let's get by, Stanhope.' I immediately knew what he wanted and how the rest of the scene should be played. That was a very good lesson, being specific and on the word, and the respect and calmness of Truffaut was another very good lesson. It's useless screaming at people. If someone screams at me, I just switch off; I don't want to know.

Journey's End is the play that Marwood's off to do in Withnail, isn't it?

That's right. It had a profound effect on me, *Journey's End*. We were enormously successful with that play; it was packed every night for month after month. It's the only time I think I've been really good as an actor. I got fantastic reviews in all the national papers and never got offered a job out of it. Peter Egan played the lead, brilliantly I remember, and I was playing this snooty coward Hibbert, a really reprehensible little bastard. In the early seventies everyone had Bee Gee haircuts and flared trousers, and because the play was set in the First World War I had a kind of George Orwell pineapple and this awful pubescent moustache which I kept having to prune so that it stayed really thin. I must have looked like I'd just got out of Wandsworth.

What do you remember about _Early Morning_, a play at the Royal Court starring Marianne Faithfull, which you appeared in after _Romeo and Juliet_?

That was a disaster. William Gaskill was the director of the Royal Court and the director of this play. On the night we were going to open we did the dress rehearsal and he went through the entire cast. That wonderful actor Nigel Hawthorne was in the play, and it was like [_nasal voice_], 'Nigel, darling, it's absolute magic what you're doing. Marianne, don't change a single comma, it's marvellous.' Then he gets to me, and he says, 'Bruce Robinson. You haven't got the right to be on these boards.' That was his critique. You think, 'Thanks a lot. We're going up in two hours.' He was probably right, too; this was the period when I would smoke the occasional joint. I played three or four different parts in this play – one of which was a ghost in a shroud – and I was always stoned and laughing. There were four of us in shrouds, four ghosts, and you couldn't see the faces, and you'd hear [_nasal voice_], 'I know who that ghost is. It's you, Robinson. You're in there. What are you doing?' Another part I played was this cavalry officer, and I had to come strutting out and then come to attention, and I did that and slipped flat on my arse. It brought the house down. The entire audience was in hysterics and I was meant to be a dignified officer. Oh God, it was so awful, and I was so bad in it.

Your second film performance was in _I Love You, I Hate You_, also known as _Sleep is Lovely_, which featured John McEnery, who had played opposite you as Mercutio in _Romeo and Juliet_.

Never came out. That was with Peter McEnery, as well. Peter, John, me and a French actress called Olga Georges-Picot. I barely remember it. Again, it was a bum-boy round the back type of part. I don't know why I was in it; I'm sure it's unwatchable. And what happened to John McEnery? He was a brilliant actor. His Mercutio is a masterpiece, the highlight of Zeffirelli's film.

Then you were in a film called *Private Road*, directed by Barney Platts-Mills.

Me and my friend Mickey Feast acted in *Private Road*. It was totally improvised. There was a shooting sequence but there was no shooting script. I'm quite good at improvisation because it's just yakking, and provided you've got enough cover you can cut a pretty decent film out of it. Robert Altman, for example, uses the technique all the time, but he can probably shoot thousands of feet a day with two or three cameras. If you can only afford 1500 feet a day it's quite dangerous, improvisation. But it was a laugh. I liked Barney, and because Mickey and I were close friends it was good fun. The other guy who was in it has become a famous film composer, George Fenton. If I look back over my year at Central, only Michael Elphick and Michael Feast are still acting, as far as I know. Everyone else is doing something different or is dead. Which *is* doing something different. Half of the movies I was in I've never even seen so I don't know what they're like. I was in one called *Brute Syndrome*.

It was retitled *The Brute*.

I remember this gruesome shot of a naked woman running, super over-cranked, and her tits going up and down like a couple of buoys outside Dover harbour. It was a mad film, and it had dialogue like [*imitates doorbell*], 'Hello, Caroline, my name's Frank, a close friend of Peter's. I'm wondering if Peter's sister Janice is in, because Janice is going to introduce me to Mary.' It was awful, and I don't think I've seen it. I've seen bits. There was another one I was in, *Tam-Lin*. God, that was a dog.

That was released as *The Devil's Widow* after sitting on the shelf for two years.

When I first met David Wimbury he was a second or third assistant director on that film. He was working his way through the ranks. It's very like the services, the film industry, in that you do get promoted. I got on well with him, then I met him once or twice later and we became friends, and sixteen years later we were doing *Withnail* together. But *Tam-Lin* was an absolute dog and was one of the catalysts to me being a boozer, because of Ava Gardner. I was meant to be playing one of her lovers, of which she had a myriad, and at six-thirty in the morning I was thinking, 'I'm going to be acting opposite Ava Gardner!' I was really nervous; she saw me in the corridor and said, 'Come and have some breakfast, honey.' She gives me a couple of vodkas, we go out on the set, get it in two takes, and I thought, 'This is the key to brilliant acting. A couple of vodkas and you can play Hamlet.' Wrong.

The director was Roddy McDowall, his only effort behind the camera.

He didn't know his arse from his elbow. Another faggot. Much gentler – he wasn't vicious like Zeffirelli – but a raver. I had no idea. Now, I can spot a faggot at 600 feet, but in those days I just couldn't do it.

Then there was *The Music Lovers*, a Ken Russell film.

That's when Ken was starting to lose his marbles. He's an enormously talented man, and he was so influential that everyone was copying him, pushing him further and further into orbit until he became a mad cliché of himself, like somebody at a party who's determined to dominate the environment. They become embarrassing. I had enormous respect for Ken, and still do; I think he was a smashing director. I don't think he makes films now, does he? It's a shame.

Ironically, after having a run-in with Zeffirelli and being directed by McDowall, you were actually playing a homosexual.

I was playing Tchaikovsky's amanuensis, i.e. his bum-boy. That script was written by Melvyn Bragg, and I thought there was a weakness in the construction. They split his homosexuality and they'd have been better off just having me, or much better off just having that dancer who was in it, Christopher Gable. The homosexual side of Tchaikovsky became diluted, and it was very potent in his life. I love those Russians: Tchaikovsky, Prokofiev, Mussorgsky, Shostakovich. It's powerful stuff. I love Russian writing, too. Fascinating place. I tried to take Sophie there on our honeymoon, and in those days Brezhnev was in charge and because I had 'Writer' on my passport they wouldn't give me a visa. Those were the days when they didn't like writers. They didn't like anybody. The first thing that any reactionary government does is round up the writers. They're the first victims.

You also appeared in a couple of commercials around this period.

I did two commercials in the late sixties, early seventies: a coffee commercial for the cinema involving this beautiful model and a £60,000 Ford GT-40, and one for Pepsi Cola directed by Ridley Scott. That one involved riding a horse in the Sahara desert, and the plot was me and this other bloke on our horses getting hot and thirsty, cut to these two models on their horses getting hot and thirsty, and they collide just in time for the Pepsi can that happens to be 2000 miles out in the Sahara desert for no apparent reason, and they all have a Pepsi and go off and shag behind some sand-dune – at least, that's the assumption.

By that time I thought of myself as a writer, and I talked myself out of one or two parts because I'd go in to read and there'd be the writer, the director and the producer, and I'd say, 'This is an awful line. Why don't we try it like this?' From their perspective it's like, 'Who is this wanker? How dare you come in here with a hole in your shoe and your hair all over the place and tell us the script's shit. What do you know about it?' I couldn't resist it. There was a film that I auditioned for called *Mr Forbush and the Penguins*, and there was a line I was supposed to read *vis-à-vis* his sexuality: 'I refuse to be a slave to the slit.' I was reading it out loud and I said to the writer, 'This is outrageous. I can't say this. Can I say a different line?' 'No, you cannot. You're here to read.' *Death on the Nile* was another one, I remember savaging that script and them telling me to piss off.

Anthony Shaffer, who wrote *Sleuth*, was responsible for both *Death on the Nile* and *Mr Forbush and the Penguins*.

Was that who wrote it? Well, we're all capable of suffering creative imbalances from time to time, and he certainly did on that. He was incensed.

John Hurt took the lead in Mr Forbush and the Penguins, and I assume that the part you almost got in Death on the Nile was the one played by Jon Finch?

I talked myself out of that very thoroughly. I was definitely getting close to that. It was about the third time I went to see them, virtually here come the costume fittings, and I started yakking about the construction of the third act. 'You do know you can do this better than this?' 'Really? What could we do?' 'Well, I'll tell you what you could do . . .' Then, of course, I'm out the door and never heard another word.

When did writing start to take over from acting?

At Central I met all these remarkable people who were much better educated than me. My flatmate Vivian MacKerrell was like a kind of teacher. He opened my eyes to literature because he'd been to public school and could speak French, Latin, Greek, the whole show. I'd been turned on to Dickens as an asthmatic kid, but the Second Empire French poets, people I'd never heard of like Verlaine, Rimbaud and Baudelaire, Viv turned me on to all of those. I've never been into drugs much, but there was a period in the late sixties where everyone was smoking dope, and there was a thing Viv used to do that he called 'The Baudelaire Principle' – savage black coffee with honey, cinammon and a nut of hashish that he'd melt and stir in. One day I said to him, 'Who's Baudelaire, Viv?' and he said, 'Probably the greatest of the modern poets.'

Next thing, I'm down Camden Library looking for Baudelaire. I couldn't find any, so I went round to the bookshop and ordered some, the Penguin book of Baudelaire in English and French, and it was like a revelation: 'God almighty, this is astonishing writing.' My first shot at a screenplay, *Spleen*, was about the life of Baudelaire. No one in their right mind is going to do the whole life of anybody, because you can't encapsulate that in a movie, but that's what I did. It was part of learning to write scripts. Over that period, I read and wrote and read and wrote all the time. I was going through a box the other

13

day and I found the book that I tried to learn French from: *Hugo's French in Three Months*. Seven-and-six, it cost.

Then I left Central and went off to do the Zeffirelli thing, and while I was in Rome I started to care about writing home to friends. I actually used to pre-write a postcard. Letters, too. It would take me two days to write a letter. That's when I was becoming a writer; I took trouble over anything I'd written. I think it was the winter of 1969 that I wrote *Withnail*, the novel, and as soon as I finished I couldn't give a fuck about acting any more. And once that decision had been taken, being a writer had no fear for me. Acting was always full of fear, thinking, 'How can I do this? How can I get through it? Will I be adequate?' With the writing, I knew I wasn't adequate, but I knew I was going to be a writer, and if it took me twenty years to learn it, that didn't bother me. That's the truth. I really felt like that.

In fact, after you finished writing *Withnail*, the novel, you continued acting for another five years or so.

I stopped after *The Story of Adele H*, the Truffaut film. I still had an acting agent, and she said, 'Truffaut's in London looking for an English bloke for his new film.' Naturally I was very interested because it was Truffaut. I went down to see him and bullshitted my way through this meeting. If you're an out-of-work actor and someone says, 'How's your horse-riding?' you say, 'Marvellous. As a matter of fact, I used to do quite a lot of steeplechasing.' If they say, 'What's your parachuting like?' you say, 'Pretty good; I'm fine up to about 16,000 feet.' You've never jumped out of a back window, but anything to get a part. Viv is a perfect case in point. He went up for this part at the BBC, a priest or something, and the director said to him, 'If you weren't an actor, what do you think you'd have done?' He immediately said, 'I would have gone into the Catholic church.' Which is complete horseshit, but anything to get the job. So it was either going to be me or Corin Redgrave, and I got it and fucked off to Guernsey and then Senegal where we shot it.

14   Truffaut was brilliant in many ways. The whole body of his

work doesn't impress me that much, and all that *auteur* stuff I completely and utterly disagree with, but three or four of his films I think are pretty tremendous, the early ones like *The Four Hundred Blows* and *Jules et Jim*. He was a gentleman and he was very kind, and I learned a lot from him. He was so respected on set that the technicians who didn't need to look at the take would turn their backs. Isabelle Adjani was startlingly beautiful – she still is – and I was terribly fond of her. Her talent does tend towards hysterical women, the archetypal role being Adele, but she's very smart and everyone's dream of what a French girl should be. At least, she was mine. I said to myself, 'If I can't enjoy working with people like this, what am I doing it for?' By then I was writing for David Puttnam, and Puttnam was paying me £2000 or £3000 a screenplay. I thought, 'I'd rather do two scripts a year for Puttnam and make £6000 or £7000 than be an actor.' I remember phoning my agent and saying, 'I'm off the books. Even if Stanley Kubrick phones up, I'm not available. I don't want to do this any more.'

Did you write any novels before *Withnail*?

I wrote two or three books before then. I wrote a novel about a love affair set against the background of drama school. There was a girl at Central who I was just crazy about, but I was a very young eighteen and she was after the big boys. I was so in love with her.

Was that written while you were still at Central?

No, it was written later. It was a sweet story about a young guy falling in love with an older girl and having his heart broken because she was basically taking the piss out of him for her own amusement. I lent the top copy to someone and I've never seen it since. What the hell was that title? Something '*Leaves*'.

Autumn Leaves?

Not quite that crass, but nearly. *Spring Leaves*, probably. I was writing all the time, and half of them have evaporated; I just don't know where they are. *Normal Things* was the first crack I had at writing a novel. It was about a manic depressive having a full frontal lobotomy and what goes through his mind in the one fiftieth of a second it takes for this lobotomising current of electricity to get through his head. I was obviously in a pretty bad state when I came up with it.

I read that you had a nervous breakdown after *Romeo and Juliet*. Did the novel coincide with that?

That's hyperbole, actually. I've never had a nervous breakdown. I had an enormous asthma attack that involved Cinemascope despair because of what had gone on with Zeffirelli, and I ended up sitting in a hospital in Ramsgate thinking what it would be like to be an accomplished failure at twenty-one, because that's how I felt. I was seeing all sorts of shrinks, and I finally ended up with a guy called Dr Dennis Friedman who got me out of the depression. I still see him from time to time to discuss plots. I go in there and say, 'This is the gig,' and he'll look at it from a psychiatric point of view. Eric's dead, and Friedman is now in his seventies, and I'm really frightened about him retiring because he's a guy I can talk to about anything. When he read *The Peculiar Memories of Thomas Penman* he said, 'I feel very much like the grandfather in this book.' He's the kind of guy I wish could have been my dad, because had he been I probably wouldn't be fucked up, probably wouldn't be an alcoholic. But I'm not blaming anybody for my boozing. I blame my mouth and the French for that.

Did you pass these novels among your friends like you did with *Withnail*?

They all used to go round, I suppose, but *Withnail* was a palpable breakthrough for me as a writer. Until then I'd been influenced by Dylan Thomas on the one hand and Dickens on the other, and I thank them all, but when I wrote *Withnail* I was speaking with my own voice. That was what I wanted to say and how I wanted to say it.

When you went on holiday to the Lake District with Michael Feast, which partly inspired *Withnail*, you were actually writing something else, weren't you?

That's right. By then I was seriously trying to write scripts, and I was attempting to write one with Mickey called *Private Pirates*. You've got four guys who all know each other, four friends, and privately they dress up as pirates. That's their fantasy, and they happen to share the same fantasy, unbeknown to the others. We were halfway through it and it wasn't going very well. Mickey saw this advert in the *Sunday Times*, 'Idyllic cottage in the Lake District – tenner a week.' So I said, 'Let's take a couple of weeks, go up there and write the screenplay.' And that's what we did. Hence *Withnail*. That's where it came from. When we came back, I was sharing a flat with Viv in Camden Town – I didn't live with Mickey at that point – and I took Mickey out of the story and brought Viv into it, even though he wasn't the one who came to the Lake District.

Did you finish *Private Pirates*?

Yeah. I've got it on the shelf somewhere. There's a box full of that kind of crap in one of the barns out there, but a lot of it is definitely lost. Around that period I wrote a spec comedy for Benny Hill, and I wrote an epic poem for children, *A Kitchen Sink Drama*, which was miles long. I wrote a whole chunk of stuff one winter. I originally wrote *How to Get Ahead in Advertising* as a novel. I wrote and abandoned *Paranoia in the Launderette*. I wrote a lot of shorts, the ones Bloomsbury want to publish, but can I bear to put them through the machine again? I don't even know what they were called when I originally did them.

Did you write anything with Vivian?

No.

He did call himself a writer, though?

He was a writer, a photographer, an artist, an actor. He really was a jack of all and master of none. In a way, he was very jealous of me writing. He used to do everything he could to stop me, like talk all the time. He used to call me 'The Bard'. At some point around this period David Dundas, Mickey Feast and I wrote this musical called *Crazee* about the Kray twins, and Viv wanted to collaborate with me on the script. I said, 'I don't think I can. I've got to do it on my own.' [*Supercillious voice*] 'Oh, I see. The writer has spoken, has he?' He didn't think I was any good, but he was annoyed that I was doing it. I can't spell to this day, and he used to correct all my manuscripts and never thought anything of any of them until *Withnail*. I remember him holding it up, saying, 'This is the one.' Because it was about him, I suppose.

What other unproduced scripts did you write in the early seventies?

I wrote one called *The Acid Vampire*. John George Haigh was a murderer who lived in the Onslow Square Court Hotel in London, in 1948. He was and is considered the greatest forger Scotland Yard have ever come across. He could look at someone's handwriting and just copy it, that was his particular skill, and his other skill was murdering people for their money. He fascinated me, this guy, and still does. He took out entire families. He'd shoot them, drink a glass of their blood, then dissolve them in a vat of acid, making all the appropriate forgeries for the wills. But he became so confident of his abilities that he started making mistakes, rather like someone in any career.

What about your television play, *The Molecatcher*?

The Molecatcher was about an old man who lives in a wood, at one with nature like an Apache Indian, and one of his activities is catching moles. He owns this land that he's nurtured all his life, and some smartarse decides that this land would be better covered in Cortinas and bungalows and lampposts, and it's his story – the white-man coming to the Indian, if you like. And, of course, he loses.

You also wrote a novella, *Nat the Wad & Alley Soper's Cake & Jumper Shop*, which you turned into another television play.

That was a comedy. Nat the Wad owns a wool shop in Swansea and Alley Soper owns a bakery next door, and they're great pals but they start to fall out. Alley walks past Nat's wool shop one day, and in the window he sees knitting needles and various wools – and a huge bugger of a cake! War is declared, and within a week Alley has got knitting needles and wool in his window and Nat has got pork pies and loaves of bread in his, and they're usurping each other's businesses. They finally compromise and run one big shop called Nat the Wad & Alley Soper's Cake & Jumper Shop. It's a political allegory.

And then there's *Dracula – Lord of the Stars*. Was that based on Bram Stoker?

No. It was at the time when all the Apollo 13 stuff was very hot, and they go off in a spaceship trying to prove or disprove Einstein's relative theory of moving through time, and they're back in time with Vlad, or something. One of those daft things.

You've mentioned collaborating with Michael Feast, but you also worked on a project with your friend Andrew Birkin.

I wrote a treatment with Andrew called *Revelations*, about a funeral emporium which was being used as a cover to import and export cocaine in funeral urns. It was a dark comedy that never went anywhere. I always found it extremely difficult trying to write with someone else. When I met Andrew, around 1970, he was several rungs up from me, a working writer who had sold things. He's one of the most fabulous guys I've ever met, and he was instrumental in giving Puttnam the manuscript of *Withnail*.

What was Puttnam's reaction?

I don't think I ever got one. I retrospectively got one. Puttnam was very generous about me in Adrian Sibley's documentary.

[*Earnest voice*] 'Marvellous piece of writing. Not necessarily what I'd want to make.' So I didn't really hear anything from Puttnam. Then he commissioned me to write a TV series called *Garrett's Guitar*. Kid wants to be a rock star and a genie lives in the guitar. Great. I wrote thirteen parts and I got paid £200. Can you imagine? For thirteen half-hour episodes. About fifteen quid a show.

Presumably you didn't have a literary agent at this point?

No. My first literary agent was Linda Seifert, and I joined her in about 1975. Andrew was with Linda at that time, he'd read some stuff I'd written, and he said to her, 'There's this guy I know who I think is a very good writer. You ought to meet him.' So I showed her a couple of things, and she said she'd like to represent me. About a year later Puttnam sent through this synopsis for a story called *The Silver Palace*. He had a development deal with Paramount Pictures, and I got about two grand for that one. That was my first proper commission.

It was based on a story by Keith Williams.

Keith had this idea and Puttnam put us in touch. It's about a little boy in the Second World War who's madly in love with cinema and uses it to escape the horrors of East End London. He can't bear the thought of being evacuated to the country, and during an air raid he goes to the only place he feels secure, which is the cinema. This cinema gets bombed, the screen falls on him, he comes up the other side and goes through a series of film adventures to solve his problems. It would have been a funny little film for kids and adults but it never got made. At the end of the movie the little boy is going down the street with three elephants, and Puttnam said, 'I love it. But fuck me, can't we have *one* elephant?' That's a very important rule for writing a screenplay, the 'Fuck me, can't we have *one* elephant?' rule, i.e. don't spend too much money. I'd love to go down to Twickenham Studios with three or four million quid and make that, and if the sets shake it would be a bonus because that's what the film's about.

Puttnam then came back to you again, didn't he?

It was a very exciting day. Ridley Scott was shooting *The Duellists,* and Puttnam called me up and said, 'Can you come down to the set? I want to talk to you.' I went down, Ridley's doing his stuff, and Puttnam says, 'I want to contract you to Enigma Productions. Whether you're writing or not I'll give you £8000 a year.' In those days that was a lot of money. So I wrote four or five scripts for Puttnam, and other things for other people, and then *The Killing Fields* came up.

I think one of those four or five scripts was *Rage*, a rabies thriller which you co-wrote with Matthew Chapman.

God almighty, I'd forgotten that.

One of your last acting roles was in a film called *Violent Summer*, which he wrote and directed. It bypassed cinemas and premièred on Thames TV.

Christ, really? I didn't even know it had come out.

There was also a novelisation of *Rage*, even though the film was never made.

In fact, when I was going through the attic the other day I found that book. It was written by a friend of mine under the name of Jack Ramsay – his real name is Gordon McGill – and it's the only copy I've ever seen.

So at this stage you were still prepared to co-write material?

I tried to co-write *A Pin in the Nose* with Matthew, a comedic piece that was a total failure. Viv told me that when he was at public school, if they didn't like somebody they'd fill a bath with water, sling the victim in, then put those wooden slatted shower things over the top. The only way this poor bugger could breathe was to stick his nose up through the slats, and every time he did they'd stick a pin in it and he'd go under again. That same scene

21

opens *High Rise*. There are two references to noses in *High Rise*. The first one is this Irish prisoner being tortured by the English army, and they're using a razor blade to slash his nose, so it's much more severe. And at the end of the film we're right up above this high-rise block, and the women get hold of the hero, a guy called Wilder, and smear superglue on his lips and up his nose. It's like Hieronymus Bosch; the film collapses into total madness. I'd love to make it, but I'm not sure it's a very fancy Friday night out for the average punter. It's very violent indeed, the only really violent thing I've ever written.

And your first major adaptation, of the novel by J.G. Ballard.

It's very different to the novel. I took the premise from the novel. I think he's a great writer, Ballard. It was commissioned by an English company, Euston Films. It wasn't a big budget, and when I was writing it I phoned them up and said, 'There's no question you can make this for £6million. I've spent £6million by Page 20. What am I going to do?' They said, 'Write it. Let's see what we get.' We got a $35million film. I've mined *High Rise* because I don't think it'll ever get made. 'If they'd hanged Jesus Christ, everyone would be kneeling in front of a gibbet,' is a line in *Advertising* that came out of *High Rise*. It's rather like a book-end to *Advertising* because it's very much an analogy, or an allegory, for what I thought was going on in society. The people at the top of the building don't like the people at the bottom coming up and using their swimming pool, and the people at the bottom of the building don't like the people at the top – including the architect who designed the building – coming down and letting their dogs shit in the foyer or the car park, so this terrible tension develops.

I researched the architectural side of it. In the sixties there was a technique of putting up high-rise buildings involving pre-stressed concrete, and every time you put another layer on the sandwich of the building you wound these cables buried in the earth so they got more and more tense. I made the building a character, and Dennis Friedman said, 'In Freudian terms, the underground carpark is the id, the middle floors are the ego, and the top floors are the super ego.' As soon as he'd given me that I found a way into writing the script. If you like, it's about Bosnia, or it's about India and Pakistan. It's about people becoming more and more intolerant of each other until they're at war. There's one scene which is particularly revolting, where the women go mad and kill this man in the swimming pool. There used to be devices powered by CO_2 with a needle in the end that you'd stick in a wine bottle to get the cork out, and the women are using these gas stabbers to blow him up like a beach ball.

Your second adaptation of a novel, also unproduced and again for Puttnam, came several years later with *David Copperfield*.

Which fell to bits. For some reason he pulled out. I don't know why he hired me, and I did a shit load of research. Apropos of novels, I feel like reaching for my Colt every time I hear someone say, 'It wasn't like the book.' You've got an 800-page masterpiece that took Dickens two years to write, and now you've got 116 minutes to tell that story, so of course you've got to take ten characters and make them one, or change names and locales. I was going to chop the book in half and finish it when David was still a little boy. If I made it people would say, 'But in the book he grows up and marries.' Well, if you want it like that, read the fucking book, then. It doesn't matter how many film versions there are of *David Copperfield*, the book will always survive.

You mentioned research. You've got one of the greatest books ever written, you've got your typewriter and you're a fan. What else did you need?

Well, for example, when David goes away Murdstone sends him off in a stagecoach. When people travelled in stagecoaches in those days, if you were inside they'd stuff straw right up to your chin, so you'd be sitting with just your head sticking out to keep warm on these dreadful journeys. The time it would take. You'd be stopping at coaching inns and doing forty miles a day if you were lucky. Edinburgh was six days from London on the fastest stage. Stuff like that. To know what people ate, how they dressed, when they washed. Dickens knew all those things

23

because he lived in that period. We don't know them any more. At those inns you used to sleep in beds with other people, and the beds were full of lice and bugs and bullshit. That firelight and warming pan routine, with the big fluffy sheets and the little decanter of brandy and water at the side of the bed, was only for the very wealthy. Most people would have to share, and these were people who hadn't washed for nine months. Stinking feet and the sheets got changed twice a year. I would need to know all those things.

Did you finish it?

No, I abandoned it halfway in. I've actually sat down and started writing screenplays and been a month in and discovered they've been abandoned but nobody's bothered to tell the writer. It's awful, and you don't get paid. After *Fat Man and Little Boy*, the producer John Calley and a producer called Irwin Winkler said, 'What do you want to do next?' I wanted to write a film about Joseph McCarthy, which I think would make a fabulous dramatic picture, but Winkler was convinced I was doing it for him and Calley was convinced I was doing it for him. I talked to them both without cementing either one, and finally ended up with neither. Winkler went off and made the picture with somebody else. I did a lot of research on McCarthy; I read dozens of books about him. I can think of half a dozen times when I've done research – and that isn't just flippantly reading a book – and then it fucks up and you find out circuitously. 'You're writing that?' 'Yeah.' 'Well I saw blah blah the day before yesterday and he told me they'd dumped it and you weren't.' 'What?' 'No, he's definitely not doing it. He's doing blah blah's film in Scotland next year.' It's a mean business, you know. As I've said before, it's not the trade of angels.

Around the same time you also wrote an adaptation of the Zola novel *Germinal* for Warner Bros, who seem unlikely hosts for a project about trade unionism.

They didn't want to do a film about trade unionism. It's a love story, a big epic David Lean-sized love story. Another fucking tragedy in my life. That was a tough story to write because of all the underground stuff. I went down a lot of mines to get that smell, to know what it's like in that environment. I'm totally claustrophobic; I really can't handle it. I can't go on the tube in London, I'm so paranoid about being shut in.

I believe you wrote it for producer Jon Avnet, who's now a director as well.

I had lunch with him one day and he said, 'Have you ever read *Germinal*?' I said, 'No, I haven't.' He said, 'It's something I've wanted to do for twenty years.' Of course, at the same time all this was going on – unbeknown, I suppose, to Warner Bros – the Frogs were doing it anyway. To keep the Frenchness of it, which is very important to that book, the obvious thing to do is reset it in French Canada where there are coalmines. The script starts with a thousand miles of rain and this guy called Etienne – I called him Kieran – walking through the countryside until he comes to the mine. In my version he was a harpooner, a whaler, walking south to Boston.

How close did the film come to being made?

I wrote the first draft, then they wanted a second draft, then *Withnail* came up and they said, 'We're not going to get in the way of you having a shot at directing.' So I made *Withnail*, then made a second pass at *Germinal*, then a very famous director, Milos Forman, came in and the whole thing fell to bits. He wanted it completely rewritten by his writer, and I had a big row with Avnet. I said, 'For fuck's sake, I've spent months and months on this, we've got a script that the people at Warner Bros are all saying is fantastic, Milos Forman shoves his snout over the parapet and you're prepared to say, "Fuck off".' There was quite a lot of that on *The Killing Fields*, and I'll always be grateful that Puttnam stuck by me and stuck by the script.

Another screenplay which you wrote for Puttnam between *The Silver Palace* **and** *The Killing Fields* **was** *The Moderns***, a drama set in twenties Paris which was later rewritten and directed by Alan Rudolph.**

That was a shame. I liked *The Moderns* more than a lot of the other things I've written. It was based on people like Hemingway and Duvine, who was a great art connoisseur, and by rights it should have starred a young Audrey Hepburn. You know, I always say that my acting career ended in 1976 with the Truffaut film, but it didn't, it ended in 1977 with a film for a guy called Carlo Lizzani, who was quite a well-respected Italian director. I went out to Los Angeles with Puttnam, met Alan Rudolph and agreed to write *The Moderns*, then came back to London and an Italian producer I knew called Gianni Cortso phoned me and said, 'We want you in this film.' It was a film in Rome, again, with this beautiful French actress Corinne Clery. By now I was a proper writer and I didn't want to act any more – I'd definitely given up after Truffaut – but Gianni brought the director to London and kept saying, 'Please. Please. We really want you in this film.'

What was it called?

Kleinhoff Hotel. I've never seen it. It was basically high-class pornography. A Baader Meinhof terrorist on the run – me – checks into the hotel to kill himself. Meanwhile, for whatever reason, this beautiful French woman in the next room is watching this man through a crack in the adjoining door, and she decides that she wants to fuck him. [*Italian accent*] 'Try and get an erection, Bruce.' I'm like, 'Fuck off! Get an erection, with fifty people standing here?' One lunchtime one of the prop men comes up to me with a box that looks like it contains duelling pistols, and there are all these fake dicks in there and he wants me to strap one on. I thought, 'Christ almighty! I've been to drama school! No!' It was a very rude film. Lots of ridiculous sex scenes that were the most unsexual things I've ever done.

I was writing *The Moderns* all night and acting in this thing all day. It nearly killed me. I did it because Gianni was a friend, and because the more you say no in this business the more they want you. But that genuinely was the last time I acted until *Still Crazy*, twenty years later. Then I turned in *The Moderns* and it disappeared off the face of the earth. God knows what happened to it. I wasn't a member of the Writers Guild of America in those days. Had I been, there is no way the movie could have been taken away from me *vis-à-vis* a credit. I've never seen it. I caught a glimpse of Alan Rudolph on TV a few months ago and he's an old man now. I always thought of him as a young man. Twenty years ago he was.

Your friend Paul Heller, who later produced *Withnail*, helped you join the Writers Guild, didn't he?

Yes, he did. That was after *The Killing Fields* and before its release. I was in LA and Paul said to me, 'You're out of your mind. You've written a major feature film and you're not in the Writers Guild? That means you ain't going to get any residuals.' And he was right, I didn't see a penny off *The Killing Fields*, which would have been quite a lucrative film. Anyway, we drove down to the WGA and they said, 'What have you done?' 'I've just written this film called *The Killing Fields*.' 'We've never heard of it.' It's one of those Catch-22s: you can't join the WGA unless you've made some product, and you can't really make any product unless you've joined. Paul amassed all this stuff, went back down there and said, 'Here it is.' So I joined, I won the Writers Guild Award for *The Killing Fields*, and from there it was all downhill. So, what did I do after *The Moderns*, do you know?

You're asking me?

I can't remember. Some of these things are so long ago.

At some point you wrote a script called *Roadie*.

Oh yeah. *Roadie* was a rock-and-roll film set against the backdrop of the Vietnam war. There's an emerging rock band, they're about to be very successful, and the lead singer gets called up. He doesn't want to go for all sorts of reasons, not that he's a coward but he wants to play with his band and doesn't approve of going out and killing Vietnamese. So he goes AWOL and tours Texas and Illinois as a roadie to escape the draft. 27

Meanwhile, his band have brought in a new singer and they've become enormous stars, and he ends up being a roadie for his own band. Obviously he goes back and plays again, and all of that. It's rather a nice little story. It was commissioned by a man called Tony Smith who managed several rock bands, one of which was Genesis, and I went on tour with them in the US for about a month. Again, it was never made. It just dissolved somewhere. There was another script I wrote on spec at that time when I was hunting around trying to get a picture made.

An Act of Love?

That's right. Unfortunately, the collapse of Communism made that film an unviable proposition. This lovely Czech girl, a gymnast, meets this handsome multi-millionaire in LA when she's out there doing gymnastics, and falls madly in love. She's carted back to Czechoslovakia, and because he's got unlimited dough he gets a friend who was a Huey Sea Cobra pilot in the Vietnam war, and they build this special helicopter to get into Czechoslovakia under the radar. Meanwhile, the pilot has war trauma. He's the best there is, but he's frightened of flying these things. So there's all sorts of tensions going on, and they head into Czechoslovakia to get this woman and when they arrive she's moved. He's in Prague, desperate, and he's got to hit certain times for this guy to get his helicopter out again. Finally, they do get to her, fly her out, and have to land because of weather problems. They're in West Germany now, so they're happy, they're free. Then they see this sign saying 'Prague – 80km', and they realise they're still in Czechoslovakia with the border to be negotiated on foot. It's quite an exciting tale. Never went anywhere, but that is one screenplay I've written that I do own. I own that, I own *The Block* and I own *Penman*, and that's it. Everything else is owned by somebody else.

When did you buy back *The Block*?

A couple of years ago. I bought it back with my own bread, which is a daft thing to do in this business. Rule Two: never spend your own money.

28

You originally sold it to Paramount, and your ex-girlfriend Lesley-Anne Down was slated to play the female lead, is that right?

She was hot at the time. That famous line from *On the Waterfront*, 'I coulda been a contender,' sort of applies to Lesley. She nearly could have been a star. All sorts of chemical reactions got in the way. The original feeling for *The Block* was Lesley and the young Jack Nicholson, but those were pipedreams. At the time you don't think they're pipedreams, but they were. There was no way that was going to happen. Jeffrey Katzenberg, who was an executive at Paramount then and is now a big wad at Dreamworks, phoned me up – I was living in LA at the time with a model – and said, 'Come in and talk about the script.' I did, and he said [*American accent*], 'I enjoyed your screenplay, buddy.' That's how he talks. 'You can write some comic dialogue, buddy.' So I said, 'Where are we going with it?' and he said, 'We've already gone,' and points to his trash can, and there's my script.

Then I tried, over a period, to reacquire it because I liked the premise – girl steals author's manuscript is a nice comedic premise – and they wouldn't sell it back to me under any circumstances. If I'd got it back, gone to another studio and made a hit, they'd have all got fired because they'd have looked like pricks. One of the reasons I got it back was that when I approached Paramount, unbeknown to me, Puttnam had also approached them in respect of *The Silver Palace*, and the fact that they were saying no to Puttnam made them think, 'We can't play the bad guy forever,' and they let *The Block* go. But they wouldn't let *The Silver Palace* go.

The idea of a blocked writer helped by a young English girl was presumably prompted by your long relationship with Lesley?

Probably. I will ever be grateful to the darling Lesley. For a young girl – which she was, nineteen years old or something – to say, 'For God's sake, I'll pay for the milk and the bread, you write,' was marvellous. By then she was probably doing TV, so I did write, and she supported me massively. In fact, the first time I ever got paid anything for a piece of writing, I think, was because of her. She sent a screenplay I'd written to the Cheltenham 29

Literary Festival and I won £200 first prize for it. It was a television play, and I forget what the title was. Anyway, it won the prize and I didn't know she'd sent it, and I got this letter saying, 'Dear Mr Robinson, please come along because you've won first prize for amateur writing.'

Lesley was quite famous, in England certainly, and she was earning a lot of money and she was in all the magazines, and I was like 'Mr Lesley-Anne Down'. Lesley went for a casting session for *Brother Sun and Sister Moon* – one of the worst movies ever made – and for some reason I had to go along and wait for her while she went in to see Zeffirelli. Of course, my career as an actor was completely in the toilet by then, and a woman called Sheila Pickles, who'd been Zeffirelli's secretary on *Romeo and Juliet*, came out and said, 'Bruce!' I said, 'Don't worry, I'm not here for an audition.' She said, 'Well, what *are* you doing here?' I said, 'Lesley is my girlfriend.' She said, 'What are you doing these days?' I said, 'Writing.' She said, 'Lighting. Oh. How did you get into that?' I said, '*Writing*.' She thought I'd become a grip, or something.

You produced a huge amount of work during this period. Between starting to write and *The Killing Fields* finally going into production, did you ever despair?

All the time. The disappointments were myriad and frequent. But all I wanted was to learn the craft of writing, and the only way you can learn it is by writing: 'If it fails, fuck it, I'll do another one.' It took a long time. There was a big première of *California Suite* in London, and the producer was promoting a film that Lesley was about to star in, so she's invited to the première with Mr Lesley-Anne Down. We're sitting at the top table, and I kid you not, surrounding us are Neil Simon, Tom Stoppard, Arnold Wesker and Harold Pinter. From the female end of it, Maggie Smith said to me, with all these writers here, 'And what do you do?' I couldn't bring myself to say I was a writer, because the next question is always, 'Have I seen anything you've written?' 'No, you haven't.' 'Are you published?' 'No.' So I said, 'I'm a typist.'

I was a typist for years. When Puttnam asked me to do *The Killing Fields* the studio did not want an unknown, untried writer on a big project like that. They didn't want me. They wanted William Goldman, or somebody. I shall be eternally grateful to Puttnam for holding out for me and saying, 'No, I think this bloke can do it.' But had he not, had he acquiesced to the studio, I may never have had anything done even now. *The Killing Fields* was the first thing that had ever happened to me as a writer apart from a few letters in the newspaper. You go from literally nothing to people offering you half a million dollars. And without *The Killing Fields*, naturally I'd never have got a shot at *Withnail*.

Chapter Two

'A great story'

The Killing Fields

You must have been delighted to land the job of writing such a prestige film, something which you could pour your visual, verbal and political literacy into.

Puttnam cast the film very well, in that sense. I knew Puttnam very well, he knew me very well, and he'd been the recipient of plenty of my rants about this, that and the other. Depending on what time of day it is, I can be very passionate about things, and I guess he thought, 'If Bruce immerses himself in this maybe he'll get passionate about it, and if he gets passionate maybe we'll get something appropriate to this kind of material.' In that, he was right: I did get passionate about it. And I did get passionate about the atomic bomb when I wrote *Fat Man*.

This was quite a step up from your previous scripts. Did you find it daunting?

They're all the same, really, stories. It was on a much bigger scale than anything I'd done before, so the added ingredient was the research. Normally one wouldn't do that, or at least I hadn't. The stuff I'd written before really required very little research, maybe reading a few books about the subject. With *The Killing Fields*, ninety per cent of what I learned about the subject obviously wasn't on screen, but you did need to know it to write the thing. I always find with writing something like that – a big thing – that I'll want to know everything, but when you strip away the dross, as one has to when one writes a screenplay, you're basically left with that central question: 'What's this about?' Well, it's about this bloke and this bloke, and this happens to them, and then it's resolved. It's no harder writing a story like that, I don't think, than writing any other story. It was certainly easier to write than *Withnail* as a screenplay, which sounds daft but it's true. *Withnail* had nothing except the relationship of these two characters, and it was much more difficult to write that kind of stuff than *The Killing Fields*, where although it's not an action picture it's got big action scenes in it.

The film was based on 'The Death and Life of Dith Pran' a newspaper article by Sydney Schanberg, but presumably that merely served as a starting point?

Puttnam sent me a copy of that article, a *New York Times* piece, and clearly anyone who even vaguely writes would have been interested in it. You couldn't fail to be. It's what they call 'a human story', a big, emotional story on an enormous canvas, and of course that was the thing that the studios wanted to go for. But it became clear to me quite quickly, having met Syd Schanberg and a lot of the people that were around him, that the story was horseshit in many senses. The story is orientated around, 'Me and my Cambodian friend Dith Pran find ourselves in this environment, I was separated from my friend, and the whole reason for my existence after the separation became to get my friend back.' In fact, that friendship existed *after* the event and not before it, and its motive as far as I was concerned was guilt that Schanberg had let Pran down somehow. Certainly that friendship didn't exist before the invasion of Phnom Penh by the Khmer Rouge. Schanberg didn't hang out with Pran. When Schanberg and the other journalists were drinking their cocktails round the swimming pool in the evenings, Pran would be out there sniffing and hustling and bribing to try and find out where the stories were.

The film was marketed with the original article in mind, though, and a number of critics were puzzled to see little evidence of this relationship on screen.

And had I been able to go further down the street that I wanted to go down there'd have been even less of it. The

Americans got into Cambodia as a big nation to bully a little nation, and that was reflected in the relationship between Schanberg and Pran, the big American giving orders to the little Cambodian.

It must have been rather disconcerting to meet the people you were going to be writing about, and for them to meet you.

The day I arrived in New York, I got in a cab at the airport and went to see Schanberg. I sat down with him and I'd written a lot of stuff but I'd never had a film made, so he was probably thinking, 'What am I talking to this guy for? Why aren't I talking to William Goldman?' I had hair down to here and a long black velvet coat, and I immediately had this chemical antipathy to him. I didn't enjoy his presence at all, as I'm sure he didn't enjoy mine. I found him very intimidating. He's a very edgy, very complex and very hurt man. I don't know what he's like now, I haven't seen him for fifteen years, but he was a mess. He was constantly washing his hands, and you don't need to be Freud's nephew to realise that someone who does that every thirty-five minutes has got something going on under the Homburg.

I remember very clearly, having lunch with Dith Pran in my hotel room, and Dith – no, it's the other way round; Dith is his surname and Pran is his Christian name – Pran was sitting there, and he's tiny, like five-feet-three tall, and he said [*Oriental accent*], 'He used to slap me, kick my arse sometimes.' I couldn't believe I was hearing this – and I was getting it on tape, too – because I was just as much into the myth about this friendship as anybody else. And why wouldn't I have been? All I'd read was maybe one book on Cambodia, and that article, and that was it. My hair was on end when he was saying this. 'He used to hit you?' [*Oriental*] 'Yeah, he hit me.' I let that go, then the next time I met him I'd slide this in again just to see if he'd corroborate it or say, 'No, he never hit me.' But because he'd said that I was immediately suspicious of the relationship. You don't hit friends.

After a couple of weeks trying to sweat a story out, which is something you always have to do on your own, I came to the 35 conclusion that a lot of this friendship stuff was bullshit, and I knew I'd have to confront Schanberg with it. Which I did. I phoned him up and said, 'I'm off tomorrow, Syd. Thanks for the interviews. But I have to say this: I don't believe you.' He said, 'What don't you believe?' I said, 'I don't believe in this friendship. None of it. I just don't believe it.' And much to his credit he said, 'Well, they've hired you to write it, you must go the way you feel is correct.' Here I come from the safety and luxury of a highly priced hotel, never so much as a peashooter pointed at me, and it took to the limits of my guts to even say this, and he was the one who'd been through it. He just said, 'You must write what you feel is right. Puttnam wouldn't have hired you unless he believed you could do it, so I acquiesce to that.' Though if he'd said, 'Fuck you, then. You're the wrong writer,' he couldn't have done anything about it anyway.

Schanberg apparently had a very dry sense of humour, yet his character barely even smiles in the film.

Schanberg's a dry guy, and I'm sure he has got a pretty profound sense of humour. If I'm very comfortable with people, if they're my close friends, I find it much easier to get on a funny roll than I do if I'm talking to strangers, because your friends know you, and you know what they're going to laugh at. Schanberg may be like Bob Hope on his own, but he certainly never was with me. It probably sounds like the opposite, but I do have a great admiration for Schanberg. All this is said in the context of his brilliance as a journalist. Whatever his motives were, he did do something incredibly brave. It would take more than working for the *New York Times* to keep me in Phnom Penh with the Khmer Rouge coming. He had an enormous amount of balls, which is another story: what was his motor-drive in his life, why was he so driven to be the one guy who gets the big story? The fallout from it was quite astonishing, and we do get some sense of that in the film.

Perhaps that's why he comes across as being rather unsympathetic. He's driven, he's humourless, he's self-righteous. In fact, he's a real pain in the arse.

I'm sure he was a pain in the arse. I'm sure he was determined to get what he wanted out of this war. I was just reminded of that thing John Malkovich says to Andy Garcia in *Jennifer Eight*: 'You wanted to be top cop.' That's what Schanberg wanted to be, top cop, and he made it but there was a big price to pay. That's not to denigrate him. He wanted to be top cop in the same way as anybody who does anything. When I sit down to write a screenplay, I want to be as good a screenwriter as I can be. 'Why is that, Bruce? Is it because your father used to smack you in the face?' Well, I don't know. Maybe. But I want to do the best work I can, for multifarious reasons about myself and my background, and that's very much what affected him.

I think as a child he was considered to be a kind of failure, never did anything, never got anywhere, always looking up to his Dad, trying to impress his Dad, and here comes the great opportunity to be a man or a mouse: the fall of Phnom Penh. Most of the journalists – and as I said, I would have been among them – fucked off prompt. Am I going to put my life on the line so some arsehole in Dayton, Ohio, can read over his Ready Brek what's going on halfway round the world? I wouldn't do it. For Schanberg, though, getting those dispatches into New York on time to hit the front page of the *Times* was absolute life and death. There's a scene where Pran comes in and says [*Oriental accent*], 'Towers got hit. Can't transmit tonight,' and Schanberg freaks out. That's what he was like. He would have gone ballistic against Pran, like it was his fault for not being able to transmit this stuff.

Do you think it was Cambodia he cared about, or the stories themselves?

That's a terribly complex question, and I bet he couldn't answer it himself. I think you would have to care, but what do you care most about? It's a kind of high for those guys: 'Yes, I care desperately about Cambodia, but if there's a war in the Congo and I'm available I'm going to be there next week.' There are degrees of care. 'Do I care about being a star reporter, the only one getting the stories out, or is my passion to tell the rest of the world how these people are suffering because of what we're doing?' What is 'care'? Something that affected me very much was a piece of film on TV showing a Vietcong insurgent being shot in the head, his brains spilling out like a soda syphon. I think it's the most shocking image I've ever seen.

Along with the little girl, the napalm victim, running down the road.

That's right. That's the great war photographer Don McCullin. You know, 'If you saw a little girl on fire what would you do?' His famous reply was, 'About 5.6 at a fiftieth.' That's part of it, isn't it? To go to that hospital you'd have to be a journalist to survive it, because if you went there without that kind of objectivity you'd be thinking, 'Fuck the story. What can I do to help?'

Whereas to get the story Schanberg did put Pran in danger.

I'm not quite sure of the mechanics of the deal that was done there. Here come the Khmer Rouge saying, 'Anyone who's affiliated to any foreign journalist has to get out. If we find you later, you're dead.' Here are Pran's wife and children going, and here is Pran, staying behind, giving his loyalty to the *New York Times*. If it was my wife and kids I'd be on the fucking helicopter, but I think Pran was so in awe of Schanberg, in the same way that Cambodia was under the control of forces out of its control, that he couldn't have said, 'I want to go.' Pran may have loved Schanberg like a brother, and I don't want to do any disservice to Schanberg, but I don't think he considered Pran his brother. He may have done after the event, but I don't think he did at the time at all. He bullied Pran, there's no question, and I think Pran may well have been in a situation where he'd been disqualified from taking that decision. To leave your wife and kids, or rather have your wife and kids leave you, is almost impossible.

In an article written by he and Pran at the time of the release, Schanberg claims that they were both interested in the human impact of international politics and military strategy, a philosophy which could also be applied to the film itself.

I would tend to be more accepting of that as a philosophy from Schanberg if those telexes coming out of Phnom Penh, and those articles going into the *New York Times*, had Pran's name on them as well as his. I think a lot of stuff was going on in Pran's head that wasn't necessarily about reporting what was going on in Cambodia. Besides, if Pran had been taken out of the equation – either been killed or buggered off with his wife and kids – Schanberg would have got somebody else instantly. Pran was eminently replaceable in that context whereas Schanberg wasn't. If the editor of the *Times* had walked up and down shouting, 'Who wants to go out and cover the fall of Phnom Penh?' there wouldn't have been too many takers, would there?

Schanberg won his Pulitzer prize for 'International Reporting at Great Risk', which is represented in the film by some sort of composite award.

A newspaper award issued by his peers. I can't remember whether it was composite or real, but it must have been a horrible dilemma accepting any award for something you're absolutely torn to pieces about. He did say what he says in the film: 'This is for him.' He didn't know whether Pran was alive, dead or what. A lot of the world's press – the ones that stayed behind – had stringers, and when they were in the French Embassy a lot of them managed to smuggle their stringers out. For example, there was a convoy of trucks, and it took something like nine days to get out of Phnom Penh into Thailand through Khmer Rouge occupied territory, and on some of those trucks there were Cambodian stringers hidden under the seats and hanging off the axles. Imagine the terror of driving 700 miles to get to the border with certain death on the cards. If they'd found these guys they would have offed the lot. I never discussed that with Schanberg or Pran. Why didn't they take that risk? How come others did and they didn't? Does Rockoff say that? 39

He says something similar when he meets Schanberg at the awards ceremony, and the reply is that Pran made the choice to stay.

Maybe that's true. There's a line at the end of the embassy sequence – invented by me, not said by Pran, but I must have had a trigger for it – where he says to one of the other journalists, 'You make racist statements against me, as though I cannot choose for myself.' I must have got that from somewhere, probably out of Pran. Maybe he did choose to stay there and see it through. Maybe the sense of great achievement that Schanberg felt about his scoop was rubbing off on him: 'I'm part of a very important machine here, and I might not be the main cog but I'm certainly one of them.'

He did subsequently become a news photographer.

When he got to New York he did. I think he was a staff photographer for the *Times*. You know, it's very easy, sitting safely in the English countryside, to talk about what motives they may have had. Certainly the motives I tried to write in the film were the motives I thought were right. But if Schanberg says that about Pran, well, Schanberg knows Pran and I don't really, so maybe that was Pran's motive, the human interest side of it. When I say there wasn't much of a friendship between them, I wasn't sitting in a hole being machine-gunned, and I don't know what feelings were going on there. I wrote it in Los Angeles, thousands of miles and several years away from the events. It was my take on it, that's all, and how do I know whether I was right or wrong? I know I was right about a lot of things that weren't in *Fat Man*, because I set out to prove them and could do that with documents. There were no documents available to prove that Sydney Schanberg was or was not a friend of Dith Pran. But if you're up to your balls in mud being shot at, there is a symbiosis between you based on survival, if nothing else. There has to be.

Did your perceptions of Schanberg change while you were writing the script?

They did. If you're writing something properly – and it doesn't always happen – you're in there with them. At its best, when I'm writing, I can smell it and hear it and taste it, and that would change your point of view because you've set up a situation when you're writing where there's guns pointed at you and you think, 'I'm going to die.' We only have our imaginations to deal with that subject, thank God. I don't know what it's like to have a sixteen-year-old boy shove an AK-47 in my gut and scream at me in a language I can't understand, knowing that these people are ruthless, merciless killers of other people. You can't really imagine it. You can get somewhere in dramatic imagination, but you can't really imagine what it's like to have that kind of fear.

In the first draft script one of the other journalists sarcastically refers to Pran and Schanberg as Pranberg, in the same way that Woodward and Bernstein were dubbed Woodstein when they were reporting on Watergate.

Asking for that, though, aren't you? Schanberg admitted as much. The reason he did get into places that no one else could get into was because of Pran.

The first act of the film, their journey to Neak Luong, is a good example of that.

I originally wrote it not as a river trip but as a trip on a plane with an Australian guy called Oscar Dougal. I got to him via Reuters. His name really was Dougal, though it wasn't Oscar, and of course I spiced it up a bit, but he literally was bashing at the aeroplane and had oil pouring out of it. You get in the plane and there's no seats, nothing, just a string of lightbulbs and cargo of a possibly dubious nature. He was on the runway, and there's air-traffic control saying [*Oriental accent*], 'You have no clearance for takeoff. Who are you? Where are you going?' And he said [*Australian accent*], 'My name's Oscar Dougal, and I'm

41

turning left.' I used that in the script, this fucked out prop plane, because I liked it more than the boat, but the boat was very romantic too. They both would have worked.

What did you find out on your research trip to Thailand?

I'd never been to the Far East, and one of the things that I always like to do is get in there and sniff it. You couldn't really get into Cambodia, so I got on a plane to Thailand and I met quite a few of the journalists who'd been there. These guys had seen bodies floating in rivers, so I wanted to talk to them and try and get a sense of what it must have been like, the horror of seeing not only bodies but books and armchairs and television sets and washing machines and everything that's in a house all floating away. What the Khmer Rouge didn't want to loot, they just chucked in. It's an astonishing thing to have witnessed something like that, so I wanted to talk to people who had. I talked to Jon Swain, the award-winning *Sunday Times* reporter, and I got hold of a lot of pictures that Swain had taken and I lied to Puttnam and said *I* had. Swain's the kind of guy who does crawl across the bridge at night to get his story. I just couldn't do it; I haven't got it in me.

Swain was a top cop, too. In Phnom Penh, when the last flights were leaving, people were arriving at the airport with bars of gold and bags of pearls to try and get themselves or their families on a flight out of there. Now here comes the last flight into Phnom Penh – the very last flight; the plane was actually strafed by Khmer Rouge machine guns as it came in – and who's lying on the floor of the plane but Jon Swain. He got on the last plane going in. Can you imagine the mentality of someone who would do that? He had to have it. He escaped from Cambodia and next thing he's a kidnap victim in the Sudan for six months. That was his next job. Something in Jon makes him go after that, I don't know what. I'd have been the one with the bag of pearls. But not him, and not Sydney.

Thailand itself was in the middle of a military coup, wasn't it?

Thailand was in the middle of a military coup, and when Sophie and I went to India there was a coup on, in Bangalore. These sorts of things happen there and half the time you don't notice, I suppose. The day after I arrived in Bangkok, the Assistant Manager of the hotel was murdered in the foyer. These two guys came into the hotel, said, 'We want to see the Manager.' 'The Manager's out.' 'Well, who else can we see? We'll see the Assistant Manager.' Out he comes; bang, right in the face, and he's dead, in the middle of this very famous hotel.

Why do you need to go to places? Well, I had it in my head that when Pran was escaping from Cambodia over the border into Thailand, I could have him dying of thirst and cracking the valve on a radiator and drinking this rusty water. Rather like he drinks the blood out of a cow, which I made up; I don't know whether he ever did do that or didn't do it, but I thought that was a good way to get protein. So I'm going to have him drinking out of a radiator, and as soon as I arrive virtually the whole country's underwater. You'd never do something like that because you wouldn't need to. And you'd never know things like that until you went there.

You mentioned Don McCullin's hypothetical reaction to seeing a girl in flames, but you actually did see that, didn't you?

I was in a taxi, screaming at the driver to stop, and he wouldn't, and in the context that we were in why would he? If you're outside Guildford and there's someone on fire in the road there's a point in stopping, because within ten minutes you'd probably have cops and paramedics and helicopters. Out there, forget it. There's nothing. They're not going to rush round to try and get someone out of the road. There are people dying all over the place all the time. And Thailand is a relatively advanced country, it's not a poor place.

When I was researching *The Killing Fields*, I took a London cab, and me and the driver were sharing the yak and I told him what I was doing. [*Cockney accent*] 'Oh yeah. Of course, they don't feel it like we do.' In other words, here's a mother with her baby, she's got malnutrition so she's got no milk to feed the baby: 'They don't *feel* it like we do.' She feels it *exactly* like we do. People are able to rationalise it by saying that they're not like us. That's why I got so outraged by that little tosser Cook

SMOKING IN BED

sending plane parts out to prolong this civil war in Africa. When you send those spares out, you're actually sending out amputated legs and mothers disembowelled in front of their children. How he can take that sanctimonious attitude towards Kosovo and at the same time be supplying the same mentality with the wherewithal to carry on doing it, I don't know. My mind capsizes at the thought of that. How can we as a nation supply those kind of bastards? It's like supplying the Khmer Rouge.

When the tanks roll into the city Pran dances for joy, prompting one critic to point out that it's hard to blame Schanberg for not knowing how brutal the Khmer Rouge were going to be if even their own countrymen didn't know.

When the Khmer Rouge had achieved their ambition to take Cambodia back, even though they'd been extremely violent during the war of so-called liberation, no one knew they were going to behave in the way they did when they got into Phnom Penh. No one knew that women giving birth were going to be kicked out of bed and told to piss off into the countryside; old people who'd just had operations; dying people. No one knew that they were going to clear the city like that. When the first wave of the Khmer Rouge came into Phnom Penh they were incredibly friendly towards the citizens. They weren't the hardcore Khmer Rouge, they weren't hardened jungle fighters, they were kind and nice and everyone thought, 'What a relief. For five years we've been thinking these were the biggest murderers on earth, and they're not bad. They're having a beer with us, they've liberated this country, the Americans have fucked off, and now it's going to get back to normal.' Cut to the Khmer Rouge arriving, the proper ones, who weren't of the same mind.

Why did they clear the city? The point is rather obscure in the film.

This homicidal, paranoid sociopath Pol Pot wanted the country to start again, and starting again means no doctors, no medicine, everyone going back to the land and re-growing the society that he had in his insane head. He called it 'Year Zero'. The calendar

44

starts today, and in twelve months it would be 'Year One'. He got up to about 'Year Four'. He told the people that they were all being taken out of Phnom Penh because the Americans were going to launch a major bombing raid on the city now the Khmer Rouge had taken it. For four years no one was in that city. A French colonial city filled with beautiful buildings, and it was empty. Every dentist's chair, every sweet shop, every restaurant was just left.

Pol Pot was insane, and his insanity of wanting to create a peasant state was itself caused by the insanity of, in my view, a pair of war criminals: Nixon and Kissinger. Part of the reason that Pol Pot did turn from a rural guerrilla into a national leader was because of what America was doing. Henry Kissinger got it into his diseased brain that the Vietcong were crossing over into Cambodia and regrouping, rearming, re-everything-ing, so here's this country that's completely neutral, nothing to do with the Vietnam war, but Kissinger starts bombing it. There's a place called The Parrot's Beak, where Cambodia juts into Vietnam, and he started bombing there, and within a year he was bombing the entire country. Not only the Khmer Rouge but no one else in Cambodia had any means of retaliating against this day-and-night aggression from the most powerful nation on earth.

Part of the motor-drive of *The Killing Fields* was this notion that I had – and I don't know whether it's real or imagined, but it would do for me – that cancer can be some kind of extreme crisis of pathological anxiety which has to manifest somewhere. Now I know that may or may not apply to cancer, but I know it applies to me *vis-à-vis* asthma. If I get incredibly uptight and frustrated, I get breathless because I'm an asthmatic. The same chain reaction could very well happen inside a body to create a cancer: there's no other way out. The American war machine dumped eight billion – not million, *billion* – dollars worth of bombs on Cambodia, and that country had no protection against this and I think it turned back: 'If we can't destroy the enemy, we'll destroy ourselves.' That's virtually what happened in Cambodia: it went on a self-destruct.

Nixons so-called 'doctrine' was not telling Cambodia that America was going to bomb, and then not telling them they were going to invade.

He didn't give a fuck about Cambodia, probably didn't even know where it was. They were just a gang of slants. If you listen to those Watergate tapes, he's unbelievable. This man was in charge of the most powerful nation on earth, and he was like [*American accent*], 'They're just Gooks. But if anyone wants to know, I didn't bomb 'em, right?' It's all that sort of talk. This is the President that nearly dropped an atomic bomb on North Vietnam. 'Wow!' is all one can say.

In one interview Puttnam is quoted as saying that the script simply blamed the violence in Cambodia on the Americans, whereas if you go back in history you find that the Cambodians were the most violent nation in Southeast Asia.

I think that's complete tosh, and probably so does he, but he would have to have briefed himself with something to say for his various interviews. You go back over a thousand years and the Cambodians are some of the most violent people on earth; you go back one hundred years and find that the British are some of the most violent people on earth; and the French; and the Germans. There is no definition amongst humanity of who is and who isn't violent; we all are. Every single nation on earth, given the opportunity and the facility to commit acts of extreme violence, has done so, and this country more than most. So for him to go back to the period pre-Angkor – which was the great renaissance of eighth-century Cambodia – and accuse them of being a very violent people . . . sure they were, but who wasn't?

He also claimed that he and Roland Joffé toned down and stripped out the anti-American elements in the script.

That simply is not true. What you got on the screen was what I had written, eight and a half to nine out of ten. The only overt anti-American reference that was extirpated was I opened with a fat American soldier in a Cambodian brothel fucking a fourteen-year-old Cambodian girl. If David ever wanted to challenge that, I'd be able to show him the first draft he ever had with my notes all over it. I'm not anti-American at all. I'm actually extremely fond of America and many of its works, but that was a particularly unpleasant regime running the country then, coming as it did on the back of another area of American politics that fascinates me, the McCarthyite period of the fifties. But to say that I don't like America because of Joseph McCarthy and Richard Nixon would be absurd.

In any case, the first important set-piece is still the aftermath of the accidental bombing of Neak Luong by a B-52, a sequence which one reviewer commented was simply designed to blame the Americans from the word go.

That's nonsense too, because it did happen. All right, we're telling in two hours a story that really happened over five years, but that did happen, and the way that it happened was the way it happened in the film, that a B-52 got fucked co-ordinates on its computers and bombed Neak Luong. The ridiculous thing is that America was dumping this explosive on the country day and night, and at the same time paying for the doctors and hospitals to repair the damage they were doing, and of course every day they did it the Khmer Rouge got stronger.

The absence of political context might account for criticisms that the film was anti-American. Most of act one is concerned with the carnage in Neak Luong, which means that we know the Americans are bombing the country but we don't know why. The Khmer Rouge don't really figure until act two.

But how could they figure, in reality or in screen terms? Nobody knew. They really did not know what the Khmer Rouge were going to do when they won. The exodus from the city – nobody knew they were going to do anything like that.

The film was also criticised for being confusing, and it could be said that this reflects the confusion in the country and the confusion of the correspondents, but nevertheless the fact that personal experience predominates over political context means that we don't really know who's doing what to whom and why.

I think there was some confusion, but I don't think it was intended. The idea is to make the story as accessible as you can, given the constraints that you've got. You're right, the majority of people who went to the movie knew fuck all about it, but *The Killing Fields* worked because it's a great story, end of the argument. We don't give a fuck who Pol Pot is, he's just a cunt, and the Khmer Rouge may as well be Comanches, we don't care. For the purposes of this movie they're the nasty guys. You pick up books to get into who Pol Pot was, but you go to the cinema to be entertained; everything else is superfluous.

When exactly did Joffé come on board?

Roland came on board after Puttnam had locked off what the screenplay was about; that was the film he wanted to make. The first guy who was going to do it was Louis Malle, who we both had lunch with, and Louis Malle saw it in a different way to the way Puttnam saw it. He wanted to open the film with B-52s and make it much more operatic. At the end of the lunch – at which I said nothing, because there was nothing for me to say; Puttnam could do what he liked, as producers do – Louis Malle left and Puttnam said, 'Well, what do you think of that?' I said, 'I don't know. It's not the way I look at it,' and he said, 'No, nor me. I've got this bloke in England I'm going to talk to.' And that's the first time I ever heard Roland's name. He took it to Roland, and next thing Roland's directing it. Very good instinct for people, Puttnam.

It was a good instinct in the context of such a political film, and interesting in the light of Joffé's penchant for rewriting, because he'd directed controversial television dramas by acclaimed writers Jim Allen and Trevor Griffiths.

48   Thank God, from my perspective, that *The Killing Fields* was

Roland's first feature, because he didn't have the clout that he rapidly acquired having made it. I was invited along to see the dailies as they were beginning to come in, and I didn't know what I was looking at. There were all these mad improvised scenes, thousands of feet of stuff, preaching and didactic. There was a very distinguished editor on the film called Jim Clark, and he actually said to Puttnam, 'For God's sake, David. You've locked off on it. I've locked off on it. We know what we want. We don't want 10,000 feet of this waffle. Please get Roland to shoot the script.' Now if I'd said that to Puttnam it wouldn't have got anywhere, but because Jim's an Oscar-winning editor I think David did say, 'Roland, shoot the script. This is what I believe in. This is what I want to see on the screen.' Consequently, Roland was shooting the script, but by the time we got to the atomic bomb he wasn't. I think that had *The Killing Fields* been his third feature he would either have rewritten it himself or brought in somebody else to do it, and I honestly think he would have fucked it up.

Did you discuss the script with Joffé?

No. I never spoke to Puttnam once when I was writing *The Killing Fields*, and I didn't talk to Roland at all.

It went through eight drafts, is that right?

The script didn't actually go through eight drafts, the third act went through maybe five. Schanberg was in the process of quite a messy divorce at the time, and David very much wanted him to be relating to a woman back in New York. I wrote a draft incorporating his wife, and he refused to have his wife in the story. Then I wrote another draft with the father, and the father refused to be in it. Then I believe it was turned into a sister. I would have personally gone for the first draft solitary side of him, because that's all he had, him and his guilt. For example, the 'Nessun Dorma' sequence to me is very potent because he is on his own, he's got nowhere else to go.

I read in an article that Roland had the idea for this sequence. Well, anyone who reads the screenplay, which was written   49 before Roland came on board, will see that the music selected in that scene is 'Nessun Dorma' by Puccini. I was driving down to see my mother one weekend and happened to hear it on a French radio station. Now it's been debased by advertising and the World Cup, but it wasn't famous then unless you were an opera buff. I didn't know what it was, but I thought, 'If ever I've heard a piece of transition music, that's it.' At the end I heard this French chick saying, 'Puccini', but I didn't catch what it was. I went through all of Puccini until I found it, and it's written in the screenplay because that sequence clearly needed emotional music to make it work.

People have very reconstructive memories about things. When the film came out, we saw it in New York, and I was talking to Schanberg about it and he was saying, 'That stuff in the embassy is so tense.' I said, 'Yeah. That device of creating the photograph really worked.' He said, 'What do you mean?' I said, 'That was a piece of dramatic licence.' He said, 'No, we did that.' I said, 'No, you didn't.' It was a device to keep the tension going, otherwise you'd have been sitting there for half an hour and either they kick them out or they don't; either they get away or they don't. I had this idea that they produce a fake passport but had no photograph, and that gives you a lot of mileage dramatically.

I'd phoned round every principal photography outfit I could find, and my brief to them was, 'You've got film and you've got a camera, but how could you develop a photograph?' and none of them could give me a solution. I finally got through to a guy who worked in the X-ray department at Middlesex Hospital in London, gave him the brief, and he came back three days later and said, 'I've done it.' He was a photography freak. 'I boiled disinfectant and was left with phenol, which I could develop with, and I used piss as a fixative.' I was over the moon. I said, 'If ever this film gets made, you are at the première!' Of course, I never adhered to that; I didn't even know who he was. So I put it in the script, and here we are with the film finished and Schanberg being absolutely convinced they did that. They didn't, and I had a bet with him. I said, 'Do you want fifty bucks on it?' Two days later he came back with the fifty dollars and said, 'You're right. I checked it out. We didn't do it.' But he was convinced that they had.

That's a testament to the verisimilitude of the film.

It worked very nicely. He knew that they had forged a passport using a spare one. They took out Swain's photograph and put in Pran's, and because Swain had a weird series of middle names they knocked out the 'Jon' and the 'Swain' to leave just 'Ancketill Brewer'. But they were doing it under incredible duress, and the passports went via the French ambassador and he immediately spotted that this had been cooked-up, which was putting everyone at risk. He said, 'I'm sorry. You can't do this.'

The opening shot of the film, a native boy wearing an army helmet sitting on a water buffalo in the rice paddies as helicopters fly overhead, is a very powerful image but it isn't in the script. I assume this, the shots of Pran and Schanberg, and Schanberg's voice-over, were all added in post-production?

That was nothing to do with me at all. As I said, my opening of the movie in the first draft, which was extirpated in the second, was the brothel. Then the airport. Those things come out of exactly what you were talking about earlier. They screen the picture in San Diego, they get the preview cards from the audience, and the audience says, 'We don't know anything about the Khmer Rouge. We don't know anything about Cambodia.' So they think, 'We'd better tell them,' and you get sixty seconds of, 'My friend Pran' and 'War-torn Cambodia' and 'I was the *New York Times* reporter', otherwise you wouldn't know he was a *New York Times* reporter. There's all sorts of ways of doing it, but probably that was the most efficient way.

The screenplay is rather unorthodox in comparison with many modern scripts, breaking down into two halves rather than three acts, for example.

It would definitely be a three-act structure, but a lot of humour got lost in the first act, which pissed me off. I think it would have made the film richer if it had been in there. I remember one thing early on, when Schanberg and Rockoff are having breakfast in Phnom Penh and someone throws a grenade. Rockoff's dialogue, I can't get it verbatim, was something about oysters: 'They put the lemon juice on 'em just to stun 'em. I can't see that makes any difference.' Then there's the explosion. But the payoff to that line was something like, 'As far as I'm concerned, an unconscious oyster is just as horrible as the fucker wide awake.' Then the bomb should have gone off. So you get your laugh which is ruptured by the bomb, rather than get the bomb in and kill the laugh. In the context of a film like *The Killing Fields*, I think you need every laugh you can get. But that was a very difficult scene to shoot. Malkovich nearly got killed in that scene. They stuffed these condoms with helium and detonated them, and they had too much of it and it blew Malkovich across the room.

Another scene – again talking about humour that was cut – was of a guy out there in Cambodia, quite a famous American television journalist. His crew would find a hole full of water with smoke and flames two miles away, he'd take off his cowboy boots, put on a pair of army boots, get in the hole, and say, 'Less than 400 yards behind me the Khmer Rouge are approaching,' and off-camera you'd see this fucker with a tape recorder playing back machine-gun fire. Schanberg told me this story and I thought it would be wonderful, in a film that really is dealing with life and death, to start the scene with this guy in the hole giving his commentary, and let the camera pull back to see the tape recorders and the make-up girls. Some of those journalists were like that, just swilling the booze and fucking the birds, and as soon as it got within twenty miles of Phnom Penh they were gone.

You also focus on Pran rather than Schanberg in the final act, which is unusual so late in the story, and whereas in other films about war correspondents the Asian characters often simply provide background colour, here their story is at least as important as that of the Westerners.

That's right, yeah. Pran does carry the third act. There are cuts to Schanberg, rather than vice versa, because the film is about Cambodia not New York, and if he's left Cambodia why do we want to see what he thinks? We know what he thinks. I was convinced that construction was the correct one. And how do you know anything as a writer except for that gut feeling of knowing or not knowing? I can't tell you how difficult that third act was to write, which is why I put in those voice-overs, because you couldn't have anyone speaking English like you could in the rest of the movie. I came up with that solution of him composing letters to Schanberg in his head that he would write if he was allowed to write. It's his take on where he's at. That was the only way, because no one says anything in English until the administrator of the village says something. Generally, as a narrative device, I dislike voice-over.

A different method of narrative voice-over is the use of Voice of America in the film to convey occasional snippets of information. Was that in the script?

It is in there, but it's not written as dialogue, it's written in the directions. The only time the journalists were listening to the Voice of America, or more likely the BBC World Service, was when they were holed up in the embassy. That's the only contact they had with the outside world. But those guys would go to the embassy to find out what was happening. They wouldn't listen to the radio so much, because they were there. The radio was getting its shit to broadcast from the people that had left. There are a couple of jokes in the embassy scenes – I don't know if they survived into the film – where the Voice of America is telling them something about themselves that's clearly horseshit. They're sitting there in the middle of it and there's somebody 10,000 miles away saying, 'It looks like the Khmer Rouge are playing the sweetheart.'

They did survive. Rockoff jokes that the BBC correspondent manages to get his copy past the Khmer Rouge by using . . .

Highly trained chickens walking across the border. I'd forgotten that. I don't know why I'm obsessed with chickens, but I clearly am. I have chickens in everything I do. *The Block* has a chicken on the loose, a guinea fowl. In *Advertising* he throws them in the   53 lavatory. In *Withnail* they eat one. I've always got them. You can even spot some chickens in *Jennifer Eight* if you look hard enough.

The village administrator entrusts Pran with his baby son, who is later killed by a landmine. Was that a dramatic device, like the fading passport photograph and drinking blood from a cow, or did that really happen?

Most of that's pretty real. Pran wasn't the only educated man in Phnom Penh. The city was full of dentists and doctors and professors and scientists, and these people were suddenly kicked out in the country, all pretending to be daft. It's quite true that Pran pretended to be an illiterate cab driver for years to survive. 'Do you speak English?' [*Oriental accent*] 'Ah, English! Taxi! Taxi!' That's how he got by, but he could speak English, French and obviously Khmer, so the chances of running into another educated man were quite high. If you wore glasses, you were executed; if you spoke a foreign language; if you were a student. One of the most frightening scenes, which Roland shot brilliantly, is in that hut with the loudspeaker saying [*Oriental*], 'Is anyone doctor? Come now. Join us.'

But the child was an addition for the film?

The death of that kid and that moment when the landmine goes off probably was. I wrote a much bigger sequence towards the end, because the people who liberated Cambodia were the Vietnamese and I wanted to dislocate the audience. When the cavalry arrives, you think it's the American air force coming, and it's not, it's Russian Migs flown by the Vietcong. I'd like to have had that, because the saviour in the soul of Western audiences is the Yanks, and I thought that would be a potent dramatic change. As a matter of fact, that journalist who I admire read the original screenplay.

John Pilger?

Yeah. He wrote a couple of pieces in the *New Statesman* saying, 'Why was this censored from the film? This is the truth.' And it was the truth. The Vietnamese went into Cambodia and sorted those bastards out. They didn't go in as empire builders, they went in on humanitarian grounds. Now, because we are so propaganda-ised about these yellow devils, the Vietnamese, we can't conceive that they would have taken food and medicines into Cambodia. But what the Vietnamese did cannot be denied; it's well documented.

Some of the reviews in the more conservative broadsheets accused the film of glossing over the North Vietnamese incursions into Cambodia, and the wider insurgence of Russian- and Chinese-backed Communists in Southeast Asia, events which partly caused Nixon and Kissinger to order the bombing.

The Communists in Cambodia and the Communists in Vietnam were as different as black and white; they weren't the same geezers at all. The Communists in Vietnam were fighting for their country. Ninety-five per cent of people in America had no idea other than what their televisions told them of what the fuck they were doing out there. They had that ridiculous domino theory: 'If we let the Commies take Vietnam, next thing they'll be taking this, that and the other, and before we know it they'll be coming up the Rio Grande river and taking Texas.'

In fact, after the Vietnamese went in and before he made his way to Thailand, they made Pran administrative chief of Siem Reap, his home town. I read that he had a khaki uniform, a Soviet-style cap and an AK-47, and had power over 10,000 people, which is almost a film in itself.

The whole thing went through a dream/nightmare stage when the Vietnamese were temporarily there. As soon as the Khmer Rouge were in shit street, it was rather like when Germany collapsed in the Second World War: millions of members of the Nazi party were suddenly completely anti-Nazi and fraternising with the Yanks and the Russians. Like the jumping up and down you were talking about earlier. What else are you supposed to do? If you wave your fists at them you're over, aren't you? You wave the flag because you don't know which way they're going to go. But we couldn't get into that. The film would have been nine hours long. What was important in terms of the film was him getting away.

If Schanberg's relationship with Pran in the first half of the film, as we talked about earlier, serves as a metaphor for America's attitude towards Cambodia, then do you think his powerlessness in the second half, as one commentator pointed out, reflects its inability to achieve these foreign policy objectives?

I suppose that's true. The richest, most powerful and most aggressive nation on earth got its arse kicked by one of the three poorest nations: Vietnam. They couldn't control events out there, and still can't. You've divided a country up, and while it's divided it'll always be at war with itself or some other country. Every civil war on earth is basically that, which is why Ireland has lasted. This show will run and run.

What was the attitude of Pran and Schanberg to the film being made?

I don't know what Sydney's attitude was. Schanberg is a very egocentric man, and if someone comes to you and says, 'I want to make a feature film about you and what you've done,' it must be a very attractive and very flattering prospect. Woodward and Bernstein must have loved it. I guess part of him loved it, and I think part of him was in severe trepidation about it, wondering what was going to happen. He did read the script and responded in a very positive way, but I don't know whether he got a lot of money, a little money or no money from it. I suppose there was a financial incentive and an ego incentive – and hopefully a truth incentive, because the film was honourably made. We weren't trying to sensationalise anything. We were trying to say, 'Given the confines and restraints of making feature films, we're being as truthful and honest as we can.' A dishonest approach would have been casting Sylvester Stallone in the part of Schanberg, and in the third act parachuting him into the jungle where he proceeds to kill 5000 slants before he gets to Pran and flies him

out again. Films are made like that, aren't they? I don't even
know what it cost, *The Killing Fields*.

Around $15million.

Is that all? I've got to think it cost more than that. Maybe it
didn't.

And Pran's reaction?

I think pre-release we went down to the NFT, where we had a
screening for all the wads, and at the end of the film we were all
supposed to get up on stage and be pious. Which I hate. Were we
all donating our fees to the Cambodian Relief Fund? No, we
weren't. We were film-makers who had done pretty well out of
this picture. Everyone was up there with their speech about how
this must never happen again, and then Pran's turn came, and
that's where one hears his reaction, because he didn't talk about
the film, he talked about Cambodia. Everyone was crying, and
he was crying too, and he was saying [*Oriental accent*], 'Yes, it's
a film, but about my country.' He came out of Cambodia after
that unspeakable tragedy and came to the worst side of America,
living in squalor among the lowest of the low with 'Get the fuck
out' written in spray paint on his wall. It would be like seeing
England torn up. Someone makes a film about England being
torn up and you're standing there in, say, New York and you
can't talk about the film, you talk about why the film was made.
And that's what he talked about. It was very moving.

When you mentioned Sylvester Stallone, presumably you were
thinking about *Rambo: First Blood Part II*, which must have put your
success in perspective.

I really learned some lessons out of that. *The Killing Fields* –
'Great anti-war film'. And two weeks later here's Stallone
rushing up the Mekong Delta with his huge tits stuck out
blowing the locals away with an M-15. It did three times the
business. Now what do you learn from that? Well, the first thing
you learn is that film is there as a medium to entertain people. 57

That's what it's for, and the message and all the rest of it is just fantasy. Puttnam came down here and was giving a speech at the Hay Literary Festival about the moral importance of cinema, saying how there's a big responsibility on the film-maker to change points of view. From the audience I said, 'Name one movie that's ever changed anything.' He came up with *The Battle of Algiers*.

Puttnam apparently wanted *The Killing Fields* to be *The Battle of Algiers* meets *Apocalypse Now*. Did he describe it that way to you?

He may have come up with that in respect of the way he talked to Roland about it but it was never said to me. A brilliant film, *The Battle of Algiers*, but how has that changed anything? In North Africa at the moment there's a terrible civil war going on that never seems to get into our papers. It's in Algeria. There are terrible atrocities, kids having their throats cut every night, and these guys aren't saying, 'I tell you what. Before we go out to cut some throats, we'd better just take a look at this, because it might change our perspective.' Films don't change anyone's perspective. They really don't. I cannot think of a single movie that has actually, palpably produced a shift in the perceptions of the people who live on this planet. I just don't believe there is one.

Puttnam isn't alone in that view, not in relation to *The Killing Fields* at any rate. William Shawcross, the author of *Sideshow*; Jon Swain; John Pilger, whose documentary *Cambodia Year Zero* was apparently shown to the cast and crew; they all believe that one film can raise public awareness and help force change.

I disagree. In the short term, if you've never heard of Cambodia and you're sitting there in Normal, Illinois, and you think, 'Fuck me, is it this bad out there?' maybe you put a penny in the sack. But it's exactly the Kosovo situation, isn't it? We've all seen the most heinous footage imaginable coming out of those camps in the Second World War, and Yugoslavia was a recipient of a lot of that, and they're doing it again a year ago in Europe. I don't believe that movies change anything. I do believe in this horrible combination of words, 'compassion fatigue'. That, to me, is reality. You get the earthquake in Turkey: 'Oh, it's dreadful!' Of course it's dreadful, and it's people's lives, and you all send your stuff out, and then there's another one. We can't face another one. Then there's one in Japan. Now there's one in Iran. How do we face all these things? A feature film has minimal impact in the context of all these earthquakes and wars.

One of the bloodiest, dirtiest Cambodia-type wars was supported by our country, and that's in East Timor. We were supplying a lot of the weapons and planes for the Indonesians to commit genocide, and they were doing it for years and years, and it didn't suit us to make a movie about that or even put it on television. It's just not there, so if it's not there it probably isn't happening. It's all totally selective, as shown by the war in Africa I was talking about which we're passively supporting with arms, ammunition and all the rest of it. What a thing to do. They say, 'Well, if *we* don't give them the bullets the French will.' All right, let the fucking French face the morality of that, then. It's like saying, 'Well, if *we* don't give children heroin somebody else will.' I'd rather somebody else did. I can't come to terms with the fact that England is the world's second biggest arms exporter. It's horrendous.

You objected to the use of 'Imagine' at the end of the film. Its naïvety seems at odds with reality, but according to Joffé that was the point. The Khmer Rouge did imagine no religion and no possessions, which is the basis of Communism, and one man's dream was another country's nightmare.

I don't believe him. I think that's after the event. I don't think he sat down and said, 'Imagine what the Khmer Rouge had in mind.' I don't know how one could apply the archetypal pacifist of the sixties and seventies to the mechanics of something like the Khmer Rouge. That's an intellectual leap I can't make. What I objected to in 'Imagine' was we'd just spent two hours trying to make our statement about what shits these politicians are, and then we wheel in John Lennon to put the full stop on it.

I liked the fact that the final images of the film are not of Pran and Schanberg walking off into the sunset but of other Cambodians in the refugee camp who are denied a happy ending.

That's right, and that's the context in which I see his choice of 'Imagine'. All the people living in the world today can be happy, but this is the reality. I thought it was a cheap shot, and Roland knew I thought it was, but it was his film so he put it on. If there is a criticism I have of him it's not about the film – no one could have shot it better – it's about his reaction to it. He became very pious about it: 'This is how we solve the problem of war.' He's very drawn to those kind of subjects, though.

Stallone might not have been under consideration but were other name actors up for the part of Schanberg?

I think there was a lot of that in the running at the time, as I remember – not that I had any say in that department. I do remember talk of that guy who was in *The French Connection*. What's his name?

Gene Hackman.

I remember him being on the cards. He's a fantastic actor. And I think Hoffman was also on the cards at one point. I wasn't party to those discussions, but I do remember those two names. If you were hawking *The Killing Fields* around Hollywood now, well, who's your star? Sam Waterston is a very good actor, but he's not an A-list star. [*American accent*] 'Is this a vehicle for Tom Cruise?' 'No, I want to make it with a non-star.' 'Who's gonna play the other part? We're gonna have to get Johnny Depp and put some make-up on him.' 'No, an unknown Cambodian doctor is going to play that part.' 'OK, we'll be in touch.' You'd never get away with it.

What were the benefits of casting Sam Waterston, an actor rather than a star?

It was a very sensible piece of casting, because the star of the movie unquestionably is Dith Pran. Roland – if it was him, which I assume it was – played a blinder there: Haing S. Ngor, in that role, was wonderful. It's lucky he was a natural screen actor. One of my criteria for an actor or an actress is this feeling of whether they stick to the celluloid. They're not slightly in front of it or slightly behind it, they *are* it. The trouble with those kind of parts is that the next time you see an actor like him he's in a James Bond movie playing the rich Vietnamese guy at the end of the roulette table who's got a pile of dollars and a couple of lines. There are very few parts for Asians in American cinema. I guess it'll get better as integration goes on. Black Americans have been about for one hundred and fifty, two hundred years in the States, and it's only in the last forty years that you've started to get black actors in pictures, and in the last thirty years black stars.

If anything, Haing Ngor had a worse time than Dith Pran. He lost his wife and most of his family in Cambodia.

Much worse. In fact, he wrote a book about it called *Surviving the Killing Fields*. I met him after the film – I didn't meet him before – but only in a social way. It seemed a horrible coda, then he gets through all that horror then some drugged-out arsehole kills him for forty dollars. It's almost unbelievable. That place where he got murdered, though, is a particularly insalubrious part of Los Angeles. Inglewood, down near the airport, is not a place you want to fuck around in. That's part of the reason Sophie and I decided we no longer wanted to be in LA: it's a scary place. You've got the richest area on earth, which is Bel Air and Beverly Hills, and literally a few miles away one of the poorest areas, South Central. Sunset Boulevard cuts LA in half. I had a friend who was a senior policeman there, and when they had the riots he said, 'We don't give a fuck if they want to burn down their own grocery stores and shoot each other. Where we start giving a fuck is when they cross Sunset Boulevard, because we are basically here to protect and serve wealthy people.' All the police cars in LA have got 'To protect and serve' written on the side. What they don't bother to paint in is, 'The rich'.

In your BAFTA acceptance speech for Best Adapted Screenplay, you confined your thanks to Roland Joffé: 'I sort of conceived the thing, but he brought it up – and did it wonderfully, in my opinion.'

Sure. Well, it's true. What pissed me off there was we were all sitting at these tables, and I can't remember the director that got the BAFTA award that year, but clearly it should have been him. It should have been Roland Joffé. Here's all these awards floating around and everyone's getting one except Roland, and I genuinely felt that was absurd and unfair. It was like a kick in the balls, in exactly the same way as *Chariots of Fire* a year or two earlier: Puttnam gets an Oscar, the writer gets an Oscar, but Hugh Hudson ludicrously doesn't get an Oscar. The director is the guy who has to stand there for eighteen hours a day and try and make it work, and Roland had made *The Killing Fields* work, and that's why I did say that. I just thought it was all wrong that Roland didn't get anything. They gave Haing two, one for Best Newcomer and one for Best Supporting Actor, or something. I thought, 'Give Ngor one, and give Roland one, for Christ's sake.'

I assume you take awards quite seriously, then?

Everyone likes to get awards. I got an *Evening Standard* award for *Withnail*. I'd been in Australia and I said, 'I'm not flying 12,000 miles to sit there and gawp,' but they said, 'You have won it,' so I said, 'All right, I'll come back.' Now for right or wrong I've got this reputation of being a bit acerbic, and this geezer comes up to me half an hour before I'm supposed to get my award and says, 'You do realise the Duchess of Kent is handing these out?' I said, 'Yeah, sure, I've just seen her over there.' He said, 'Well, you must defer to her. When you go up there you must bow and call her "Your Royal Highness"'. I said, 'What are you telling me? Do you think I've got no manners? Fuck your award. Give it to somebody else.' Then he's like, 'Oh, Mr Robinson . . .' and I said, 'Fuck it. I don't want it,' and I refused to go up there. Now they're in a two-and-eight because it's got my name engraved on it and they can't give it to anyone else, so Richard E. Grant's sitting on the other side of the room and they go whining over to him, 'Would you collect Bruce's award and tell the audience he's in Australia?' He says, 'All right,' goes up and collects my award, and meanwhile there's a close-up of me watching him take it. I just thought they were so rude. Did they think I was going to go up there to meet the Duchess of Kent with my cock hanging out? Of course I would have been polite to her. It was all this bowing bollocks: I wouldn't have bowed, and I won't.

The precedent for this was *The Killing Fields*, where I became *persona non grata* because at the Royal Performance here's Princess Anne coming down the line, and here's Roland and Puttnam – who wasn't a knight then – throwing themselves onto the carpet in front of her, and here's me saying to myself silently, 'What are you going to do, Robinson? You've always said, "Bollocks to this. You ain't going to bow to anybody." Will you bow?' And the voice in my head's saying, 'No. I will not bow to her or the Queen or anybody else. I will be polite and shake her hand.' Which I did, and when the contact sheets came in of that night, it hadn't happened: every single picture with me and her in was blacked out. I thought, 'All right. If that's what they think.' How can you bow? It's like imperial Japan. As a matter of fact, I have great respect for the old Queen, and bizarrely, considering my politics, I'm a supporter of the Royal Family. Not so much them, but I'm terrified of what might replace them. I'd rather they were there than President Blair. But I'm fucked if I'm going to bow to them. If you're after a knighthood then perhaps it's incumbent upon you to eat the carpet, but what do I want to look down her cleavage for?

Were you disappointed when you lost the Oscar for Best Adapted Screenplay to Peter Shaffer and *Amadeus*?

Well, I never thought I was going to get a nomination. That was very nice. Certainly a film that I considered very ephemeral, the Mozart film, is not a good contender to lose to. I would much rather have lost to something I really respected, like *In the Heat of the Night* or *Mississippi Burning* or something. I just thought it was a crummy movie, but there you go. It was phenomenal to

63

get that far: to have my first screenplay – or produced screenplay – get an Oscar nomination. I must have a look at the film again; I haven't seen it for fifteen years. I've got the video but I've never watched it. I'm confident enough now to look at it. I've been very critical of Roland over the years for various things, but I've got to say he made a marvellous job of *The Killing Fields*. I can't imagine anyone could have done it better. He is a brilliant film director. What he isn't is a writer, and if only he'd come to terms with that I think he'd start making brilliant movies again.

In the acres of press coverage of the film, articles and interviews and reviews, Puttnam and Joffé were both mentioned far more frequently than you.

Of course. Puttnam does have a respect for writers that a lot of producers don't have, but by the time they get to make the film the writer's long gone, usually writing something else. Because it was my first film, it came as quite a shock. To coincide with the film somebody called Christopher Hudson did a novelisation of the screenplay and after two years of absolute toil I wasn't even invited to the launch party. I didn't get a copy of it either.

The Killing Fields **allegedly made you the highest-paid screenwriter in Britain.**

I don't think so. I mean, we had Pinter and Stoppard and all those guys. I probably made the highest jump as a screenwriter – to £250,000, which I got paid for *The Killing Fields*. Until then, I'd taken great comfort from writers that I like who had a bad time getting their stuff done. I still do. The great thing about the ones that get away, whether they're hits, misses or in the middle, is that sometimes you go to the movies and you're glad to be in this business. What's the guy called who wrote that book about his time at Goldcrest, *My Indecision is Final?*

Jake Eberts.

Yeah. We were at a dinner party at Terry Semel's house in Los Angeles, which is like Blenheim Palace. Semel was running

Warner Bros, and I think he still does. We were sitting there and clearly audiences were going with *The Killing Fields*, and Jake Eberts was saying to me, 'What are you going to do next, Bruce?' I said, 'It looks like I'm going to write this atomic bomb film for Warners, but what I'd really like to do' – and I wasn't talking about me as a director – 'is get my little film made.' He said, 'What is your little film?' – i.e. 'Bring it to us' – and I said, 'It's about two out-of-work actors in London in the sixties.' He said [*American accent*], 'Fuck! I gotta tell you this. I just had this script over my desk about two out-of-work actors in London in the sixties.' And he proceeds to tell me about *Withnail*. 'It's the most godawful unfunny thing I ever read. I don't know what yours is about, but let me tell you if it hadn't been recommended I'd never have got through it. It's just shit.' I finally said, 'Yeah, that's my story.' So there you go.

Chapter Three

'A fascinating paradox'

Fat Man and Little Boy

How did you come to write the original script for _Fat Man and Little Boy_?

It was when David Puttnam and Hugh Hudson were very close. Hugh wanted to do a film about the atomic bomb, and David sent me an awful novel about its development. The writer was so misinformed that he didn't dare call the character Oppenheimer, he called him Bamburger. I said, 'This is ludicrous. I can't possibly do this novel, but clearly the subject is of great interest. Give me a few months to see if I can find a story.' A guy called Peter Goodchild had just made a series for the BBC about the development of the atomic bomb, and I thought, 'If that's what the story is, what's the point of going through all that again in a feature?' Goodchild portrayed the army guy who ran the Manhattan Project, General Leslie Groves, as a sort of bumbling idiot, and that's the way Groves has been portrayed in a lot of the literature about The Bomb. It's expedient to do it. He had absurd lines like [_American accent_], 'Tell me, Dr Oppenheimer, are you a Communist?' Groves built the Pentagon; this guy was no idiot. He was a highly intelligent, incredibly capable and very devious man.

There was a BBC series simply called _Oppenheimer_, in which Sam Waterston coincidentally played the title role.

That was probably it. Anyway, I was looking for a story that wasn't like the BBC story, and they gave me a research budget which I started carving into. I was in Los Angeles and the first thing I did was what the scientists had done: get a train to Albuquerque and start at Los Alamos. For the next two or three months I read everything I could, and I couldn't really find anything that was new or original until I suddenly got this breakthrough. It went on like a lightbulb, *viz*: the race for an atomic bomb between Nazi Germany and the Allied Powers was bullshit. It was a piece of opportunism that has always been sold to us as an historical fact. The Germans were building the most destructive weapons they could, as were England and America, but the 'race' for The Bomb between the three nations was a lie, and it seemed to me a fascinating paradox that the most secret and most expensive project in the history of mankind – bigger than the pyramids – was premised on a lie.

I thought this was strong enough to sustain a story about the Manhattan Project that hadn't been exercised before. Little did I know that this was the very tip of the iceberg. I thought *that* was the secret, but it wasn't. You can see from my shelves that I've read virtually every serious book that's ever been written about The Bomb, and some of them are considered definitive, and without question they've all got it wrong in one of the most important areas. I know that sounds ludicrous, but they've all got it wrong.

Did you do more research for this than you did for *The Killing Fields*?

Oh, infinitely. As soon as I got this idea assembled, that there was no arms race, I had to go about the business of proving it. Almost without exception the senior scientists who built the atomic bomb were Jews on the run from the Nazis. Hitler kicked them all out, including the greatest Jew of them all, Einstein. Hitler called nuclear energy 'Jewish physics'. The world experts on it, people like Edward Teller, Leo Szilard and Enrico Fermi, had fled to America, and ultimately Groves and his ilk thought, 'Let's herd all these guys in and tell them we've got to build a bomb because we're in a desperate race with Hitler.' There were just one or two world-class nuclear scientists left in occupied Europe: Niels Bohr in Denmark – and he ended up at Los Alamos – and Carl Friedrich von Weizsacker and Werner Heisenberg in Germany. When two German scientists, Strassman and Hann, achieved fission in 1939, they published this startling breakthrough in *Nature*, and if you're about to start a war and you're looking for a nuclear weapon it's not too smart to put what you've discovered in an international science magazine.

Once I was onto this, I started hassling the Atomic Energy Commission and the various Army departments with requests under the Freedom of Information Act to begin the painful business of extracting a confirmation. Normally how the Freedom of Information Act works is it's like playing poker with a multi-millionaire: they'll always win because they can always up the ante. You ask for a certain thing and they send it back all blacked out, saying, 'Should this not be sufficient, you must write back enclosing a research cheque.' We had the funds, and I or my assistant were writing back saying, 'No, this isn't sufficient. We want Document blah blah, 1942,' and two weeks later that would come back all blacked out, with, 'Should this not be sufficient . . .' We played the same game as they were playing with us, because we could afford to do it.

And because you could afford a research assistant.

Yeah, because it was Warner Bros. And we did ultimately get the information. Man A over there will give you half the information about where the treasure's hidden, Man B over here will give you the other half, you put A and B together and then you make a re-application to a new Department of State in Washington or wherever – it's all over the country – to get what you need to know. In short, that the US and British governments categorically knew by Spring 1943 that the threat of a Nazi atomic bomb was over as far as the Allies were concerned. By January 1943 they *knew* the Germans weren't building an atomic bomb, and they didn't begin the Manhattan Project until March 1943, so if there is no threat from Germany in January what are you building the atomic bomb for in March?

Then here comes the popular fable which was filmed as *The Heroes of Telemark*, with the commandos going in to blow up the so-called heavy-water plants in Norway. It is true the Germans were taking small amounts of heavy water from Norway, but they were using it as a medium to try and build a nuclear reactor for their U-boats and there was no way they were taking enough to sustain a chain reaction. Szilard talks about the Americans producing a ton of heavy water a month and it wasn't nearly enough. I subsequently discovered, and the cynicism is quite astonishing, that the reason the Rujukan plant was blown up was to protect the patents of the DuPont Corporation, who wanted to exploit the domestic use of nuclear energy after the war. DuPont had acquired the rights to the exploitation of nuclear energy postwar for one dollar and didn't want any competition. Their trade-off was to put in enormous amounts of money during the war to assist in the construction of the uranium facility at Oak Ridge, Tennessee, and the plutonium facility at Hanford, Washington.

There was a cyclotron in Japan that was destroyed in 1945 by the American Army under the instructions of Groves for the same reason: they didn't want anyone else to have it. A cyclotron, at its simplest, is a device wherein something called uranium 235 can be manufactured. When you mine uranium ores you get 238, which isn't explosive and can't be made to fission, but 238 will produce minute amounts of 235 – and that's what was used in the 'Little Boy' bomb. The whole of American industry was involved in one way or another and none of them knew why they were doing it. The word used was 'compartmentalisation'. The people in Oak Ridge didn't know what the people in Los Alamos were doing, and the people in Los Alamos didn't know what the guys at the cyclotron in Berkeley was doing, and so on. So all that was fairly fascinating, but . . .

You were still looking for the story.

I was still looking for the story, and the story started to develop out of Oppenheimer and his relationship with this woman called Jean Tatlock. I knew that Oppenheimer had this ex-lover and I wanted to find out about her, so I went to Berkeley where she was a student and virtually everything relevant to her had vanished. I knew she had come from Berkeley, so I went to the San Francisco library and I got out a 1938 telephone directory and I looked her up. Her address was up in the Heights, a very salubrious area indeed, and I think, 'At least I can start there: knock on a couple of doors and hopefully find someone who may remember Jean Tatlock.' I get a cab up there, and here are all these expensive houses with one house locked and abandoned, the windows painted black on the inside. So here I am, standing in front of this house, totally and utterly bemused. It said in the phone book this is where she lived, and here's this rotten tooth in this row of gleaming dentures. Now it's back to the library to get the microfiche out, and I start researching what may have happened to her.

Oppenheimer was liberal to the point of being considered a Communist. He was a liberal and his then girlfriend Jean, who he was very much in love with, was a liberal. When the war came along and Groves was looking for a scientist to run the Manhattan Project, he knew that Oppenheimer could be his man, but no one in the security services would countenance him. Groves faced an enormous dilemma: 'How do I prove that Oppenheimer is safe?' And I repeatedly asked myself that question: 'How could Groves have been so sure?' So I proposed a hypothesis for myself and then desperately tried to destroy it, because it was far-out at the time and still is pretty far-out now. My hypothesis was this: 'No-one wants Oppenheimer, and I'm General Groves and I do want him. What am I going to do? I know what I'd do, I'd test him out.' Cut to what actually happened, a famous event called the 'Chevalier Incident'.

In 1943, before Oppenheimer went to Los Alamos, he was having cocktails with his wife Kitty and a close friend, Hakon Chevalier, at Eagle Hill, which was Oppenheimer's house in Berkeley. Oppenheimer is fixing drinks in the kitchen and Chevalier comes in and says in a roundabout way, 'Can you give me some information on this nuclear thing which I can pass back to our war-stricken allies, the Russians?' Now, this project was so new and so secret it was unbelievable, so how does Chevalier even know about it and know how to ask the question? He asks it because a man called George Eltenton, a so-called union activist at the Shell Oil plant in Emeryville, California, and ostensibly a Soviet agent, approached Chevalier to approach Oppenheimer. Oppenheimer tells Chevalier, 'No way. I'm not going to give anybody anything, particularly the Soviets, and how dare you ask me.' Chevalier goes back to Eltenton and says, 'He said, "Absolutely not. Under no circumstances can I hand over anything to you or the Soviet Union.'"

Eltenton now knows Oppenheimer ain't talking, but he doesn't go and tell the Soviets, he goes via a circuitous route and tells Groves, because Eltenton was an MI6 spy. In the Second World War the Shell Corporation was a vehicle for putting MI6 all over the world. Now Groves is a hundred per cent certain that Oppenheimer is safe: if he isn't telling his best friend, Chevalier, he isn't telling anybody. What Groves didn't do – and it ended in tragedy for Oppenheimer and Tatlock – is tell the Army Intelligence Unit, namely a man called Colonel John Lansdale who was in charge of G2 Security, that he'd made this test. Lansdale is still very anti-Oppenheimer, always questioning his past and his loyalty, and to get round and cover up the 'Chevalier Incident', Oppenheimer says, 'I may have been approached by somebody.' 'Who?' says Lansdale, and naturally Oppenheimer can't say, 'My best friend,' for fear of the consequences, so he says, 'Three scientists may have mentioned something to me.' 'Who?' 'I can't tell you that.' 'Why not?' And so it went on. Of course there *were* no three scientists.

Why didn't Groves tell Lansdale that?

Groves was the most secretive man I've ever come across. He had one gang of secrets with Lansdale, one gang of secrets with Oppenheimer, one gang of secrets with the President of the United States and the Secretary of War, Stimpson, and one gang of secrets with the British. He ran the atomic bomb programme on a need-to-know basis, and he didn't think Lansdale needed to know. Lansdale went to Groves and said, 'I want to know who these three scientists are.' Groves said, 'There's no problem with them. I know they're safe and I trust Oppenheimer.' Lansdale isn't satisfied and sometime later goes back to him and says, 'Is one of them Oppenheimer's brother Frank?' Trying to avoid the question, Groves says, 'In the strictest secrecy, I'll tell you: it's possible.' To which Lansdale replies, 'Bullshit. I know it isn't Frank Oppenheimer. I know what time Frank Oppenheimer shits. If you won't tell me who these guys are I'll have to take this thing further.'

Meanwhile, Oppenheimer is at Los Alamos with Kitty, building the bomb, but every time he comes back to San Francisco on official business he's going off and fucking Jean Tatlock. She's now training in Berkeley to become a child psychiatrist at the Ann Arbor Hospital in Michigan. What Oppenheimer didn't know is that Jean had other boyfriends: Mason Robertson, a black Communist journalist on *The People's Daily World* – a left-wing newspaper in California championing the cause of the Spanish Civil War and the cotton pickers in the southern United States – and the black singer Paul Robeson, who was also a very well-known Communist.

Groves knows Oppenheimer is safe; Lansdale doesn't. Groves knows Tatlock is safe; Lansdale doesn't. He asks, 'Is Tatlock one of the people who approached Oppenheimer?' Groves stonewalls, and despite the threat of a court-martial for nagging at this, what Lansdale does is override him. Groves, and everyone down from Groves, is controlled by G2 Security, but Jean Tatlock is a civilian, under the jurisdiction of the FBI, so Lansdale goes to J. Edgar Hoover in Washington and lays it all on him via two agents called Tamm and Whison. Paraphrasing him, Hoover says, 'Fuck this. Oppenheimer is not only committing adultery, which I don't like, but the girl is a Communist, which I don't like even more. I don't like Communists, I don't like adultery, I don't like blacks, and we've got the most secret and expensive project in the history of mankind that could win us the war. This bitch is the perfect Soviet letter-box. We've got to take her out.' Four days later Jean Tatlock is dead. She supposedly writes a suicide note, takes a bunch of chloralhydrate, and drowns herself in her bath. Apparently she was manically depressed and she'd been seeing a psychiatrist.

Now we start taking that apart. Until this point, by the way, I'd never seen a photograph of her; they seemed to have disappeared from any of the places one would expect to find them. So me and my assistant, Anne Gardener, sit in my little office at Warner Bros with every phone book in the United States, and call every Tatlock in America. It took us four days. We didn't know who or why or what. We're in New Mexico, we're in New York, we're in wherever. Finally, phone call three thousand, nine hundred and forty-six: 'This is Warner Bros . . .'

'She was my sister.' This guy lives in Vermont, and that was where we got the first photograph. Now I'm after any and all information about this woman because I'm so suspicious. I assemble as many facts as I can, and because I'm a storyteller not a historian I throw them up in the air and see how they come down. My assistant said to me, 'You're going too far. They wouldn't have killed her.' I said, 'I'm telling you they did.' To prove that they did another six months' research is involved.

I got her autopsy reports to Professor Keith Simpson, a leading forensic pathologist in this country, and he looks at them and says, 'These are bullshit.' If someone with the importance of Oppenheimer's lover drowns in the bath the authorities are going to do a very detailed autopsy, because perhaps she was killed in a botched hit against Oppenheimer, by the Russians, the Germans or Christ knows who. Of prime importance, one of the first things you do when someone's drowned is a thing called a diatomaceous test. Diatoms are tiny one-celled organisms that live in water, and if someone's dead in the bath you take fluid from the lungs, the brain or whatever, and check for diatoms because maybe they were drowned in a river and slung in the bath to make it look like suicide. No diatomaceous test was done. It didn't take long to prove that the whole autopsy was an inadequate invention. Then we go after the psychiatrist and the 'suicide note'.

'She'd been seeing a psychiatrist for two years because of depression,' said the newspapers. In actual fact, she'd been seeing a psychiatrist for two years and paying to have lessons with him for her forthcoming job in Michigan. We found her friends who were still living. 'Jean depressed? No way. She was a good-time girl. She loved life.' Piece by piece we get to the point where, had I been the cop I would have made the arrest. The G2/FBI people had her murdered. They gave her chloralhydrate to knock her out, slung her in the bathtub, faked a note, and within a day or two – because her father was a very prominent man in the Berkeley area – there are newspaper reports talking about Jean Tatlock's suicide. I've got a tape somewhere of me confronting Colonel Lansdale, who was now an old man, and you should hear his astonishment that someone had finally busted it.

Groves must have realised what had happened.

Oh, he knew. He absolutely knew. It's indicative that in Groves' postwar account of the Manhattan Project, *Now It Can Be Told*, he mentions neither Chevalier, Eltenton nor Tatlock, yet these three were among the major players in Oppenheimer's subsequent destruction at the hands of the Atomic Energy Commission. In the 1954 hearings, Lansdale was asked, 'Why did you go to the FBI?' Fighting sudden and uncharacteristic amnesia he said, 'I went there about Frank Oppenheimer because he was a leftie and we were worried about him.' But In reality Frank was a co-ordinator in the Manhattan Project – he would travel to Washington, Los Alamos, Oak Ridge, anywhere he needed to – and he was also constantly supervised by G2 Security. I actually have a staggering letter from Groves sent towards the end of the war congratulating Frank on his invaluable contribution to the project. In any case, there was huge competition, a turf war, between the civil and military authorities, they didn't even share information, so there was no way on earth Lansdale would go to the FBI about Frank Oppenheimer, because Frank was already under his jurisdiction. It had to be a civilian. Groves must have gone apeshit, not because he was worried about the death of Jean Tatlock, but because he was worried about the effect this might have on Oppenheimer, and indeed the news wasn't immediately made available to Oppenheimer.

I believe this ruined Oppenheimer's life. This doesn't end in 1945 with The Bomb. The security system that had been put in place rears its head again. Oppenheimer drops the gruesome duo on Japan, then he goes to the new President, Truman, and he says, 'We've got blood on our hands.' The President doesn't like this at all. Oppenheimer wouldn't readily build the Super-Weapon that Teller wanted to develop all the way through Los Alamos – they're all trying to make an *atomic* bomb and he's constantly talking about the *hydrogen* bomb – and they think, 'Oppenheimer won't do it, so we'd better get rid of him.' Which they did. He was a moral man among immoral men, a dangerous pearl in the oyster. Teller takes over from Oppenheimer because Teller is enthusiastically prepared to build the Super-Weapon. Then they use the affair with Tatlock, who they'd murdered, and the 'Chevalier Incident', which they'd set up, as an indication that Oppenheimer is not to be trusted with highly classified information, and Chevalier has to flee to Paris where he subsequently lived in exile.

Eltenton wasn't a Soviet spy. He was working for MI6, whether he actively knew it or not. He was in the process of applying for US citizenship when the US Government decided it was time to go for Oppenheimer, and Eltenton is out of America overnight. He's gone, disappeared. And where had he disappeared to? He'd disappeared to the Wirral, just outside Liverpool, where he carried on his job for Shell Oil in England. Here's Klaus Fuchs, a senior theoretical physicist at Los Alamos, serving nine years in jail for conspiring to supply information to the Russians, and what does Eltenton get? He gets his job back at Shell. When I was trying to find out about him, a letter was forwarded to me from the then Home Secretary, Leon Brittan. I couldn't get anywhere, and a Tory MP that I knew rather well – who was quite close to Mrs Thatcher – became fascinated with this and wrote a personal note about Eltenton to Brittan. Brittan said, 'I'm afraid I can't talk about this. It's totally inappropriate.' He'd probably had his civil servants check it out and found that this guy was MI6. Even though this is historical stuff it's very volatile. None of it was in the film.

Volatile enough for your phone to be tapped, a story which David Puttnam gave to the *Daily Mail* in this country.

Yeah, he did, and that's a reflection of his and my security system. I did the research in Los Angeles for eighteen months then I came back to London to write it, and my phone was tapped here and in the US. Warner Bros were renting me this house in LA, and how the phone system works in America is you phone up Bell or Western Union and tell them what you want and they say, 'Come down and collect them, take them back, wait an hour, plug them in, and they'll work.' So I go and get my phones and give them my American Express card, which says 'Mr B. Robinson'. A couple of months go by and I'm making a lot of Freedom of Information requests and calls to various government departments, and someone out there puts two and two together and makes three and a half. I get this call and they say [*American accent*], 'Mr Robinson, you're making a lot of long-distance calls here.' I said, 'That's right.' They say, 'We're just phoning to check on your service.' I said, 'It's absolutely fine. I'm terribly busy. I'll let you know if it doesn't work.' They say, 'Sir, could I just confirm your name? It is Mr Bruce Christopher Robinson?' I said, 'Yeah,' put the phone down, was sitting by the swimming pool reading, and that's when I figured out someone was onto the phone, because Christopher is a name I *never* use.

By the time we got back to England – and Sophie will corroborate this – they *wanted* me to know they were listening. Conversations I was having with my researcher and various other people in the States would literally be interrupted, and a voice would be on there saying [*American*], 'Sorry, I'll put you back to the Operator.' They were trying to freak me out, and indeed they did freak me out, which is why I used to copy all my letters to Puttnam. I made sure that everything I was finding out he was finding out, because if they were going to give me a bad time they'd have to give him one too.

Did the studio give you a deadline for turning in the script?

Originally, but it went straight down the nearest toilet. John Calley was in charge of this project – and had formerly been in charge of Warner Bros – and Calley is a very smart man. I guess they got to the point where they thought, 'We're not going to get this until 2006,' but Calley was sufficiently interested in what I was uncovering to leave me alone. The same with Puttnam.

The project eventually became a Tony Garnett production of a Roland Joffé film for Paramount, rather than a David Puttnam production of a Hugh Hudson film for Warner Bros. How did that come about?

It all got out of hand. It was originally scheduled to be shot by Hugh, then he was elbowed and Roland came in on the back of his success with *The Killing Fields*, then when I delivered I got elbowed. When I put the draft in Calley was over the moon with it; he was so complimentary it was ridiculous. Then I didn't hear a word from anybody until I ran into Roland at a preview screening of Hugh Hudson's film *Revolution*. Roland comes up to me and says, 'Did you know we're making The Bomb?' I said, 'No, I didn't know that.' And that was it. That was the last contact I had with Roland on that script. Not, 'Come in and sit down, I want to talk to you about some of these scenes, and why this and why that and why the other, and can we do this, can we do that, can we do the other?' Nothing. No one had even phoned me and said that they were doing it. It's unreal.

Meanwhile, he'd had a whole legion of idiots who knew nothing about this subject fucking around with the screenplay, culminating in him fucking around with it, and he was like one of the passengers suddenly flying the 747. He had no idea, and that's what I find unforgivable, and that's why I fell out with him in a big way. I've got nothing against him personally, but he was an arsehole as far as the atomic bomb was concerned. Anyone in their right mind wanting to make a film that complex after the work I'd put in at least should have scheduled a weekend with me. I'm an absolute mine of knowledge on the atomic bomb. They weren't. I'd spent two and a half years working on it. They hadn't. So why not ask me rather than hire some prick living in the San Fernando Valley who probably reads two quick paperbacks before he starts hacking at it? I was almost insane with this. I can't tell you the amount of effort involved in researching and writing that script.

Garnett gave the impression in an interview about the film that he and Joffé didn't come on board until after the script had been rewritten several times.

Under the auspices of whom? That simply is not true. There was *one* screenplay – that I'd written, that John Calley had – and Roland came on and started hiring different writers. There were four or five writers on this, and any screenplay that has more than one writer has an automatic arbitration by the Writers Guild. Even if I said, 'I don't care,' they'd still arbitrate. These scripts were coming in via the WGA with people seeking credit on this film, and they were unreadable they were such nonsense. We were back to the Peter Goodchild horseshit: 'Tell me, Dr Oppenheimer, are you a Communist?' As if. Here's one of the most intelligent men in America, the guy who built the Pentagon. He's now been entrusted with the development of the atomic bomb, and he's going to ask Oppenheimer if he's a fucking Communist, and if Oppenheimer says, 'No, I'm not,' he'll say, 'Oh, good, I just wanted to clarify that.' Roland's intention, which is one of the reasons I was outraged by him, was not even to give me a credit at all, to say that it was written and directed by Roland Joffé. By then I didn't want a credit on the thing, but the WGA had arbitrated and if you look at the credits on *Fat Man* you'll see that it's 'Screenplay by Bruce Robinson and Roland Joffé, Story by Bruce Robinson'. They gave me two credits; I didn't ask for them.

Why did all this happen if John Calley liked your draft so much?

He thinks that a massive error was made. You've got to remember the circumstances. Roland had just come off *The Killing Fields* and was the blue-eyed boy; then he won the Palme d'Or for *The Mission* in Cannes and what Roland said went. 'I want to do this.' 'All right, Roland. You do it.' I think the tidal wave of ego on which he surfs didn't serve this project particularly well. Retrospectively, people like Calley have said, 'What the fuck did we do?' John's actually said that to me. I'm incensed even now, fifteen years later, about what happened to that film.

In any case, its release coincided with Japanese corporations like Sony buying American companies such as Columbia, so the mood in America may not have been right for a film saying The Bomb shouldn't have been dropped on Japan.

I think it played four days in New York before they pulled it. They changed the title because everyone thought it was a comedy. It was too late to change it for America, but they called it *Shadow Makers* in this country. It was the most expensive flop that Paramount had ever made: I have that on good authority.

According to the various interviews, Joffé and Garnett did roughly two years of research before making the film.

The amount of research time that someone like Roland can put in is minimal. He's not going to sit there like I would sit there, out of bed at six every morning working until midnight seven days a week, reading all this stuff trying to find out where these things developed from and why it went like it went. Roland probably starts researching from the script, and he's not going to find out anything that I haven't spent months investigating before I delivered. He gets the script, and because he doesn't realise *why* it's written in the way it's written he thinks, 'I could change that,' rather than asking me, 'Why did you do it like that?' or 'Where did you get this from?' which he ultimately did try and do.

The law in America is that you can libel the dead, and they had areas of this story which, unless they could prove them, were consequently libellous. They wouldn't have been uptight about these elements, for example the murder of Jean Tatlock, if they'd had the evidence to prove it. Roland didn't know how I'd got to that, so they came to me via my lawyer saying, 'We want all your sources and workbooks.' I sent a letter back saying, 'You've stolen my car. Don't expect me to buy the fucking petrol.' My job was to supply them with two copies of the finished screenplay. How I got there was my affair. Of course, had I been involved in the film Roland would have had access to every single piece of research that I'd done. There are boxes and boxes of it. I've got Groves' diaries; I don't imagine many people on earth have had access to those. There's nothing I put in my screenplay that I can't prove. Nothing at all.

Roland seemed to be more interested in the mental patients who were impregnated with radioactive isotopes, and all that kind of stuff, which is not material to the story, but as he said in Sibley's documentary, it depends which way you look at it. We're all different, and we're all different writers, and we're all different directors, and if I'd sat down with a very handsome film star, albeit in his sixties, like Paul Newman, I couldn't in a million years have seen him as Groves. Roland could and I couldn't. I have great respect for Paul Newman as an actor, but to cast him as Groves seems to me to be absurd. He's completely the wrong sort of actor, and that's not just the weight thing, the fact that Newman isn't fat. If you're going to cast Paul Newman as Groves you need a star to play Oppenheimer, you need

Redford or Hoffman or Pacino. I've never heard of the guy who plays Oppenheimer.

Dwight Schultz.

Oppenheimer was a star and should have been played by a star. The reason that Groves wanted Oppenheimer is because he was so charismatic. The scientists working out of Los Alamos would have gone anywhere for him. He'd have been trusted, respected and admired by the scientists who trained under him and by the whole scientific community. He'd get on trains and planes and go into these labs and say, 'Please do this.' He had French, Italian, Hungarian, English and German guys there and he could talk to them all in their own language. He spoke several languages fluently. He taught himself Sanskrit as a hobby. He was an astonishing man, Oppenheimer, with an astonishing brain.

If Groves had gone barging into the offices of those scientists he wouldn't have got anywhere because scientists distrusted secrecy. Now there's a symbiosis between scientists and secrecy that never existed before, for example with genetic engineering and people patenting the asthma gene. If your kid's got asthma and you can afford the forensics that are going to come out of these patents, then they'll knock out the gene, but if you're a poverty-stricken kid in India you're not going to get this medicine. That isn't how science worked prewar. There were no patents on penicillin and other breakthroughs. Sir Alexander Fleming wasn't trying to monopolise a market to make loot out of it. You discover penicillin and within five minutes the information is everywhere. It isn't like that any more, and The Bomb is one of the reasons it isn't. That's where all this stuff started, keeping discoveries secret.

There were a lot of scientists more innovative and brilliant than Oppenheimer who wouldn't have taken on the job because of their innovative brilliance. Groves hit on a specific weakness that Oppenheimer had. Oppenheimer was a great scientist but not an innovative scientist. If you'd lined up Fermi, Teller, Oppenheimer, Szilard and Einstein, you could have gone down the line saying, 'Nobel Prize; Nobel Prize' – got to Oppenheimer – 'No Nobel Prize; Nobel Prize; Nobel Prize.' Groves knew that this guy wasn't going to win the Nobel Prize, but what he could do was 'win the Second World War', and that's bigger than any prize there is. By the end of the war, magazines would just put his hat on the cover and everyone knew it was J. Robert Oppenheimer. That's how famous he was.

Garnett says that he and Joffé took Faust and Mephistopheles as their image, which is quite rigorously worked through in the film.

But you don't need to be Freud to work that one out, do you? Of course it was Faust and Mephistopheles, which is why I called it *Fat Man and Little Boy*. Based on that Freudian principle 'Nothing happens by accident', it's very bizarre, and subliminally the core of the screenplay, that those bombs were called 'Fat Man' and 'Little Boy', and this enormous army guy Groves and his obedient scientist Oppenheimer who he manipulated to get them. There was a documentary called *The Day After Trinity*, and it was called that because someone asked Oppenheimer what he thought should have happened in respect of the atomic bomb, and Oppenheimer said, 'We should have stopped the day after Trinity.' Trinity was the codename for the first test in the Alamogordo Desert, and there's a famous photograph of them at the site wearing *Withnail*-type bags on their feet. You can see the fat man and little boy relationship; it's like Oppenheimer is saying to Groves, 'Is that enough? Have I done it for you?'

A little boy who got littler. Oppenheimer lost a tremendous amount of weight in the course of the Manhattan Project.

He was like a skeleton by the end of it, in a terrible condition, because he was such a moral man. The point at which he found out that the arms race with Germany was bullshit was basically when it was perfectly apparent to everybody, i.e. Germany's surrendered: 'What are we still building this thing for? You told us it was for Germany, and now that Germany's collapsed we should stop.' Half of the scientists did. I don't know whether it's in the film or not, but half of the senior scientists at Los Alamos formed this committee, went to Washington and said, 'We want out.'

A petition is discussed towards the end of the film.

That was it. Towards the end, before the Alamogordo test, Oppenheimer chaired a lot of discussion groups about the morality of this thing and whether it should or should not continue. One argument was, 'If we do use it against Japan shouldn't we have a demonstration explosion on an island in the Pacific?' and the counter argument was, 'If you designate an island, they're going to move all the American POWs onto it.' These meetings went on for three months because they didn't want to know about dumping it on anywhere else, but by then it was out of their hands anyway and Oppenheimer had come down on the side of Groves: 'We have to let this thing off.'

Dwight Schultz, who does give a fine performance, pointed out from his own character research that although in the film Oppenheimer expresses the view of scientists who wanted to stop the project after Japan surrendered, in reality he dismissed colleagues who held that view.

By the time Oppenheimer was presented with that final dilemma he was so wasted that he had nothing to say either way. If you read the contemporary accounts, Oppenheimer was saying, 'We've got to do it,' but I believe internally he wished that he was a million miles away. He was now the little boy, echoing the official government line, i.e. Groves, Stimpson *et al*, but he didn't want to drop that thing. If you want to use the analogy, Faust says in the original translation of Goethe, 'The cost is considerable,' and the cost was considerable for him. He lost everything. He lost his career, he lost Jean – who I believe he was very much in love with – he lost his family, he lost his friends. You could argue that he lost his life because of this. He died relatively young, of throat cancer, though he did smoke like a Catholic church.

How did he lose his family?

His marriage was fucked. He married Kitty when he was still in love with Jean after Jean gave him the boot. His daughter hanged herself. Oppenheimer had the weight of the world on his shoulders, as far as I understand it. He was racked with guilt over all sorts of things – not least, of course, Jean. He may have had his suspicions, I don't know; he's been dead a long time. When I met Frank Oppenheimer at Stanford University and obliquely referred to the subject of Jean he burst into tears and had me thrown off campus.

The most powerful image in the film, Oppenheimer's features contorted into a grotesque mask by the blast which is reflected in his protective goggles, fits in with Joffé's idea of Oppenheimer as the flawed hero in a classical tragedy.

Sibley showed that in the documentary, didn't he? Even that, to me, is completely wrong. The shot starts with him going to put a cigarette in his mouth, and I know a film is different to reality but there's no way he was casually lighting up – although he did casually light up eighty a day normally. The tension in that bunker was beyond belief. Oppenheimer was on the verge of unconsciousness when that bomb went off, he actually thought he was going to collapse. He knew what it was going to be used for if it did go off, and he was terrified that it would and more terrified that it wouldn't. They had a piece of Tchaikovsky playing over that.

The Nutcracker Suite is playing on a ground channel and they can't get rid of it. I thought that detail had to be true, otherwise the irony of it being that piece of music was too convenient, but the scene isn't even in your original script.

Because it had no relevance, and it certainly wasn't playing at full volume over their ground post. It's true that part of their communication system kept getting interference out of somewhere like Albuquerque, a radio station playing Tchaikovsky, but it wasn't coming in over loudspeakers in the way it's portrayed. It's a perfectly legitimate thing to do as a film-maker, to bump that up, but I wouldn't have taken that decision.

The youth of many of these scientists seems to have led to a childlike naïvety about the uses of what they were building.

You spend three years trying to make a car and suddenly you've got the petrol; do you mix the petrol with the car and see if it will go? Of course. They were scientists. They were enquirers. They had to let it off. Also, this information that I became party to was much more available to me fifty years later than it was to these guys at the time. They didn't know any of this stuff. They'd never heard of Eltenton and Chevalier and Tatlock. They didn't know what the hell was going on in Washington. They knew Groves and they knew his subordinate, Colonel Nichols, but Groves and Nichols were always on the road, they weren't there. Richard Feynman said 'I was a twenty-six-year-old child who was suddenly given anything I wanted. Of course I was going to do it.'

Feynman came up with the mathematics in respect of the Coulomb Barrier. They thought they'd set the world on fire, that the chain reaction would impact on the air and the sea and everything else and the whole world would become an atomic bomb, and Feynman said, 'It won't.' They didn't know. There's a line in the script that was actually said by a guy called Serber: 'What we're doing is designing a motor car before the invention of gasoline.' They literally were. Theoretically plutonium existed but nobody had ever seen it, so there was a commitment of $2billion by the US Government to build this monstrously expensive device without even knowing that they'd have, if you like, the gunpowder to put in it.

Could you explain how the two bombs worked?

The 'Little Boy' bomb, dropped on Hiroshima, was a uranium bomb, and the 'Fat Man' bomb, dropped on Nagasaki, was a plutonium bomb, and they used different methods of detonation. The 'Little Boy' was basically an artillery piece with a chunk of uranium, a sub-critical mass, at one end of the gun barrel, and another chunk of uranium, with a conventional explosive behind it, at the other end. They're both very unstable, and when you put these two together the instability of that mass, which is known as the critical mass, will cause the thing to become violent and release energy. They drop the bomb, and when they want it to go off, a mile and a half above the city, the conventional explosive fires that piece of uranium down into that piece and it goes critical and happens.

The 'Fat Man' bomb was much more complex. It contained plutonium and couldn't use the same detonation system, so they had to crush it. The detonation method was devised by a man called Tuck, an English explosives expert who had designed armour-piercing shells. He built explosive lenses all round it, to crush that amount of plutonium into that amount of plutonium so it'll go critical, which is why it looked like a fat sea-mine. The lens method would work if you could detonate all the explosives simultaneously, but if one was a few milliseconds out the bomb wouldn't go off. That's why they tested it. They didn't test the 'Little Boy' because they were absolutely sure it was going to work; they only tested the 'Fat Man'.

Most of the scientists thought of it simply as an academic problem, didn't they? They were collectively in denial about what solving that problem might lead to.

It was a problem, but I think that a lot of people were very well aware that a lot of other people were going to die from this thing. The atomic bomb killed 120,000 people in Hiroshima and Nagasaki combined, but just before that the Allies had killed over 80,000 in fire raids on Tokyo. This was a war, and people were dying all over the world every day; that was a given. I think they were very used to that: 'We'd rather they died in Tokyo than in New York because they are the enemy.' It's very hard for us now to imagine the hatred that must have existed for the enemy, and I don't think that they gave too much of a fuck about who was going to die.

This was one armament, don't forget. Meanwhile, all over America, there were other outfits developing other armaments. Here in England we had Barnes Wallis building the Grand Slam – curiously, he called his bomb 'Tall Boy' – up to the atomic bomb the most powerful bomb dropped in the Second World War. Barnes Wallis developed the Bouncing Bomb and this one, a ten-ton bomb that he had to modify Wellington aircraft to carry, designed to penetrate eighty feet into the earth and then explode. Which it did, and it killed thousands of people. Look at the damage done to London in the Blitz, and London was intact compared to Berlin or Dresden or Cologne. All those cities in Germany were completely levelled. So I don't think anyone was particularly worried about killing them. They were worried about them killing us.

In any case, secrecy prevented them asking difficult questions.

That's right. There were no interdepartmental questions. Compartmentalisation was Groves's absolute dictum, the first commandment of running that project. The need to know. And very few people did know. It was only the higher echelons of security and the scientists and the politicians who knew anything was going on. Oppenheimer did get his way and have interdepartmental discussions between the senior scientists – one of whom, of course, was Klaus Fuchs – and Groves, the eternal pragmatist, must have considered that very carefully and come to the conclusion that it would hasten him getting what he wanted. But we're talking about an enormous project, the scale of which is almost beyond belief: $2billion would be $200billion or something now. Hundreds of thousands of people were involved in the Manhattan Project, most of whom had no idea what the end product was. The scientists were maybe five per cent of the citizens of Los Alamos, and all the rest were there as services to The Bomb. It developed into a self-contained town with barber's shops and laundries and gas stations, and the majority of people there, carpenters and metalworkers and plumbers, were required to keep the town running. The nucleus of it was the scientists, and all those areas were out of bounds; there were very selective passes.

The next President up was Truman, the Senator from Missouri, and he had little or no idea. They swore him in, hauled him into a meeting and said, 'Mr President, we've got this mother of a weapon,' and that was it, and of course he greenlighted using the thing. Imagine being presented with that as your first real decision as President. Imagine being presented with that decision at any point in your career as President. Someone like Barnes Wallis, by the way, wouldn't have known what was going on in America. The atomic bomb started here in

England known as the Tube Alloys Project, and the reason it had to move to the States was there was no way it could have been built in this country. There wasn't the money, there wasn't the manpower, and you couldn't have hidden it from the Germans, as indeed the Germans couldn't have hidden it from us. Had they wished to copy the K-25 uranium complex at Oak Ridge, they'd have had some difficulty in disguising it from our aircraft because the roof would have covered sixty acres. You couldn't have built it in Germany; it would have been impossible.

Anyway, even if anyone remotely thinks they were building this bomb to be dumped on Germany, how come B-29s were practising their runs over Cuba? Germany doesn't look like Cuba. What does look like Cuba, of course, is Japan. Hiroshima, Nagasaki, Kyoto and two or three other sites in Japan were kept as virgin targets. They didn't have so much as one hand grenade dropped on them, because the Americans wanted to see what this weapon would do to these cities. There were no virgin targets in Germany. The Allies didn't say, 'We'll keep Hamburg, Dusseldorf and Cologne for the atomic bomb.' No city in Germany was spared the USAF and RAF attacks day and night. But if you didn't know bollocks about the atomic bomb, maybe you'd think it was to do with Germany. The pilot flying the bomber towards Hiroshima had no idea what it was until the last moment. The components for the 'Little Boy' bomb were brought to the island of Tinian in the Pacific, where there was a secret enclave keeping the airmen apart from everybody else. Meanwhile, the pilot who flew the 'Fat Man' plane over Nagasaki, Claude Eatherly, came back to America and went crazy with guilt, and in the fifties the US Government put him in a nuthouse: 'The man's mad.' Why is he mad? He was mad because he was saying, 'It's a terrible thing that I've done – that *we've* done – dumping this stuff on Japan.'

In the context of the German nuclear effort, you've mentioned something called the 'Alsos Mission'. What was that?

The 'Alsos Mission' was another part of the enormous pantomime engendered by the atomic bomb. 'Alsos' means 'groves' in Latin.
Groves wanted all these security people who were chiselling away

at Oppenheimer off his neck, and one of his principal annoyances, a guy called Boris Pash, was sent to find out 'where the Germans were at' with their nuclear programme. Groves knew very well that they had next to nothing. Pash couldn't seize much to do with the atomic bomb because it didn't exist. He rounds up all these German nuclear documents and brings them back to the US, where they get dumped in a basement at Oak Ridge. David Irving – who's taking someone to court in London as we speak, claiming the Holocaust didn't really happen – wrote a book called *The Virus House* about the German nuclear effort, and you've never read such claptrap in your life. Irving got his research material from the 'Alsos Mission'. He comes across this material and thinks, 'Eureka!' But Groves may as well have thrown it in the trash. It wasn't even classified. It was forgotten because it was crap. We had a serious spy network in Europe, and if there had been a genuine and lasting concern about the nuclear endeavours of Germany, that would have been priority number one for our agents, as it later became with the V-2s. The reality is, in the entire Second World War, the Germans spent on nuclear research what the Manhattan Project was spending every day.

If you were to phone up the Ministry of Defence and say, 'Could you tell me everything that you knew about the German bomb in the Second World War,' every single piece that they'd give you would be post-1943. 'You must have been very concerned about Germany's nuclear activity in 1939, 1940 and 1941?' 'Of course we were. We thought they were going to build an atomic bomb.' 'OK, could I see some of the documents pertaining to what your spies found out about the German nuclear programme in 1941?' 'No. Classified.' The same pertains in America. Anyone can get hold of what they knew in 1943, 1944 and 1945, but ask them about the German atomic bomb in 1942 and it's classified. Because what they found out is the Germans weren't building a bomb, and if they stood up and said, 'Sorry guys, the Germans weren't building a bomb, and we knew it,' we end up with this paradox of spending enormous sums of money on these weapons and creating international nightmares all based on a lie.

The whole Cold War was predicated on this bollocks, because if the West had not built that bomb in the Second World

War, it's arguable that the Soviets wouldn't have built one. They were busted flat by the war. They'd lost over twenty million dead, the whole western side of the Soviet Union was destroyed, and they didn't want to spend all that money on an atomic bomb, but they had to. It would be extremely embarrassing, at minimum, for the US government and the British government to say, 'You're right. We knew they weren't building it.' It's an important point. If you read the official history of the Manhattan Project, somewhere towards the beginning we gather that in 1943 we were in a vicious arms race with Germany, and several volumes later we read, 'By the beginning of 1943,' – i.e. *before* Los Alamos – 'the German threat had receded.' Because it's an official history they have to bury this in ten million words of waffle and bullshit so that if anyone like me comes along and says, 'You're a gang of liars,' they can say, 'No, it's in the official history. We did say that the threat from Germany had receded.'

In other words, the war provided the scientists with a timetable which they would bend over backwards to meet, which meant that they provided America with the biggest stick in the playground when it was over.

Absolutely. Various companies made billions out of this thing. It was very good news. Hence this disease of McCarthyism, pretending among other absurdities that the Russians had 'stolen our bomb'. The Russians did have intelligence officers in the US, of course, but they didn't need Klaus Fuchs to tell them about the atomic bomb. The Russians had nuclear physicists in the same way that the English did, the French did, the Italians did. There was a Russian scientist called Kapitza, for instance, who worked out various formulae which helped the Americans at the beginning of the Manhattan Project. Teller was a Hungarian, and he knew about the potential for a hydrogen bomb, so are you telling me that it stopped at the Russian border and Teller knew in Budapest but they didn't know in Moscow? There was an international community of scientists and, just like Strassman and Hann published their discovery of fission in Berlin in 1939, these scientists shared their information. At the famous Potsdam conference between Attlee, Truman and Stalin, Truman confided, 'We've got this weapon,' and Stalin knew all about it. As a matter of fact, in 1945, before the bombs were dropped, the Soviets declared war on Japan, and the big fear was that when Japan was levelled the Soviets were going to march in and take it. They were due to begin hostilities on August 8th, and the Americans dropped the bombs on the 6th and the 9th, conveniently timed to send the Russians a very clear message.

Men like Teller were invested with enormous power, particularly by Ronald Reagan. Teller was very involved in the whole Star Wars weapons system nonsense. I remember talking to him; I forget the university, but it was very difficult to get in there. You're vetted before you're allowed to talk to him, to see what your political point of view is and whether you're going to attack him because of his past, so naturally you lie to get in: 'What do you think about apartheid?' 'I think it's a bloody good idea.' Then you get in there, and he says [*in the manner of Dr Strangelove*], 'We have an interview for one half of an hour. I will ask some questions, and then I will answer them.' That's it. You sit there in silence while he says, 'Why did we decide, in 1949, to build the Super-Weapon?' Then he'd tell you. It was the most bizarre thing, the most bizarre man to meet. In Budapest, when he was young, he fell over a tram line and a tram came along and cut his foot off. In my interview with him he had a transparent sock over an artificial foot that he'd swing like a yo-yo while he was talking, and you'd see the mechanics of his foot swivelling round. Most disconcerting.

Did meeting these old scientists help you to write them as young men?

As I said about *The Killing Fields*, I try and research a hundred per cent, and ninety per cent I wouldn't use. The way one develops character with real people is in the way we talked about with Schanberg and Pran. You read everything you can about them, get as many opinions as possible from people who know them, talk to them if they're available – obviously Groves and Oppenheimer weren't – and formulate what you believe their characters were like given the environment and the situation they were put in. Feynman was apparently a very witty guy, but I don't know what he actually said. I don't know what Groves said or what Oppenheimer said, and I would never use that even if I did. Even if there was a tape-recording of the whole thing, I wouldn't use it. Feynman was a funny man, that's all I knew about him, so the whole description of the atomic bomb in my script is in his manic behaviour. If it's going well for you as a writer they start talking, and if I have a talent as a writer that's what it is: I start listening.

You've said that you heard Oppenheimer as clearly as you heard Withnail.

Oh, yeah, I did. The two most potent characters that I've ever heard as a writer, one was Withnail – he was just going in my head like Tchaikovsky: 'Take this music out of my brain' – and one was Robert Oppenheimer, talking all day at me. And Groves. I could hear him clear as day. He was a 'This is God's country' type of guy, believed Jesus was born in Cincinnati, that kind of stuff. He spoke the American language like John Wayne. He was ultra-conservative, and the only thing that I absolutely agree with Goodchild about was that Groves did keep chocolates in his safe. He was a pig.

The explanation of nuclear fission which you gave to Feynman in your script is delivered in the film by Szilard. Groves visits him at home to confirm some kind of report on the potential for an atomic bomb and arrives to find him in the bath, where this old scientist uses a sponge to demonstrate the principles involved. It's like Archimedes, except Groves substitutes 'Hallelujah!' for 'Eureka!'

Szilard and Einstein wrote a famous letter to Roosevelt saying, 'We're very concerned that the potential for building a nuclear weapon is in our hands and also in the hands of the Nazis.' Einstein went to his grave regretting writing that letter. It was Einstein, basically, with Szilard, who kicked this thing off. When it first started, no one was really interested. Fermi was given a grant to try and get a chain reaction going at the University of

Chicago, which he did, but there was not much interest from the military or the government in the beginning. Then it suddenly took off. Einstein himself said, 'If we don't get rid of this thing, day one after the end of the Second World War will be day one preceding the Third World War.' Now everyone says, 'It's fifty years ago. These things will never be used.' I don't agree with that. I think somewhere somehow we will have a nuclear war on this planet. The proliferation of these things is terrifying. Pakistan and India and Israel, people like Saddam and the rest. Sooner or later something is going to happen. The development of the atomic bomb happened bit by bit, and it's still happening bit by bit. It's off the agenda at the moment, but it's still there. It's just that we're not talking about it, like we're not talking about the Congo. It doesn't mean to say that people aren't still dying.

The final act of the film bears the closest resemblance to your original script, and both involve a fatal accident during a sensitive experiment at Los Alamos which historians claim didn't happen until after the war.

That's true, which is why there's only one character in my script who has a fictitious name, and that's Merriman. What I wanted to do, because I couldn't show the effect of The Bomb falling on Hiroshima or Nagasaki, was to show what nuclear poisoning does to people. I created an artificial character based on a man called Szlotin who was exposed to radiation after the event, and everything that happened to him happens to Merriman so we can see what this bomb's going to do to human beings before the event. It's quite true that did happen in 1946 and not before The Bomb; or at least if it did happen before The Bomb it's not known and was hushed up. I'm sure Roland knew that as well as I did.

And Merriman's romance with an Army nurse?

That's all true. I just moved it forward six months and changed the names. Everything that happens to him happened, including Groves saying, 'It must be a nice way to die.' He actually said that when this terrible accident took place. What they were doing is allowing something to go super-critical for a nano-second, and for no apparent reason the apparatus stuck. I don't know whether Roland used it in the film, but this guy hit it with his fist, got drenched with radiation, and went to the blackboard and worked out mathematically that he was going to die.

It is in the film. Joffé remarked that about thirty to forty per cent of the shooting script is yours, but it must be closer to seventy per cent in the final act.

Yeah, but it's not mine. Excepting Merriman, he either followed the historical reality of it or he didn't. Film-makers can choose what weight to put on these things. It's potentially unfair of me in some ways, and I admit that, to be so antipathetic towards what Roland's done with the film because I haven't seen it. I saw the first twenty minutes on video. When they premièred the film in New York they didn't send me an invite, and my name's all over it. I didn't get pissed off about that; I couldn't have given a fuck. What I did get pissed off about was this butchery of historical reality. Just before I turned the video off, there was a scene with an aeroplane parked in a hangar with its engines going – I suppose to stop any bugging devices – and Groves and Oppenheimer in the cockpit, and I thought, 'I haven't spent two years of my life trying to be as factually accurate as I can, to see this.' It wasn't even dramatic licence, it was just ludicrous. So I stopped watching it. I'd read parts of various drafts and all of the draft that Roland finally shot, and I was incensed. I remember throwing the script across the room thinking, 'How can you do this?'

From an outsider's point of view, though, the scene is punchy and dramatic. The same applies to an earlier scene, where Groves is placed in charge of the Manhattan Project instead of being given a front-line command, which is shot through frosted glass so you get two silhouettes arguing with each other.

Which in itself is complete bullshit, by the way. It isn't true that Groves resisted being in charge of the Manhattan Project. The common folklore is that this enormous man the size of Uncle Monty wanted to go out there with a machine-gun and blow some Krauts away. Groves knew he was going to be in charge and wanted to be in charge. But you say that the film's a good film; I'm prepared to believe that. Maybe it is.

Whose idea was it to put all these scientists in one place? The film credits it to Oppenheimer in the aeroplane scene.

Everybody who was involved at the top would have come up with the same idea because it was the only way to make it, but the reason you would get Oppenheimer credited was because he knew the Sangre di Christi Mountains and the Los Alamos Boys School. He'd had a lot of riding holidays down there and he was aware of this area being very difficult to get at, miles inland in the middle of nowhere. He took Groves down there, Groves approved it, and they started building a road into this cliff. It was on a mesa with no road, no contact at all. The weird thing about the Los Alamos Boys School is that William Burroughs went there as a child, sitting where fifteen years later The Bomb was going to be built.

Both your script and the film depict the US Army clearing the Trinity test site by shooting a whole herd of healthy cattle, a historical event which is powerfully emblematic of the madness and slaughter endemic in the Manhattan Project.

I believe anything and everything would have been sacrificed to this thing, because it really was – and it sounds like hyperbole – the Devil's work going on here. This is to do with God, this kind of stuff, if anything is. Oppenheimer's got a line in my script where he says to Jean, 'There are fifty-six elements on this planet, and out of that God makes everything from the forget-me-nots to the stars.' These fifty-six elements, put together in a particular way, make a daffodil, and in another way make an elephant, and in another way make a Mars bar. By implication, because plutonium doesn't exist as an element, you're into God's work: man-made elements that had never existed until then.

Joffé's stated intention was to show that if The Bomb can be made by people it can be unmade by people. That's quite a lofty ambition.

Yeah, but that's all part of his hands together and bowing when we were doing *The Killing Fields*. I agree with Roland in some ways, and I think he genuinely believes certain things like that. I mean, we can't disinvent cancer but we're spending billions of pounds every year trying to find a cure for it. We can't disinvent The Bomb but we'd like to get rid of it. I think that's what Roland means, but it's naïve because it ain't going away, this thing. We'll cure cancer a long time before that thing's buggered itself into oblivion. Because of the film Roland made, what we're talking about now is sort of in the public domain, but get into a cab in London and say, 'Do you think Hitler was building the atomic bomb?' and you'll hear in all sincerity [*Cockney accent*], 'Do I think? I know it. He was ready to put them in his V-2s and fire them at America.' One hasn't really busted the myth around this thing at all.

I've said a lot of derogatory things about Roland but I don't harbour any personal animosity towards him at all. I think he's making a film now and I sincerely hope it's marvellous, because he's a very talented director. I may sound vitriolic towards him but even after all these years I do care intensely about this story. If Roland and I had sat down for two days, two weeks, two months before this film was made, at the end of that he might have said, 'Well, thanks a lot, Bruce. I'm not going to do it like that.' That's his prerogative, he's the director. But not to have tapped into this amount of research I find ludicrous. Surely he would have got something out of discussion with me? I could have talked him through it and given him the documents. It wasn't me that ran away from him and refused the stuff; he virtually told me to fuck off until they ran into trouble. 'Can we have this, Bruce?' 'No. Now you can fuck off.' In the documentary I say it's the biggest hole in my life creatively, and it is.

You've also said that it's the best thing you'll ever write.

I still feel that, but when I say, 'the best thing', how can one qualify it? What's the best piece of work that I'll do? What's the best piece of work any writer will do? It's certainly the most important thing I've ever worked on; though, as I've said, cinema is about entertainment, and if I want to make people aware of my take on the development of the atomic bomb perhaps the medium for it is in a book. The atomic bomb is a story, of course, but it's made up of lots of stories. I imagine if you sat down for a day with a piece of paper and said, 'Right. The atomic bomb. We're not doing Oppenheimer and Groves. What else can we do?' you'd get a hundred approaches. You could do it from the point of view of some of the people we've discussed. What did Mrs Einstein think about it? There is a bomb in the story, but in a way the more bomb you can shave out of it the better it is, because audiences react to people. You were talking about, in the context of *The Killing Fields*, Schanberg being America and Pran being Cambodia. Well, the 'Fat Man' was the government and the 'Little Boy' was the people. We've all been conned. Oppenheimer was conned. Everything that happened to him, the lie that destroyed him, is the lie that has fucked us.

This whole nuclear energy thing was Pandora's Box. When I was a kid they used to sell the domestic advantages of nuclear energy. It was going to feed the world and turn deserts into gardens. 'Electricity too cheap to meter' was a common expression in the fifties. We built a domestic nuclear plant because the Americans, particularly Groves, were prepared to exploit the British as needed inside the Manhattan Project but wouldn't give us atomic bombs after the war. We had to create our own fissile material up at the place whose name was changed every time they had an accident. It started out as Calder Hall, then they had a terrible accident in 1959 – not quite Chernobyl, but very serious – and they called it Seascale, then Windscale, then Sellafield. It's had four names. Nuclear energy has to lie to survive. I grew up in the fifties thinking I was going to get fried by the Chinese, and subsequently we find out they hadn't even got the money for a garden rake. That bogeyman's dealt with, now let's invent another fucker. I saw an American guy being interviewed on TV the other day about what is tantamount to Star Wars all over again. 'Why do you want to build Star Wars when the threat from Russia is massively diminished?' This guy says in all seriousness, 'The threat from Russia may have diminished, but we do have Iraq and we do have North Korea.' And so it will go on until they say, 'Well, the Icelandics are looking a bit dangerous.'

Do you regret agreeing to write *Fat Man* for Puttnam?

I'm glad I know what I know about the atomic bomb, but it was a very bad career-move. I could have written three or four screenplays back to back rather than doing the atomic bomb that took two and a half years of my life. Paul Heller, being a producer, was very well aware of this, and he said, 'You've got to stop all this fucking around, marvellous as Puttnam may have been, and get an agent out here.' He phoned CAA, I went down there, and was faced with one of those marble tables that go from here to Margate with 200 agents sitting around it, all apparently keen to represent me because of *The Killing Fields*. Third on the right was this bright-looking Jewish guy with a beard, Rand Holston, and every time I said anything I was addressing myself to him, so I thought, 'This must be my agent,' and he has been ever since.

The thing is, I'm a very obsessive person. If, for example, I read a book about building the railway across America, I'll read everything I can get hold of about the railway across America. Then there'll be adjuncts to that, like how the Indians reacted to the railway, and I'll read all those books about the Indians. I've always done that. I can't read one book about Jack the Ripper, I want all of them. A lot of those atomic bomb books were incredibly difficult to track down. Some of them took me five years to find. You'd see them referred to in a footnote, and then one day you're in a bookshop in the middle of nowhere and there it is. I spend too much time doing that, as a matter of fact, but I can't help it. I obsess.

Chapter Four

'A timeless quality'

Withnail & I

Withnail & I was based on your novel, but is it true that the novel was based on a diary you kept?

It wasn't based on a diary, but I used to keep a diary because those were bleak days. The reason Lesley and I lasted so long is there was no internecine jealousy between us. If there had been it should have come from my end, because we were both actors and she was doing well and I wasn't. But there wasn't any of that, so I used to vent spleen into this diary.

For a time you lived with friends in Camden Town, including Michael Feast, David Dundas and presumably Vivian.

We were all there together. In the second year at Central, David, who was much more wealthy than the rest of us, bought this house in Albert Street. We all moved in, the whole lot of us, until there were so many blokes in there that he moved out. He bought himself another flat in Hampstead, and in his infinite generosity didn't kick our arses out and sell the house. Then we finished drama school, I went off to Rome to be in *Romeo and Juliet*, and I came back with nowhere to live except Albert Street, by which time David had left. There were no unoccupied bedrooms, so I was in the bathroom on a mattress. Over a period of about a year or so, the other blokes would get a girlfriend and go and live with her, or they'd get a job and go up to Edinburgh, or whatever. They all filtered away through 1968 and into 1969, until there was just Viv and I left, which was the genesis of *Withnail*, this intense two years that he and I spent together.

So by the time you went to the Lake District with Michael Feast he wasn't living in the house any more?

No. By then he'd married his agent and gone to live in Primrose Hill. It was just Viv and I in there, and David didn't throw us out, but he did sell half the house to a guy called Christopher Bowerbank who took over the downstairs and converted it into a flat. We used to rob him blind, because he was a working architect so he used to keep booze and food on the premises, and we were always down there. When they came round to cut our gas off, at our instigation they cut him off, and at one point bailiffs took everything but his bed because they were after our stuff but we misdirected them. Viv and I were together for two years, and it gets very intense, that, if you haven't got any money. My life with Viv was one of paradoxes, of loving and loathing. [*Gestures to the wall beside his desk*] There's a picture he drew of me up there. It says, 'Bruce Robinson – aged 47'. He drew that in about 1969, I suppose. The one thing we had in common was we were smart, and we would sit up all night talking about whatever. It was a marvellous time in my life, even though I was absolutely destitute.

Didn't he come from quite a wealthy background?

He came from the kind of background that would have an uncle like Uncle Monty: affluent, drowning-upper-class – 'shabby genteel' as Orwell used to call it. He was into wills, Viv. He was always praying that some aunt on Bodmin Moor or somewhere would croak so he'd get ten grand – and they did. He was constantly fascinated by the physical condition of his distant relatives. That was the worst side of Viv; he was totally materially orientated. He cared more about clocks and tables and chairs than he did about people.

He did have a lot more money than me, but we both used to get National Assistance, which involved taking a bus from Camden all the way down to Victoria where you'd sign on. It was the most humiliating experience. Rows of winos and Irish and actors. There was a guy down there once and they said, 'You've had your money. You're not having any more.' [*Irish accent*] 'I've got a wife and four fuckin' children waitin' for me at home, I've got to have some fuckin' money!' I think they gave him an extra two quid, and he turned round to me and said, 'There's goin' to be some drinkin' done tonight,' and fucked off. A bunch of other actors were always there as well, with their frayed cuffs and soiled shirts, whining, 'Laertes is coming up, my agent has assured me I've got the part, and, er, could I have a fiver?' 'No, you can't.' 'Well, um, what about a quid?' We were down there all the time, and it was very formative for me as a writer, this sea of stuff coming in which I used to shove into my diary.

Withnail is such a self-dramatist that you get the impression he wouldn't have much left over for auditions. Do you think that applied to Viv?

He was a lousy actor. He was one of those people born with the silver spoon in his mouth. He was doted on by his parents and he was very handsome when he was younger, so by the time he got to drama school he was some sort of young Marlon Brando figure. The sun shone out of his arse as far as Central School was concerned, particularly in the first year, even though he was awful. It came as quite a freight train of shock to him as he was getting older that it hadn't worked, and consequently he got stuck in 1968 for the rest of his life. One would see him in the eighties and he'd still be playing the Rolling Stones all the time.

You deliberately excluded major female characters from Withnail, to emphasise the emotional poverty of the male leads.

Yeah. They can't afford girls, as indeed we couldn't. You used to get the odd shag, I suppose, but when my relationship with Lesley took off it was her financing it, not me.

In fact, during the period you were writing about, you were already going out with Lesley, weren't you?

Withnail was retrospective in that sense. I met Lesley in the winter of 1969. She was invited to Ava Gardner's birthday party which Roddy McDowall threw and it was love at first sight, so to speak. She was fifteen, I was twenty-three. Viv and I were still living in Camden, and she'd come to stay occasionally and the cops would get sent round because her parents freaked out. At the time I didn't understand it, but now my daughter's thirteen I can.

Didn't you write a letter to Lesley from the Lake District saying something like, 'We're having an awful time but I've had a great idea for a story'?

I've still got the letter somewhere. The cottage depicted in the film was positively luxurious compared to what Mickey and I actually found when we arrived. It really was a bucket by the bed with rain coming in and so cold you could hardly see. The only source of heat was one room that had this kitchen range in it, and we ended up burning everything to try and keep warm. We got a bed down from upstairs and we used to sleep together, not in a fag way but just for heat. There was a sixteenth-century oak spice cupboard in that room, and we couldn't tear it to bits because it was made by somebody who intended it to last. That was one of the only things that survived, and thank God it did. But the chairs all went on, tables, the whole lot.

I remember running down the hill with polythene bags on our feet when we saw a coal lorry coming up the side of the lake. Polythene bags were not amusing to us, they really weren't. We were saturated day and night, and that was the only solution because we didn't have any wellingtons. The chicken scene actually happened. We whacked this chicken with an axe and it didn't go down, it just stood there with no head, so we had to hit it again to kill it. The Jag didn't survive the trip. Lesley had bought this fucked old Jaguar like the one in the film, and when we were driving up to wherever it was – it wasn't called Crow Crag – we drove it into a ditch. The farmer came by – Parkin, which is where I got the name – and he connected it to his tractor and pulled the entire front of the fucking car off. That was our holiday.

This would have been in the spring of 1969?

Something like that. I haven't specifically got a date, but it was around the winter of 1969/70 that I wrote *Withnail* because Viv had gone.

Leaving you in the position of Withnail.

That's right. No money. No work. I wouldn't by any stretch of the imagination describe myself as a good actor, but I would also say that I am not a bad one; I can do it. But that five, six months with Zeffirelli completely destroyed me as an actor, the desire to do it and the ability to do it. He made me terrified of directors, because he was the first professional director I'd ever had and he treated me like shit. Whenever I got a job after that I would assume that I was going to get this kind of treatment, and either become over-defensive towards the director or try and make him like me. I'd do everything wrong, so the first few years of my career were a disaster and I couldn't even act to the level of ability that I had.

'He's got a pretty face, but he can't act,' was kind of it for me. 'Four floors up on the Charing Cross Road and never a job at the top of them' was very much my life. For years you'd sit there waiting for the telephone to ring, and then when they'd cut off the telephone you'd have to tramp out to the call box over the road. 'I've already put two shilling pieces in.' That used to go on all the time, phoning the agent. 'When's he coming back from lunch? Well, would you tell him I called? Bruce Robinson. No, Bruce. B-R-U-C-E.' I used to get that. I was at some crummy party somewhere, and here's my agent talking, and he says, 'So what do you do?' I said, 'You're my agent!' I'll never forget him saying that.

Viv had managed to land a part, though.

In some play by that awful writer Shaw. Viv went tramping off round the provinces, it was a particularly vicious winter and here I was with no heat, an Oxfam overcoat and a lightbulb. I used to swipe abandoned vegetables off Camden Market. There'd always be apples and turnips hanging about when they'd shut up on a Saturday. It was fucking awful. I think they used to give you eight pounds a week National Assistance, and eight pounds a week – particularly for someone who likes a glass of wine with their turnip – isn't a lot of money. It was impossible to live off, and I used to start the day, if I'd been up all night, with a pint of somebody's milk from up the street and probably their *Financial Times* which was stuck in the letterbox. [*Posh voice*] 'Where's my paper?' 'I delivered it, sir.' 'Well, you say that, but this is the third time in a week I haven't had my *Times*.'

Nemesis, when it struck, was shutting that front door for the last time and throwing my key down the drain as I crossed the road heading for the tube to go back to my parents' house in Kent. It was like seven years – from 1963, when I decided to be an actor and go to drama school, to that winter of 1969/70 – was a chunk of failure. It was Lesley who got me back to London and back into Albert Street – by now Viv's back – where I lived for another two years until about 1972. Then Lesley and I got a flat together and that was the end of the Withnail days.

An interview with Michael Feast in the *Observer* suggested that Withnail was based on him rather than Viv.

Mickey sent me that, with a sort of apologetic letter. Mickey's a very old friend and I absolutely believe him, but the implication in there was that I had based Withnail on Mickey, which is complete nonsense. Mickey had a massive impact on the writing of *Withnail* in the sense that we went on holiday together, but he had no bearing whatsoever on the relationship between Withnail and the 'I' character. Withnail is basically me and Viv, an amalgamation of the two, but I didn't sit there with a tape recorder and a notepad writing down what Viv said. I just took his acidity, his pompous cowardice, and his very pungent sense of humour, and wrote that character.

I offered the part of Danny the Dealer to Mickey but he turned me down because he'd been there and back with drugs and alcohol and it was too near the knuckle. Mickey was a very good actor and was getting plenty of work around that period. He was playing opposite John Gielgud at the National, Ariel to Gielgud's Prospero, and he did the first night and then fucked off. Same when he was in *Hair*. The booze and drugs got hold of him to the point where he was crashing into Chinese restaurants in Gerrard Street out of his skull demanding heroin and stuff. It took him a lot of years and a lot of AA, but he's a distinguished actor now and he's doing the work he wants to do.

Withnail also got one or two of his characteristics and his unique surname from a friend of your father, is that right?

Jonathan Withnall, his name was. He was an upper-class ne'er do well and he had an Aston Martin, which is why I always wanted one and finally got one. Total alcoholic. The last time I heard of him he got arseholed and backed his Aston out of a pub carpark straight into the side of a police car. Then, as I understand it, he emigrated to America. He was a real yellow-cravat-and-cavalry-twill rogue, and when I was a little boy he took me for a drive in this Aston, completely fucked with booze. He was driving along, opened the door, puked into the gutter, slammed the door and drove off, happy as a sandboy. I was eight, and I thought, 'This guy's extraordinary!' Years later, when I was coming to write *Withnail*, this name came up in my head, Jonathan Withnall. I go through all sorts of titles normally, but that was always the one it was going to be for that book. Because I can't spell, I spelled it Withnail, which is a more appropriate name. It sounds like he is, vicious and bitter, which I guess is why Richard used it for his book *With Nails*. The name doesn't exist. If you look in the telephone directory in London there isn't a Withnail in it.

Where did Danny the Dealer come from?

There were two sources for Danny. The voice came from a hairdresser at Pinewood Studios who did Lesley's hair for something. She was somewhat thick, and she'd say things to you followed by, 'Do you understand?' The other source was another hairdresser – strange that they should both be hairdressers – a bisexual bloke whose name was Danny, who I heard is now a whizz in the city with grey silk suits and a Porsche. He used to walk round in a top hat, a stove-pipe hat, a thing we called a pelt, which was like a wolf skin, and clogs, and he'd be virtually naked other than that. He'd turn up at our doorstep in the snow in the middle of the night with his pelt and his top hat and these terrible waxen pin-like legs with clogs at the end of them. He became Danny the Dealer. He did deal, I think. He didn't deal as far as we were concerned. He was one of those pieces of insanity that used to shuffle round London, and he really impressed me as being a character. At the fag-end of the sixties there were a lot of freaks about the place. It was post-*Sergeant Pepper* and the whole culture was very weird and spaced out. I went to Rome in 1967 wearing a blazer and a tie, and when I came back in 1968 everyone had long hair and was dropping acid. It was known as 'The Acid Summer'. The city had completely changed; it was a different place.

Since you were already writing scripts, why did you write Withnail as a novel?

Because I had no idea it was a movie. I just thought, 'It's a story.' As soon as I'd written *Withnail* I thought, 'Bollocks to acting. This is what I want to do.'

What was it like adapting the novel into a script?

It was terrible. *Withnail* as a book was a dream. It was one of the few times in my life I feel I was inspired. I was writing it so fast, and crying with laughter as I was writing. I wasn't earning my living writing; I certainly never thought it was going to be published. I wrote it purely for the joy of writing, and I sat there in penury having one of the best times I've ever had. *Withnail* as a screenplay was my biggest nightmare outside the atomic bomb. What happened was, I'd given the novel to friends and people were photocopying it – like that *samizdat* that they had in Russia with illegal books and stuff. A surprising number of people who I'd never met would say, 'I read your book.'

A friend of mine, an actor called Don Hawkins, had a friend called Moderick Schreiber – Mody – whose father ran a big oil company. Mody had piles of money and, I suppose, aspirations to be involved in the film industry, and Don gave Mody the book to read. Mody came back to me and said, 'This would make a good film. Let's do it as a script,' and he gave me a few thousand quid to try and turn it into a screenplay. Half the dialogue was there, but I really struggled to write it as a film. It's like the first time you taste a really great wine: you can't replicate that. I'd had my share of pleasure out of writing *Withnail*, and by the time I got to it as a screenplay I knew more about writing and it was just a headache. I nearly jacked it in. It didn't make me laugh, didn't give me any joy at all.

There was also no guarantee at that stage that it would be turned into a movie.

No, and indeed it was not. I wrote it about 1980 – I was living in California by then and I broke up with my date out there about 1982, so it had to be before that because I wrote it in her house – and it wasn't until 1986 that it was made. So if my memory is right and the book was written in the winter of 1969/70 – and I've got to think that's right – it was seventeen years later that it got made into a film. That's what's so bizarre about it: it's thirty-one years old and it's still playing. By accident rather than design it has a timeless quality that all writers love to have built into their work. Perhaps it's easy to identify with if you're a twenty-one-year-old male with not much money living in squalor, which you tend to do at that age, because it isn't pulling punches or being condescending towards that life. Also, it can be said, 'Twenty years later Bruce Robinson's made a film about it, so it may be awful now but it won't be awful later. We'll all be Marwood; we'll all escape.'

A lot of its fans think they're Withnail, though.

Oh God, yes. When I was tramping around the place doing publicity for *Penman* there were all these Withnails coming up with coats and scarves and joints: 'Can we have a photograph of you smoking this joint and me standing next to you?' As Jack Straw might say, I was minded to protest. Firstly, I don't smoke grass. Secondly, I don't want to be known as someone who does. Thirdly, I've got no interest in being photographed with them or anybody else.' They were *Withnail* fanatics.

Didn't you meet four of them on a trip to Wales?

It was ten, fifteen miles from where we are now. David Wimbury was staying for the weekend, and we went to this really remote rural pub for a drink. We were sitting in the garden with ducks all over, and there were these four boys. I didn't know them, they didn't know me, and I said to them completely out of the blue, 'Do you know what kind of ducks those are?' All four of them said, 'Raymond Duck! Four floors up on the Charing Cross Road and never a job at the top of them!' They were really aggressive, and they were Withnailing it after that, and I thought, 'That's quite astonishing. Here I am in the middle of nowhere, up a hill with these four wankers and ducks everywhere, and someone's quoting my own lines back to me in a pejorative way because they think I'm not even worthy of hearing them.' When we left I forced Wimbury to roll the window down and shout, 'Scrubbers!' at them out of the Range Rover.

Do you find that sort of thing flattering, or alarming, or both?

I don't find it either, actually. I'm just bemused by it, I suppose. There seem to be thousands of Withnails out there. Very weird.

What was the role of Paul Heller in helping set up the film?

Paul encouraged me to direct *Withnail*. I wouldn't have directed it had it not been for him. We're sitting by the proverbial pool, and he'd read it and really liked it, and I said, 'I'm looking for a director.' He said, 'Why don't you do it?' I said, 'How am I going to do that?' He said, 'If I raise the money will you do it?' I said, 'Sure.' Two weeks later he had half the money from this fabulous guy he knew called Lawrence Kirstein, a property developer in Washington, and half the money is halfway up the ladder.

How much did it cost?

£1.1million – now we're in London with half the money, speaking to Wimbury, who took it to Ray Cooper at HandMade Films. Ray really liked it, there was some vacillation from Denis O'Brien, and the script ended up on George Harrison's lap, first class on his way to New York. He read it and said, 'We'll make it,' and he obviously had the executive power to say that. Next thing I'm a film director. It really was as simple as that. It'll never be that easy again.

Am I right in saying that you were paid a token amount of £1 for the script and £80,000 for directing it?

Yeah.

£30,000 of which you ploughed back into the film to cover the scenes which HandMade wouldn't shoot?

Thirty grand I never got. I got fifty grand for *Withnail*, end of story.

What made you decide on Richard E. Grant and Paul McGann?

Paul and Richard, Richard particularly, both really suffered to get cast. I hired Paul and then I fired him before we started. He would not lose that Scouse accent. I kept saying to him, 'You've got to dump it, Paul. You're meant to be a lower-middle-class boy who's gone to drama school, and you can't speak like that.' I got rid of him then reinstated him because he promised me he'd get rid of it, which he did. Paul was very generous in the film. He doesn't have the fireworks like Grant, he doesn't have the laughs; he's setting up the laughs for Withnail all the time.

Richard had to come back four times, and I knew he was shitting himself. Mary Selway kept saying, 'This bloke hasn't done anything but I think he's got something about him.' I said, 'I'm looking for Byron, not a chubby Dirk Bogarde.' He swears that he was never fat, but I've got the pictures. When he came along I said, 'Half of you has got to go.' He says in his own book that he phoned up Gary Oldman and asked, 'How can I lose weight quickly?' and Oldman told him about some protein drink you buy in Boots. He lost all this weight and he's never put it on again. When we were shooting the film he was a rampant carnivore, shoving beef and sheep in, and now he's virtually a vegan, purer than the driven snow.

What convinced you that he was the right man for the job?

109

One line: 'Fork it!' It was bang on, exactly the way I heard that line in my head, and I thought, 'If he's got one and we go about it properly, he can get the rest.' That, basically, is why he got the part. When I finally cast him and Paul, I phoned Sophie and said, 'Come and meet the actors,' and she came along and had a look, and when we were outside she said, 'Are you out of your mind? What are you doing with him?'

He mentions in his film diaries that Daniel Day-Lewis had already turned down the role of Withnail. When did you offer it to him?

Long before, when it was still a pipedream and Dan was clearly on the up as an actor. He didn't so much turn it down as time passed and by then he wasn't available. Bill Nighy also gave a very good account of himself in the auditions, but that was in Bill's drinking days and I thought that one drunk on the set was going to be enough.

I believe you offered the part of Marwood to Kenneth Branagh but he turned it down because he only wanted to play Withnail.

This was before Kenneth Branagh took off. He's an excellent actor, Branagh, and he could have played Withnail, but it would have been a podgy Withnail. I don't mean that physically, but Ken's very mannered and I don't think he'd have had that splenetic depth that Richard's got. Richard's a vicious old tart, and he obviously had the wherewithal to play Withnail otherwise he wouldn't have done it like he did. Withnail's quite a nasty guy in many ways. He's a thief, a coward, and – the ultimate treachery – he's prepared to sacrifice his friend to get what he wants. Withnail was a timebomb ticking in Richard for many years, I think. Withnail was the detonator to allow that side of his personality to come out, and he's fundamentally changed. He is thin, he is demonstrative and he is witheringly verbally aggressive towards other 'thesps' as he calls them. Paul remained the same, just lovely.

He also mentions that you offered Marwood to Michael Maloney,

Which in terms of his subsequent career was probably a mistake. He phoned his agent and said, 'Even if they offer me the part I'm turning it down.' I don't know why. It certainly isn't anti-gay, it certainly isn't anti-black and it certainly isn't anti-Irish. But when I was living there, Camden Town and Kentish Town were heavyweight Irish areas, and these were nice enough guys but when they got tanked they'd go for you. I remember having to run for my life on a Saturday night. [*Irish accent*] 'Come here, you cunt! Come here!' You'd start running, and twenty minutes later, bang, bang, bang on the front door, there'd be one of them standing out there, bleeding all over the place with his teeth smashed, saying, 'Have you got any glue?'

There was a cafe there, the Parkway Cafe, that we used to go into when we had the money, and I was in there one morning, sitting in front of the window eating a poached egg on toast, and I looked up and there was an enormous Wanker – we called them 'The Wankers' – with a red beard staring in at me. I was instantly uptight and didn't know what to do, and I went like this [*pantomimes taking a big mouthful and rubbing his stomach in satisfaction*], and he thought I was taking the piss and came crashing through the door. I sprinted up this cafe, knife and fork still in my hand, through the kitchen, out the back door, over the first garden wall, second garden wall, third garden wall, which was our house, and got in the back.

I used to nail my door up every night because I was paranoid about The Wankers. Viv and I had freaked out one night with hammers trying to eradicate pustules that were coming through the plaster in the bathroom, and we knocked the back wall of the house into the garden. The bathroom had a piece of blue polythene on the back of it, and anyone could have got in. Behind Gloucester Terrace there was an enormous building, what would have been a workhouse in the nineteenth century, divided up into rooms for The Wankers to live in. There were a thousand Wankers in there, and they'd all come out and drink down the Mother Black Cap. When arseholed, which was always, they were a pretty scary mob.

You mentioned offering Danny the Dealer to Michael Feast, but it's difficult to imagine anyone in that role but Ralph Brown, and of course the film wouldn't be the same without Richard Griffiths as Uncle Monty.

At least eighteen months before *Withnail* was even on the cards Sophie and I went to see *A Private Function* – another Hand-Made film – and Richard's in that, and I said to Sophie after the film, 'If I ever get a shot at making *Withnail*, that's my Uncle Monty.' When we came to make the film I said to Mary Selway, the casting director, 'There's no actor I want in England except this one,' and in he came, face like a cherub. He sat down and I said, 'Have you read it?' He said, 'No.' I said, 'Here's the script. If you want to play the part, it's yours.' And he fucked off. Then he phoned up and said, 'I'd love to do it,' and that was that.

Ralph came down to Shepperton in all his rig, dressed like Danny the Dealer. Ralph's got very short hair, and he had this long wig and bare feet and looked quite unconventional. I think he'd read the script, and from what he said subsequently it seems that in the seventies he was at the back end of that sort of stuff anyway and knew quite a lot about it. When I saw him for Danny, Ralph brought that quality of intense seriousness about absolutely nothing, like when he pontificates at the end of the film about politics and hippy wigs in Woolworths and the fact that the sixties are now being marketed rather than lived. We did a lot of work on the voice because I was very specific about how I wanted it to sound.

The casting of Grant and McGann was quite apposite. Grant had been out of work for several months, like Withnail, and whereas Marwood is about to play the lead in one First World War drama, *Journey's End*, McGann had just played the lead in another, *The Monocled Mutineer*.

It is strange, that. I'd never thought of that. Around the time Viv and I terminated our relationship I was in *Journey's End*, and that's why he's in it.

How did they get on?

I don't think they liked each other at all. As long as I was getting what I wanted I couldn't have given a fuck what they were doing off set, but on location actors often dine with each other and I don't think there was much of that going on. Richard's got a thing about drinking – he's got a very alcoholic personality, which perhaps is why he's so antipathetic toward drinkers – and the night we were shooting the arrival at Uncle Monty's, Paul was a bit pissed and scraped the Jag. Richard leaped out the car, slamming the door, saying, 'I'm not working with that drunken fuck.' Didn't bother me; I was drunk too. I'd never directed before, though I'd been on film sets as an actor, and I was so afraid. It's a massive responsibility to have thrust on you. A lot of directors come up through the ranks, and I'd gone from being an actor and a writer to being a director, and it's quite scary. I used to booze my head off, but I didn't ever get drunk because the adrenalin levels were so high.

It's hard to believe that Richard Grant was and is teetotal.

The scene where he's arrested by the cops is the best drunk acting I've ever seen, I think, because it's restrained but Richard's face is completely drunk. He is totally drunk, but he isn't. He mocks the notion now, and I don't know whether it's mockable or not, but could he have done that without going through the process of sitting up all night and drinking vodka and champagne? He said, 'Look, I've never been drunk,' and I said, 'Richard, you've got to do it, just once, and remember what these feelings are like, of losing control but trying to keep it.' People who are drunk think that other people don't notice, and the reality is that two or three glasses of Scotch are like a neon sign on top of their heads: 'I've been drinking.' The cops know from fifteen feet when someone's been drinking. They smell it, they sense it.

So we got Richard drunk, hauled him in the next morning to read through the scene, and he spewed up through the French windows. He's often told that story, but he never bothers with the rest of it, the part where I have to clear the stuff up, which was awful. Then we threw him in the back of a car and he went home and slept for twenty-four hours. And did that help him to play drunk? I know it didn't hurt. There can't be anything wrong with knowing what you're up to, but it's the writer's job to do as much work as he can for the actor. I don't necessarily believe in Method acting, because if one was applying the Method to that particular film you'd have to have said, 'Go and live in a dump for a month and learn what it's like to have no money and no food.'

You always like to rehearse first, don't you?

Very much so. Not up to performance, because if you let the actor perform in rehearsal that's probably the best it's going to be. You've got to get it nine out of ten rather than ten out of ten. It's an instinctive thing of knowing when to say, 'All right, we're not doing that any more,' because you can sense that on the day, with the adrenalin pumping and the camera rolling, they'll hit that. Then you can go on. We had so little money we had to know what we were going to do when we got out there; we couldn't fuck about rehearsing on film, which American actors like to do.

Your experience of performing helped you write the screenplay, but did it also help you direct the actors?

It never crossed my mind. I was never worried about how to direct them, I was worried about getting what I had in my head. For example, Richard would say, 'I'm *in* a park and I'm practically dead.' Well, had I not written the line, as a director I may have let that go, but there's no laugh. 'I'm in a *park* and I'm practically dead.' Funny. The line 'Get in the back of the van' is only funny if it's said like Goebbels at high dudgeon. The same thing with the other policeman. In the rehearsals he used to say, 'Out of the car please, sir.' Not funny. The humour is the pauses. 'Out of the car. Please' – and he can hardly bear to say it – 'Sir.' Then you get your laugh.

The thing about being an actor and then being a director is

that because I wasn't a brilliant actor I know how bloody difficult it is. If I've got two actors in here reading a scene, that's one thing. Now you've got sixty people staring at you, and that's another. There's a camera here, and you're in a rage or you're in love with someone or you're going for a laugh, and it's a terribly difficult thing to do. I never mastered it as an actor.

Did you find directing easier than writing?

Physically it's not. Physically it wipes you out. But when you're directing a film you've got 75 to 150 people standing around you, all of whom are experts in their field. If you're on the set and the scene is difficult or you don't know how to approach it, you can turn to them and say, 'How am I going to do this?' These guys do this all day every day, whether they're doing it for a commercial or a feature film, so you've got all this advice which the writer simply hasn't got. As a writer you're totally on your own. There's you, the ashtray and a piece of paper. If I'm writing a comedy, how do I know it's funny? It's funny when I laugh. That's the only judgement I've got. I may sit here all day in the deepest gloom and not laugh and yet still know there's something inherently funny about that particular thing, but I can't say, 'Do you think that's funny?' because there's no one in here to ask. Occasionally I'll bombard Sophie with things.

What happened when you shot the first scenes, the arrival at Crow Crag?

The film kicked off in the first week under the most inauspicious circumstances. On a movie, particularly on a low-budget movie, if Scenes 31, 51 and 97 are in this room, even though they'll be broken up and put all over the film, you're going to shoot them back to back. This room happened to be as black as your hat and dripping with rain with a gale blowing outside that you couldn't hear because it wasn't on the track yet, and HandMade got the shits because they could barely see it. It was all wiped out with black edges and eyes glinting, because that's how I knew it had to be in the context of the picture, but all this darkness disturbed them.

George Harrison and Denis O'Brien were seeing the rushes in London while you were shooting in the Lake District?

They were seeing them before I did, because the rushes would go back to London for processing and then straight over to HandMade. I didn't see any footage for five days. The hours were too long and the facilities were too limited. Meanwhile, there was rumour, innuendo and the physical presence of HandMade on the set saying, 'We can't do this.' Apart from all this pitch-black shit, they'd seen the first scene I shot with Uncle Monty. Withnail comes out and says, 'He sent me to tell you the coffee's ready,' and in the shooting script Marwood and Withnail go back into the dining room and Monty says, 'Ah, Baudelaire', etc, etc. When we came to cut the film together we realised that '*Laisse-moi respirer*' was great but it was so much better to junk that scene and put it over the walking scene. When they watched it, all they saw was this fat guy at a table quoting Baudelaire and waving his arms above his head, and they hated it. That's when they said, 'He's got to be made into a camp homosexual.'

Then they saw the chicken scene and thought it was as a funny as cancer. It didn't make them laugh at all. I said to them, 'Of course it doesn't make you laugh, because you haven't got them in context. I do know once we've set these guys up, and you see them contemplating the death of this chicken, this is going to be extremely funny.' They didn't buy it. They thought, 'This isn't going to be funny, so what can we possibly cut?' and the first thing that they wanted to cut was the bull scene. I was shooting 2500 feet of film a day, which is nothing. Most adverts will shoot about 15,000 feet a day. So I just said, 'Fuck it. What time's the next bus?'

How long was the shooting schedule?

Thirty days.

And how far into the shoot was this?

Three days in. Denis O'Brien and the great Ray Cooper, who's a pal of mine now, came up, and Ray was hired by Denis to do the dirty work. We're walking round on the back of this hillside and Ray's saying, 'The thing is, they don't find it funny, they think it's too dark and they don't think Monty's going to get a laugh unless he's an effete faggot.' And I said, 'I do this my way or I'm not doing it at all.' And Ray, God bless him, was instrumental in getting Denis out of there. Because the film was so cheap and they'd gone this far, they left me alone and just thought, 'Fuck it, we've blown a million quid.'

Where did David Wimbury fit in?

He was basically line-producing, and it's a fantastically complicated job. You're up a hill in the middle of nowhere, and where's the rain, or where's the bull, or where's the food for a hundred people? All that has to be taken care of by the line-producer. Considering I'd never done it before, I was very lucky with people like that: Ray, Wimbury, and indeed Paul Heller. In the first week, the night before we started shooting, I couldn't sleep. We had a five o'clock call, and at two o'clock I'm still sitting in this closed-up bar with a bottle of vodka, not trying to get drunk to get drunk but trying to get drunk so I could get some sleep. I was quivering with terror, and Wimbury sat there drinking with me until about three in the morning. That was the night he said something about film-making that has really stuck in my mind. He said, 'It doesn't matter how good your script is, how good your actors are or how friendly the weather is. If you haven't got luck on a picture, you haven't got anything.' And that's so true.

In the opening titles of *Withnail*, and also *Advertising*, you give a primary credit to the camera operator, Bob Smith, in addition to the director of photography, Peter Hannan, which is unusual. What did they each contribute?

Hannan basically lights the film; he puts the lamps up. We discuss the scene and he asks, 'How do you want this? What mood are you going for?' But the first person actually to see the film is the camera operator because he's looking through the frame that's going to go on the screen. Your first question at the end of every take is not to the director of photography, it's to the operators: 'What do you think, Bob?' and he would answer not from a director's point of view but from a technical point of view. Because I hadn't done it before, I'd say, 'How was that, Bob?' and he'd say, 'Great,' and I'd say, 'Really? I didn't like that,' and it was a while before it sunk in. He said, 'I'm not making judgements about what you're making judgements about. If you think it's great and I say it's crap, I'm talking technically.' Bob gets a primary credit on both films because he deserved it. I'd say, 'Let's have the camera over here,' and he'd surreptitiously nod towards another part of the room, and I'd say, 'Oh, I meant there.' He helped me massively, and obviously I know more about it now than I knew then, but if I do make *The Block* I want Hannan and Bob.

The production designer, Michael Pickwoad, also worked on both films.

Pickwoad came out of the HandMade woodwork; he'd worked on some HandMade films before. He's terribly eccentric and very tense, wearing bow-ties and a grin. I liked him enormously from the moment I met him, and I think the casting of the crew is as important as the casting of the actors. I was incredibly well served there by Wimbury, because he knew me well and he brought in people he thought I would work with well. When we had our first technical read-through, a guy who was something to do with properties said, 'At the cottage we can always use candles with lightbulbs at the end.' I looked at him with astonishment, and as I was looking away I saw Wimbury looking at me, and this guy got fired five minutes after the meeting. Wimbury knew I didn't like the sound of that, and if I didn't like it we weren't going to do it. How could you have them walking around with lightbulbs on the end of candles?

You still had some technical problems with the tea-shop scene, didn't you?

A close friend of Hannan's had died, and because he was upset he got all the stops and everything wrong on the camera. It was a good piece of acting that had been going on that day, but when the dailies came back he said, 'We've got to shoot it again.' I said, 'No way. I can't reshoot that scene because we're not going to get that edge back.' We'd rehearsed the scene without the expletives, so those local old ladies who were sitting there had no idea what they were going to get when they got it. We stuck the camera on them and played the scene and their shock was genuine, we couldn't have got it back, so the lab fucked with the negative to bring it up to a reasonable quality because I wouldn't shoot it again. If you look out for it, you'll see there's a lot of darkness in the tea-shop that shouldn't be there, but it plays great.

Richard Grant kept cracking up, too, on one particular line.

'Liven all you stiffs up a bit,' I left it in. They're not meant to know that they're funny, not in any way. I kept saying, 'Please don't laugh, Richard. Please don't laugh,' and we went again and again and again. Every time he hit the line he laughed. He just could not do it without laughing, and I figured, 'Fuck it. He's meant to be totally drunk and for once he's made himself laugh.' So it's in the film. I think it's quite funny.

You were superstitious about the crew laughing, weren't you, because scenes shouldn't be funny out of context?

No, they shouldn't. Bob laughed on that line where Marwood comes back from trying to get fuel and wood and Withnail walks through in a blanket and says, 'Jesus – you're covered in shit.' Bob laughed behind the camera and I said, 'Cut!' I knew it would be wrong. I couldn't get it, and it still doesn't get the laugh from the audience. It's one of the few laughs that should be there that you don't get. It's weird, that. The only moment I laughed on the film was when Grant does that grin with a piece of pastry stuck in his tooth, and that was by accident. I did laugh at that, and I still think that's an incredibly funny image.

The supporting characters were all perfectly cast, for instance Noel Johnson as the pub landlord and Llewellyn Rees as the tea-shop proprietor. How did the older actors respond to this very offbeat script?

In a very positive way. As a matter of fact, that old guy in the tea shop wrote me this very sweet letter, terribly charming, like it was 1932 at the Oxford Repertory Theatre. He only worked for a couple of days on it, but he said what a nice two days they were and that he really enjoyed himself. Noel Johnson was a radio star in the fifties; he had his own show, something like *Sexton Blake*. It's so autobiographical that I absolutely knew what I wanted, down to the tea-shop lady and the old girl who opens the door. We saw a lot of people for those little parts, many more than we did for the big parts. The tea-shop lady, of course, I offered to Mrs Thatcher, but her agent said the money wasn't good enough.

The sixties are seen as a time of sex, drugs and rock and roll, but in the film there's no sex, very few drugs, and the only rock and roll is on the soundtrack.

No, there's a paucity of all of those. They never listen to music. There's virtually no drugs. It's always Marwood who doesn't want drugs, and that was how I was. I was really spaced-out by this point in my life anyway, and if I had taken drugs I'd have freaked out. One of the great advantages of alcohol is that you can pre-judge the effect from the dose. You know what that much booze is going to do, but that much LSD or that much grass you don't know what's going to happen, which is why I'm not fond of it. I don't like that feeling at all, of completely losing control. Drugs are referred to when Marwood says, 'Speed is like a dozen transatlantic flights', but they don't take Danny's 'phenodihydrochloride benzorex', and they only smoke one joint, the Camberwell Carrot, that Marwood gets the horrors off. That was one of the toughest scenes to shoot, principally because it was so difficult to get the hysterical side of what being high is like. Danny says, 'That is an unfortunate political decision, reflecting these times,' and you cut to Withnail, sitting in a chair, who says, 'What are you talking about, Danny?' and Danny says, 'Politics, man,' and the whole rhythm of the scene shifts badly. In fact, it should have been reshot, but you get away with it because they're stoned. Richard never did laugh like that. We recorded it, then re-recorded it again and again in the lab.

Their main recreation is drinking, hence the popular student game where you drink what they drink when they drink it.

When I was doing *Journey's End* I used to supplement my forty quid a week as a touring provincial actor by going to auctions, buying things for a tenner and selling them for a hundred in London. We went to one in Alderley Edge, and there was nothing in it, but there was a boarded-up hotel opposite that they were about to demolish, and the only thing left open was this little bar. The actors who had gone to the auction trooped in, and they all wanted a pint except me and my friend Steve who wanted a glass of wine. The barman said, 'I can't sell you a glass, but I can sell you a bottle for a quid.' We said, 'Really? What have you got?' He said, 'I don't know. Come and have a look.'

We go into the cellar, and all the best vintages of the twentieth century were down there, stuff that even in those days was worth fifty quid a bottle. 'A pound a bottle is it, mate?' 'Yeah.' So we were plundering fifty-three Margaux, 'best of the century', as Withnail says, well over £1200 a bottle now. We had £200 between us, and me and Steve bought two hundred bottles of wine. The landlord said, 'You do know this wine is old, don't you?' We said, 'Yeah, but we don't mind that. We'll have another dozen of those sixty-ones, please.' The plan was, take it back to London, where we were literally on our uppers, and knock it out at Sotheby's, which would have made us several thousand pounds. We drank the lot in two weeks. We were literally sitting there with fish and chips, saying, 'Shall we have the Haute-Medoc or shall we have the Margaux?' And I'm so glad we did drink it because there's no way you could drink that kind of wine now.

Danny is the only representative of the decade in the film. Without him it . . .

Could be any time, yeah. Except for the cars. But there's plenty of modern cars in there if you want to look. The money wasn't there to be able to navigate that. We had to get out on a road with spotters saying, 'You've got a gap,' and try and shoot. We had old cars surrounding our car, but you couldn't control a hundred yards behind that on a slip road. The arrest scene was on the M25, but nearly all of the country road scenes were shot in Ealing Broadway, and if you'd moved the camera two feet sideways there would have been greengrocers shops and houses. We had to do it so fast. There was just no dough. Guys were out looking in London rather than being able to get in the country, which would have taken another four hours.

Is it true that as you were shooting the drive out of London, Grant and McGann were pursued by the police because of the condition of the Jag?

That's right, they were, and Grant jumped over someone's garden wall and rushed through the herbaceous border to escape. And he always accuses me of cowardice!

And the return to London by motorway was . . .

When HandMade wouldn't finance the scenes. They said, 'You don't need them,' but not to have shot that drive back would have been a hole in the film. Marwood would have said, 'Get your kit together, we're leaving in half an hour,' cut to them in the hallway in London. It would have been awful. And then we'd have had to have cut the piss-bottle scene, because what's the point of setting that up if it's not going to be used? And then we'd have had to have cut it in the car: 'This is a device enabling the drunken driver to operate in absolute safety.' It would have been difficult and it would have been detrimental to the movie. You'd have lost part of that insanity, and that's the whole point of the film.

I notice that the 'Accident Black Spot' is in the London Borough of Finchley, which was still Mrs Thatcher's constituency when you made the film.

It had to be Finchley: 'They're throwing themselves into the road gladly.' One in one thousand people will have got that reference, and that's enough didacticism in any film. Some people may get it, and those that do will quietly grin to themselves, and those that don't, it doesn't matter. The obverse of that is ramming it down people's throats like I did in *Advertising*. It's a hard-learned lesson. What is the point of *Withnail*? It's not a political film, it's a film to get people laughing for a hundred-plus minutes. That's all I care about.

Although the film tells a personal story rather than a political one, its end-of-decade atmosphere does lend it an element of social comment. Did you sense a sniff of something new in the air during the sixties?

The whole generation, kids of the sixties who are now cabinet ministers and Prime Ministers, did think that there was something new and that it couldn't possibly revert to the old order. It did feel for a while that something fundamental had changed, like at Grosvenor Square, 150,000 young kids out saying, 'Fuck the war in Vietnam.' And then, of course, it all fell to bits and turned into Margaret Thatcher. Until the sixties, young people tried to look like their mums and dads. The girls wore pleated skirts and court shoes and the boys wore ties and sports jackets, and suddenly this sixties thing happened and it was a phenomenon. I remember being very excited about it all. It was so pungent it rubbed off on everybody; everybody got a bit of the excitement.

It's interesting, though. Without Danny, the film would have no timeframe at all. He is very much anchored in the age and they are not. 'Why's he wearing that old suit?' Well, he did wear old suits, Viv, and was heavily into tweed. Viv and I used to wear second-hand clothes; old waistcoats and corduroy trousers and polished brogues. We didn't dress in the period of the sixties at all. Uncle Monty has got nothing to do with the sixties, has he?

A character like him could easily exist . . .

In the thirties or the eighties. I envisaged him as this bumbling homosexual, but I got a fix on his specific look because one night Sophie and I had been invited to dinner at someone's house – a well-known art dealer – and we were talking about paintings, and at this dinner there was a Monty-esque figure who was Head of Classical Art at the Royal Academy. He said to Sophie and I, 'Why don't you come back and have a drink with me?' We go back to his house, two hundred yards from where we were, and there, two years later, is where I shot Monty's room. We went in there and it was like a museum. He was very much into the notion of set-dressing his life, and when we came out I said to Sophie, 'That's Monty's house.' When we were in pre-production I phoned him up and said, 'How do you fancy us shooting in your drawing room?' and because he needed the dough he said, 'OK.' I wouldn't let a film crew into my house for all the tea in China, but we went round there, Hannan stuck the lights in, we turned the camera on and that was it.

Monty also came from a book in a junk shop, didn't he, which included various poems and a photograph at the front?

Of a naked kid, yeah. *Rondeaux of Boyhood*. I still have it somewhere. It was privately printed in Putney or Hampstead, I can't remember which, in 1922. You can imagine some old queen coming up with these ridiculous poems, stuff like 'In trousers now my boys arrayed' and 'Come into the woods and strike my conker, oh bend, I conquer you' and 'We all got laid at the Dog & Duck in the morning'. The influences on Monty were very much *Rondeaux of Boyhood* and my experience with Zeffirelli.

Monty drew criticisms of homophobia from some critics, despite the fact that he's an extremely sympathetic character. As soon as he arrives at Crow Crag the whole place comes alive.

That's the thing Withnail loves about him being there: warmth, cleanliness, fabulous booze – all the things they haven't got arrive with Monty. That was the only time I did anything cinematographically: I changed all the lenses. Everything to do with Monty was shot on a 35mm lens, just this side of being a wide-angle, and it was sort of encompassing, whereas Withnail's view was all shot on a 50mm, so narrow that he never saw anything but what he was looking at. Withnail may as well be in Clapham High Street. He never once makes reference to the countryside, except, 'We've gone on holiday by mistake.' He's got no interest whatsoever. The river isn't beautiful, it's to be shot at to get 'flesh'. Everything about it is hateful and loathsome and terrifying to him. Monty spreads warmth and spreads light, so we changed into 35mm then back in 50mm when they go back to London.

Do you think there is an element of repressed homosexuality in the relationship between Withnail and Marwood?

No, I don't. I think that the character of Withnail is so self-obsessed and self-absorbed that he'd be incapable of making love with a woman, a man or a fucking elephant. His love was for himself. I think if there was even the remotest hint of that in *Withnail* there would have been the remotest hint of it in my relationship with Viv, and there wasn't. Neither of us were vaguely homosexual. But for anyone to call *Withnail* homophobic is ludicrous. It's not even taking the piss out of homosexuals. I have two close friends who are homosexual, actually, and I couldn't give a fuck.

Monty's a tender character, much nicer than Withnail. He happens to be a homo, and there's no way that a homo of his type would come on to Marwood unless Withnail had primed him. If Monty had said off-camera to Withnail, 'I do think your friend's awfully charming,' and Withnail had said, 'Yeah, he's got this most beautiful girlfriend he's madly in love with,' Monty would have said, 'Really? How marvellous.' But Withnail says, 'I hate to tell you this, Monty, but he's got a lot of problems.' I think it would have been very funny if I'd shown Monty and Withnail going off into some little boudoir somewhere, but if we'd had the scene in the film it would have blown his arrival at the cottage, and the only reason I put that poacher in was to confuse the audience. Marwood and Withnail thought that the poacher had come to get them, and so did the audience. Elphick's part is completely redundant other than for that, except to rev up the paranoia a bit.

He was bloody good in that, Mike, wasn't he? He was so pissed. When he arrived, he'd been up all night boozing, and like all boozers within twenty seconds he knew where the stash was hidden, so he made a beeline for the wardrobe van and was in there glugging. Now he's on the set, so wasted he could hardly stand up, and we shot thousands of feet. I didn't even bother with cuts and takes and stuff, I just kept shouting at him, 'No, Mike, you've got it wrong.' Those out-takes would be interesting, wouldn't they? 'What do you mean I've fucking got it wrong?' 'You're saying the wrong lines. You're in a different film, mate.' 'Fuck off!' 'Keep running. Start again.'

He played the part as a favour, didn't he, because you were in the same year . . .

At drama school, yeah.

Like your friend David Dundas, who composed the music.

I had terrible problems with the music. David saw the film, I went round to his studio one night, he put it up on the click screen, and my toes were curling because track after track was completely wrong. For example, he'd bring up this piece of music over shooting the fish in the river which was like bongo drums. He was getting more and more fraught because he could see I didn't like it, and I was getting more and more fraught because I kept saying, 'No, no.' We went through the whole catalogue of the music he'd done and I didn't like any of it, and then he put on that last track, 'Withnail's Theme', played on a kaliope, which is a little steam organ, and that was it: it was brilliant. Thank God. I said, 'That's it, David! That's the music!' He had absolutely one hundred per cent caught the essence of *Withnail*. So he was delighted, and I was delighted, and we just threw all the rest away and that became the focus of the score.

It's lovely and it's haunting and it's memorable, and it really segued in beautifully at the end when he walks across the park back to exactly what he's been all the way through the film except half of him is gone.

The score is actually credited to David Dundas and Rick Wentworth.

What happens is that David improvises the themes on a piano, then Rick, who trained under a really famous English composer whose name escapes me, writes it up and orchestrates it. David obviously knows a hell of a lot about music, but he doesn't know much about the technical side of it. I don't know if he can write music, or even read it. Rick would do all that, and actually produce the written sheets.

The music over the opening titles is equally striking, 'A Whiter Shade of Pale' featuring King Curtis on saxophone.

It's such an eclectic film, and it developed over so many years. A friend of mine told me about this piece of music ages and ages before we made the film, and when I heard it, I thought, 'This is the opening music.' King Curtis was murdered the night he played it. He came out of the concert hall, got into a row in the carpark, and the guy offed him and fucked off. Never caught him. It's sublime, that music, isn't it?

It's a live track, and the sound of the audience is the only indication in the film of that sixties hedonism, with the exception of Danny.

That's right. It's the only time that there is an enjoyment of the sixties, that opening music with the sax playing. It's what the film should be, so sweet and so sour. From the departure of Monty right through the third act you keep laughing, but you're aware of this fracture happening. For that period of their lives there is a symbiosis. They need each other to function as individuals, which is what makes it so tough at the end for Withnail. Unless you felt very strongly that the symbiosis between them is over, it wouldn't be moving. There's something awful about this guy in the rain acting his heart out to these animals, and that's the biggest audience he'll ever get.

The original ending was even more bleak, wasn't it?

It was too dark, that's why I dumped it. Originally the Shakespeare scene didn't exist. They part in the park, Withnail goes home, then you cut to the 'I' character in a dressing room about to go on for *Journey's End*. He's got a letter from Withnail which is very optimistic about his life, then you cut back to Withnail and he's got the shotgun and one of Monty's fifty-three Margaux that he pours down the barrels, 'Chin-chin,' and blows his head off. I was never happy with that, and other people who were involved in the film thought it was over the top. It didn't need it. You know what's happened to Withnail. He's a loser. Then that idea for the Shakespeare speech came up, I stuck it in and it seemed to work.

Monty talks about Hamlet in his first scene and Withnail says that he intends to play the part, which he does.

To a pack of wolves on his own. I can't remember whether I stuck that line in the Monty scene after I'd written the final scene – *I'd* written! After William Shakespeare had written it and I'd appropriated it – or whether it was the other way round. When Uncle Monty stands up in that scene, 'It's gone. We do it wrong, to offer it a show of violence,' that's from *Hamlet* too. There's a lot of *Hamlet* references in there.

Not only is their relationship coming to an end, together with the whole decade, but the city itself is literally coming apart, crumbling under the wrecking ball.

It's permeated with decay, and at the end the 'I' character leaves with some hope but there's no hope for the other bastard. There's none. There's nowhere to go. He hasn't got anyone to play off. He's going to spend his life drinking himself to death, which is exactly what Viv did. I've never seen anyone as badly affected as Viv. Years later when he came to stay with us, he'd wig out on the sofa with his shoes and coat on, and you'd come down in the morning and there he would be, wigged, in his brogues and green tweed, still in the same position, fucked with alcohol. He'd get up, come into the kitchen, and the first thing he'd do is pour himself a shot of Scotch. Our bodies can tolerate an enormous amount of punishment, but not that much. He walked like an old man with the shakes. It was really sad.

You said he read the novel, but did he read the script or see the film?

I took him to see the film when he was dying. He didn't know he was dying, but he was fucking ill. When did it come out, 1987? He died in about 1990. It was throat cancer, the most terrible thing. They'd sewn his throat up and he couldn't swallow, so he had to spit into this enormous cauldron. He had a pipe coming out of his stomach which he was fed through, and he was pouring neat Scotch straight into it.

What did he make of the film?

I think he liked it. He laughed quite a lot.

It must have been quite a shock to see someone living out events from his life.

I suppose it was, to see someone else playing you. It wasn't a shock to see Paul McGann playing me because I cast him in the part, but Viv had no notion of how Richard was going to interpret those early years together. Some of the funniest nights of my life were spent in that house. There would be four or five of us round there, and maybe it's memory playing tricks but I remember tirades of wit and people crawling on their hands and knees trying to escape the laughter. It's the difference between being broke and being poor. There are people with a lot of money in the bank that I consider poor, because they're poor in spirit. We weren't poor, we were just terminally broke.

There are other scenes in the script which aren't in the film, such as Withnail and Marwood fixing up the Jag and stocking up on booze.

Didn't need them. Once they had decided to go, the best thing is to get them gone, otherwise you'd have cut from Uncle Monty's not to that ball swinging but maybe to an off-licence, and I think it would have slowed it up. There was a scene that I cut where they fence in a Shakespearean manner that I've re-used in *The Block* in a different way. Withnail's smoking a cigarette inside his fencing mask, which is something that Viv did in one of our classes at Central, this beehive with smoke pouring out and the teacher saying, 'Are you smoking in there?' That was so funny. I always wanted to use it, and I tried it in *Withnail* and it didn't work, so I've stuck it in *The Block* and hopefully it'll find its feet in there if it gets done.

Alan Strachan was the editor on both the HandMade films – a really nice guy – and in those days you used to cut the film manually on a Steenbeck. When we were doing *Withnail*, I was sitting in front of the Steenbeck working on the return to London, trying to get a Savile Row suit out of remnants, literally using bits before the clapperboard went in. I was going on and on and on at him about this sequence, and he was standing behind me, and I said, 'If we did this, wouldn't that . . . ?' and I turned round and he was like [*stands up, hands outstretched, leering maniacally*] a sort of horrible wizard wanting to strangle me. God it made me laugh, that.

Another change is that in the screenplay Marwood packs a notebook in his suitcase at the end which has *Withnail & I* written on the front.

Has it? I wonder why I changed it. In the film it's *À Rebours* by J. K. Huysmans, and *David Copperfield*. You see, that would be the way to turn someone on to something, if they came out of the movie and said, 'What were those books he shoved in his case at the end? One was *David Copperfield*, what was the other?' Maybe they see it another time and they say, '*À Rebours*. What's that? Why would that be going in?' Then they go to a bookshop and say, 'Have you got a book called *À Rebours*?' That's the best way to turn someone on to something, not as I did it in *Advertising*.

The first preview screening over here didn't go to plan, did it?

That was the most nightmarish piece of stupidity that I've ever been through. The people who were employed to recruit the audience – the kind of young audience that we thought would like the film – recruited a load of students who couldn't speak English. If you can't speak English you don't get *Withnail*. Even if you can speak English fluently but it's not your native tongue you don't get it. I've got a couple of French friends who are absolutely ace at English but they don't get it because to a French ear a line like 'We've gone on holiday by mistake' probably sounds perfectly reasonable. To an English ear, 'We've gone on holiday by mistake' is something that can't possibly happen. How do you go on holiday by mistake? So these Germans are all sitting there and they don't know what day of the week it is with all this yak coming at them, and all they see is two ludicrous blokes tramping about in polythene bags with a tirade of dialogue that's meaningless to them. They got fired, those publicity people, and quite rightly so.

In fact, on its original release, the film did better in America.

Yes, it did. It played at the Carnegie Cinema on Lexington or Fifth – one of those. I went with the editor to New York, my agent flew up from LA, and there were Denis O'Brien and a few of the wigs from HandMade there, and we previewed it at the Carnegie with a street audience. I didn't know whether the Americans would get it, but by about thirty minutes in there were two girls three rows down from me standing up to laugh they were in such hysterics, and I thought, 'We've cracked it.' I was so thrilled. I was sitting next to my agent and I said, 'I'm not going to watch. I'm going for a drink.' Then we got the preview cards back, and all the cards unequivocally said, 'It's got no legs at all. It wouldn't play for a week.' I said to O'Brien and my agent, 'I don't believe it; that audience was really digging this movie.' When I came back at the end of my boozing session they were all clapping and I knew that it would work for America, as indeed it did. It was packed for six months, and then they took it off to put on a film with Paul Newman and his wife, Joanne Woodward.

Mr & Mrs Bridge?

That's it. It played eight days and went, which was a shame for *Withnail* because that could have stayed there.

One critic suggested that the film went down so well there because it caught the spirit of Hunter S. Thompson, whose books are on your shelves.

Fear and Loathing in Las Vegas I liked very much when I first read it. It's very dated now. *Withnail* does have elements of *Fear and Loathing*; it's not that dissimilar. Two blokes taking off to go somewhere and then coming back. That's the plot of his book and that's the plot of mine. It's the S.J. Perelman three-act thing: 'Put a man up a tree, throw rocks at him, bring him down the tree.'

But you wrote *Withnail* before he wrote *Fear and Loathing*.

I believe so. When did he write *Fear and Loathing* – 1972? Something like that.

Withnail found its audience on video in this country, which was consolidated by the re-release. Why do you think it wasn't more successful first time round, given that it's so English?

It's very curious, that. Americans are always embracing novelty, which they indulge much more than we do, and I suppose a lot of English people who saw *Withnail* just thought it was depressing. I've seen the film many times, but not that many times with an audience. I didn't see it when it came out again a couple of years ago.

The video features Ralph Steadman's drawing of Withnail and 'I' on the front. That was actually done a long time before the film was made, is that right?

That was done about 1980/81. The script had been finished, and I suppose it was the guy I was talking about earlier, Don Hawkins, who went to see Steadman or sent him the script or whatever, and begged, borrowed or stealed Steadman's talent to do us a picture. And it's a brilliant picture. The brilliance of the picture, to me, is the Marwood character, who's just standing there knowing that it's pointless even moving: 'There's nowhere to go and nothing to do and I may as well just stand here for an hour or two, or longer.' He's magnificent, Ralph, in the inventive league of Goya and J. J. Grandville. Some people are confused by his drawing, but I happen to think he's a genius. He totally captured that sense of what it was like in Albert Street in 1968: moaning and spewing and standing.

Tell me about the recent Withnail & I gala night in London.

I've never seen the film look so good, and Richard raised about £100,000 in one night for his charity, to fund these African kids who can't get an education because there's no money to fund them. £100,000 is like £1million in Swaziland.

That's where he was born, isn't it?

Yeah.

Was it just a screening of the film?

There was a screening then an auction of Withnail memorabilia, and because they were all Withnail fans in the audience they sold £40,000 worth of stuff. We got out the sign 'Crow Crag Farm' that's been holding up the door of the chicken hutch in my barn for six years, wire-brushed the duckshit off it and sold it for £600.

Grant's script with all his notes on it got about £5000. There was a poster which got £2500. Even some crummy old T-shirt of mine got £300. The first manuscript of *Withnail*, the novel, got £6600, and it was bought by Richard Curtis, of *Four Weddings and a Funeral* fame. A week later he sent it back to me with a note saying, 'I think you should keep this,' which is one of the sweetest gestures I've ever had happen to me. He's a real gentleman, Mr Curtis, and one day I'm going to send him a bunch of white gladioli.

Where did all this take place?

The Odeon Leicester Square.

The auction as well?

The screening, then the auction, then there was a question-and-answer thing which I couldn't handle. I don't want to answer any more questions about *Withnail*. You may have the dubious pleasure of being the last person I shall ever talk to about it. I had a letter the other day from a guy who wants to do what he called 'The definitive book on *Withnail & I*'. I just thought, 'No,' with a lot of 'o's. It's talked out, I think, and there are no anecdotes left to hang it with. What else is there to say about it? I hear they're opening it again in the Odeon Leicester Square, in one of the smaller screens. Oh, well.

Why were you unhappy with the re-release in 1996?

I liked the fact that *Withnail* had come out in the way it had, and people discovered it and it kind of became their own. In the sixties I used to go and see French movies and they'd be like a discovery. The reason that they re-released *Withnail* was they thought, 'Maybe we can wring another few hundred grand out of this movie.' Then there was all the rest of the exploitation. Oddbins, a major chain owned by someone like Sainsbury's, had competitions all over the country for the best *Withnail* window. I thought it was a fucking cheek. No one had referred to me and said, 'Do you mind this happening with your work?' It wasn't that I was asking for any money out of it, although money would have been nice, but if they'd said, 'Can we do the Oddbins thing and give ten per cent to Save the Children?' I'd have been a lot happier.

But just take money out of the equation for a second. *Withnail* was very much about me and my life, and if I'd only done one thing for my desert island of course it would be *Withnail*. It's a very important piece for me because I lived it and wrote it, then wrote and directed it, and then I was completely *persona non grata* except if it suited them in their marketing, and I just thought that was wrong. I don't think it should have been re-released in the way it was at all. On the material side I didn't like it because I was still owed thirty grand for directing it. I don't know who owns it now. The video's got a Paramount logo on it. This thing is playing all over the world all the time, and neither I nor the producer nor the actors have ever received one penny in residuals. So you think, 'You're going to re-release it. Why would I be jumping with joy? As a matter of fact, I'm not.'

Especially since you're so antipathetic to advertising anyway.

Sure. At the same time, Criterion in New York were doing those big laser discs of the movie. How these things work is if the 'bull scene' comes up you can flick the button on your controller, and instead of watching the scene you could be looking at me or Richard Grant standing there saying, 'I remember we had a terrible time because we auditioned twenty bulls and this was the only bull that would paw the ground and when we got it there on the day it wouldn't do it and we had a set of cardboard horns on it that fell off and we didn't have the time to get the horns back on,' and all that kind of stuff. Then they flick it again and they go back into the picture.

It's very prestigious to be on Criterion, it really is *Taxi Driver* and *Citizen Kane* type of stuff, so it was very flattering to be asked. But Richard said to Criterion, 'What do you sell these things for – $90 a piece? Do you have to pay a royalty?' And they said, 'Of course we do. Every copy we sell, $15 dollars goes to Mr X.' They weren't going to pay us. We thought, 'Why are we doing all this work promoting this movie for other people to be constantly taking the money? They don't even send me a fucking birthday card.' So I refused to do it and Richard refused to do it, and it's the only Criterion disc that hasn't got all the yak on it.

Still, every cloud has a silver lining. *Empire* magazine did give you one of their film awards that year.

Yeah. Best Cult Film, or something. The actual monument is on the stairs. [*Actor's voice*] Next to my BAFTA.

Bruce in Broadstairs, aged about fourteen. *(Bruce Robinson)*

Bruce as Benvolio, opposite Leonard Whiting as Romeo, in Zeffirelli's *Romeo and Juliet*. *(Ronald Grant)*

Bruce as Lt Albert Pinson, opposite Isabelle Adjani as Adele, in Truffaut's *The Story of Adele H. (Ronald Grant)*

Bruce as Brian Lovell, with Billy Connolly as Hughie and Hans Matheson as Luke, filming a scene from *Still Crazy. (Columbia TriStar)*

Sam Waterston as Sydney Schanberg and Dr Haing S. Ngor as Dith Pran in the Warner Bros. release *The Killing Fields*. *(Ronald Grant)*

Bruce with David Puttnam and Roland Joffé publicising *The Killing Fields*. *(Ronald Grant)*

Richard E. Grant as Withnail (left), Paul McGann as 'I' (above), and Richard Griffiths as Uncle Monty (below), between takes of the HandMade film *Withnail & I. (HandMade Films)*

Richard E. Grant as Dennis Bagley in the HandMade film *How to Get Ahead in Advertising*. *(BFI)*

Rachel Ward as Julia Bagley in *How to Get Ahead in Advertising*. *(BFI)*

Andy Garcia as John Berlin, opposite
Lance Henriksen as Freddy Ross (left),
Uma Thurman as Helena (above), and
John Malkovich as St Anne (below), in
the Paramount film *Jennifer Eight*.
(BFI/Ronald Grant)

Bruce directing Richard E. Grant, Richard Griffiths and Paul McGann on location for *Withnail & I. (HandMade Films)*

Bruce directing Richard E. Grant on location for *How to Get Ahead in Advertising. (BFI)*

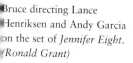

Bruce directing Lance Henriksen and Andy Garcia on the set of *Jennifer Eight.* *(Ronald Grant)*

Paul Newman as General Leslie R. Groves and Dwight Schultz as J. Robert Oppenheimer in the Paramount film *Fat Man and Little Boy*. *(BFI)*

Vince Vaughn as Sheriff and Anne Heche as Beth in the Polygram film *Return to Paradise*. *(Ronald Grant)*

Annette Bening as Claire Cooper and Aidan Quinn as Paul Cooper in the DreamWorks film *In Dreams*. *(Ronald Grant)*

Chapter Five

'An expression of how I felt at the time'

How to Get Ahead in Advertising

How to Get Ahead in Advertising might almost be the modern equivalent of a satirical pamphlet by Swift.

I think there are elements of that, because being a pamphleteer was the most immediate and accessible way of communicating one's outrage and a lot of people did it. Every day you pick up your *Guardian* and there's a Steve Bell cartoon about a serious subject that can make you laugh out loud. Comedy is the greatest weapon there's ever been for dealing with politicians. I'd be sitting there with a boiled egg, saying, 'How can people not see what's going on?' I thought I was looking at reality, and I suppose I wondered why no one else was. If you rant and rave like I used to and you haven't got an outlet for it, people think you're a nut. That's when they say, 'Just lie down. A little bit of the old liquid cosh and you're going to feel much better.' I don't do that any more. Sophie says the first time I took her out to dinner I made an hour and a half speech about Margaret Thatcher. That was our first date. She told me that after about twenty minutes she just cut off and nodded. And that's what became of the film: most of the audience cut off and nodded.

What was the difference between the film and your original novella?

The novella was much more psychological, in that he did a lot more thinking in it than he could do in the film. If I look back   137 now I can't remember where this came from. The only thing I remember is taking photos of myself in the Sherry Netherland in New York and double exposing them to give myself two heads. But that didn't mean anything in terms of *Advertising*, it was just something I did when Lesley was doing press junkets and I was in the hotel with a camera and a bottle and nothing to do. I guess that notion was in my head, together with Thatcher, her government and everything in general, and somewhere they fused to make a story.

Was it 1987 that Mrs Thatcher got back in? A watershed year. That was her third election triumph, and nefarious is an inadequate word to describe her repeated successes; clearly it was fucking ludicrous that she should have been voted in for the third time. *Advertising* was my way of dealing with it, right or wrong. It was all bollocks. It was all spin. It was all what we're getting now, as a matter of fact. The National Health: 'What crisis?' I'll tell you what a crisis is: people are dying in one of the richest countries in the world because we're too blind or too mean to put the money in. I very much had the feeling around that period that this was the end of politics in England. Then they kick her out and here comes John Major, the man I used to call 'The Hyphen' because he was that which came after Thatcher and before what was going to come after him. That's all he was, a political hyphen.

The irony of using cinema to attack the capitalist system is that it costs a lot of money to make and market a film.

I'm not some mad beard in a loft who repudiates the notion of money, or even advertising. There's nothing wrong with saying, 'I grow potatoes. Do you want a pack?' It's the interlocking behind it that I find distressing. It's so insidious. Look at the BBC, for example. I remember phoning their news desk one night – this was before Mandela was released – when they said, 'The ANC went on the rampage into Angola and shot up two police stations with their AK-47s.' AK-47, i.e. Russian guns, i.e. Communist guns. Why mention the guns? When the South African police murdered a bunch of rioting blacks they didn't say, 'With their Colt automatics,' i.e. American guns. Virtually every news item contains that kind of manipulation; it's an example of perverted truth.

The whole news selection process is phenomenal. 'Here's the news.' It's not the news at all, it's what the editors and owners and advertisers have decided we're going to see. Some nights there may be five hours of news worth exploring and other nights there might be sixty seconds, but there's half an hour a day and 'This is the news.' It's a constant reiteration of crisis and tragedy all over the world. Some bus has gone over the edge in Bangladesh and twenty people have been killed. That isn't news. It doesn't really impact on us. All it does is to subliminally reinforce the power of the authorities. Keep telling us we're living in a nightmare and we will turn to them for our protection. What would be news is the fact that two in five children in this country are living in abject poverty. You occasionally get a *World in Action* tossed at you, but that's not actually news, that's television.

I was reading the other day that those missiles the Jaguar aircraft were raining day and night on Serbia, Kosovo, whatever, are between £28,000 and £46,000 a piece. That plane fires four missiles, that's £100,000 gone in ten seconds. How can we afford that? How is it we can't afford to get our own railways together yet we can afford to go out there and fuck up theirs? How come we can't build new hospitals but can afford to bomb theirs? I know it may be considered a bizarre way to look at it but I think it's a reasonable question to ask. There's thirty-six people dead at Paddington: 'We need this new signal system.' 'How much will it cost?' 'A billion pounds.' 'Christ, we can't afford that!' No way, because we've just had to spend a billion fucking up their communications system out there.

East Timor is a perfect example of selective news-gathering. Indonesia invaded in 1975, but it only became news when they withdrew last year.

They chose to ignore it. Why? Because we were the biggest supplier of weapons to the Indonesians. The carnage going on was like a *dozen* Kosovos and had been for a long time. 'That isn't news.' 'Why not?' 'Well, we spend six million on advertising with you, and one of our side divisions manufactures small arms, so if you fuck us about over East Timor we're going to retract our ads.' And so it goes. If we were really treated to the truth of what's behind what finds its way onto the television, we'd be in trauma. The biased attitude towards Europe is another good example. Protecting our 'sovereignty' is a concept out of *Alice in Wonderland*. How can you talk about British sovereignty when you're driving an American Jaguar and stuffing a McDonald's down your throat? The truth is, if we had closer ties with Europe, the British establishment would get found out. In general, other European countries have better education, better transport, better architecture, better health, better food and better weather. Were we to join the Single European Currency, people might want to know why, for instance, a pensioner in Germany pockets three times as many euros per week as a pensioner over here, and perhaps that would stick a pin in this preposterously inflated fantasy of 'Rule Britannia'.

The apogee of this was Mrs Thatcher, and the whole period outraged me. Things like the nation's 'jubilation' that she had committed an international war crime, sinking the *Belgrano*. Naturally she would support Pinochet, a mass-murderer, because in effect she did the same thing and lied about it. That boat was *not* going in the direction she said it was, it was going in the opposite direction and it was full of sea cadets, boys. She murdered 250 young men to get herself a war. Before the election she was absolutely loathed, so she did what they all do: rush out and kill a few foreigners. A woman called Diana Gould put her on the spot on television. She said, 'You're lying, Mrs Thatcher,' and Thatcher said, 'No, the *Belgrano* was heading into the Exclusion Zone.' 'No, it wasn't. I've got the facts in front of me and you are lying.' It was the only time I've ever seen Thatcher completely nonplussed. She could not answer this woman because she could not deal in truth.

Thatcher could still be in power if she hadn't gone mad. She actually lost it. She was sending submarines down to Argentina with nuclear warheads on board. Did it cross her mind that she might have to nuke Buenos Aires? Surely there was some way she could have come to terms over that island. Surely it was ridiculous to allow a pile of rock covered in penguin shit to escalate to the point where the *Sheffield* copped an Exocet missile, cremating two hundred men. Waste of money. Waste of life. 'A couple of bald old men fighting over a comb,' as I heard it described. If the same thing had happened in Hong Kong there's no way Thatcher would have sent the navy out there because the Chinese would have bum-rapped them from a thousand miles away. Francis Pym was sacked by Mrs Thatcher because he said, 'You're out of your mind,' and he was right. Just because she had a political mandate doesn't mean she was exempt from the normal rules of human behaviour.

The Bomb is mentioned more than once in the film, the fact that to sell it you need to sell fear, and the fact that it also has a health-giving ingredient: peace.

Obviously that came from my interest in The Bomb, but also that thing Bristol points out, which is really phenomenal. In London, on The Mall heading west towards Buckingham Palace, there's this huge statue to the Royal Marines. There are bronze plaques all the way round it, and one of them commemorates the 'Shanghai Campaign – 1898', with pictures of Brits shoving bayonets into Chinamen in their own country. If I was in China and I saw a statue featuring the 'Hampstead Campaign' with Chinese soldiers bayoneting British people I'd be absolutely shocked. But here we are knifing and shooting slants and hottentots all over the world. We were a very bellicose nation. Still are. Every scrap there is, we can't wait to get our six Harriers out and start dropping cluster bombs – internationally illegal, incidentally – which our country was using in the former Yugoslavia.

The whole show out there was ludicrous. The American public was antipathetic towards that war and Clinton was already in the shit domestically, so he said to Blair, 'I can't carry the can for this, but you'll get away with it. I'll back you up.' There's no way someone like Blair can be as bellicose as he was without the sanction of the United States, but it was sold to the British public as Blair the intransigent 'war-leader'. The Americans had 180 combat aircraft out there and we had six. Six clapped-out planes and a wheelbarrow and that was about it.

Radios that didn't work, rifles that didn't work, bombs that couldn't hit the right target. Not the way it's sold, though. It was at the time of Thatcher that politics and propaganda started seeping into each other all the time. What was the name of that guy, one of her senior ministers, who said he'd been 'economical with the truth' over the Peter Wright spy thing? That is a perfect epitaph for that period: 'economical with the truth'. The truth didn't come into it.

Thatcher's approach to dissent was that if you didn't go along with what she said you were anti-British. You weren't. *She* was anti-British, in my view, because she was prepared to kibosh millions of working people to satisfy her Year Zero concepts. And they never got us anywhere. It's a cowardly and creepy way to conduct politics to say, 'If you're not in total agreement with me then you're anti-British.' I've never been anti-British. I am overtly anti-her. She used to tramp around these wastelands up north with her handbag and say, 'We're going to revitalise this area,' and some journalist would point out, 'You were here three years ago, Mrs Thatcher, on this patch of land, and you said it was going to be a hospital.' 'Oh, you're such a Moaning Minnie.' She was an *enormous* liar, which is why the Conservative Party fell to bits without her. Do you remember 'The Economic Miracle'?

As built on North Sea oil revenues.

Certainly. Where has the populus of this country benefited from that bonanza? It's been squandered. It's all owned by foreign multinational corporations who are taking the profits. We pay the highest fuel taxes in Europe. To fill our Range Rover is forty quid, and thirty-six of that is tax. If there were alternatives, like cheap trains and regular buses, one would use them, but there just aren't.

The Boil accuses Bagley of being a Communist, and he replies that he doesn't want to take anything away from anybody, he just wants to give them a choice of something better. Trains instead of cars, for example.

[*The Boil*] 'You Commies don't half talk a lot of shit.' That was good fun, being The Boil. I used to read The Boil in, and we were going to do it later with Richard's voice, but I liked my Boil voice better than his so I kept mine. [*The Boil*] 'I hate trains.' Thatcher was on record as saying she wouldn't travel on trains; she didn't like them. The wonderful thing about trains is that you can have a big chunk of countryside and 1600 people go whizzing through at ninety miles per hour and two minutes later the butterflies are back. With cars it's a perpetual visual, aural and atmospheric polution. I don't watch television much, but every time the adverts come on they've got cars on beaches, cars up mountainsides, cars on deserted freeways. Under the Trades Descriptions Act that should not be allowed, because cars aren't like that. No matter what it is, a Ford Fuck or a Toyota Twat or whatever, cars are sitting behind another car with another one behind you. How many times have you driven a car along a beach with a waterskier behind you and waves crashing over it? It's such horseshit.

When you were doing publicity for the film, you claimed you'd never knowingly buy anything that you'd seen advertised.

It's almost impossible to buy things that aren't advertised. You'd have to walk round in a hair suit eating raw potatoes. Using the word 'Advertising' in the film was a mistake; that wasn't what it was about. When we did *Withnail* everyone hated the title. They thought no one was going to want to see a film called that. It had the effect of making me over-confident, because when *How to Get Ahead in Advertising* came up everyone hated that and I said, 'But you all hated *Withnail & I*, so I'm going to keep it.' And they were right. I was right with *Withnail*, but they were right with *Advertising*. It shouldn't have been called that because it primed the audience or the critic or whoever was looking at it to think that this was some maniac raving about advertising, and it wasn't. I don't give a fuck about advertising. For me it was more like *Nineteen Eighty-Four*. Orwell said Big Brother will watch you, and the truth is we watch it. We come in every night with our gourmet supper from Marks & Spencer, stick it in the microwave, dump arse on the couch, and sit there of our own free will being told by somebody with a vested interest what's going on out there.

It's actually about standard of living versus quality of life. Thatcher was fixated on material advantage whereas Bagley is concerned with spiritual growth.

I think that's true. The quality of our lives is astonishingly important, and why should we wake up every morning thinking about the new Toyota when our air quality is visibly deteriorating? The writing is on the wall. Do we know more about all these natural disasters, or *are* there more of them? I tend to think the latter. Half of the south side of the Alps has heated up a couple of degrees, and it's thought all that's going to start sliding because the permafrost is melting. Meanwhile, let's pump out another 300,000 Toyotas. I'd rather give those scientists who say 'We're treading a very dangerous path,' the benefit of a very big doubt. This is an organism we live on, we're part of a living system, and we are fucking it up. So what do you do? I have friends who are very concerned with that kind of thing, and when they bend my ear about it I think, 'Give me a break.' But they're right. They're right to do it. Obsessives do tend to lose their sense of humour, though, don't they?

Well, that's the main problem with the film. When you were publicising *Withnail* you told one interviewer that the problem with cinema today is that it frequently tries to say something about something. When you came to make *Advertising* you fell into your own trap: it tries to say everything about everything.

I did indeed. There's still a lot in there that I like very much, still some good laughs, but it becomes too didactic, too much of an earful, and therefore it's self-defeating. The problem with cinema today is you can't make two or three films to learn how to make a film. Chaplin cut his teeth on dozens of shorts, and some of those films are so bad they're unwatchable, but he learned from his mistakes: 'That one wasn't too good, we'll make a better one next week, and the week after we'll make two better ones.' Now cinema is so expensive that unless you've been through the television route you haven't got that facility. You really don't know what you're doing when you're making a film. You know that you're trying to make it as seamless as possible, but when you put the first assembly up it can be a big shock, either very pleasant or very unpleasant. When you're writing the script, you don't write Scene 96, then Scene 24, then Scene 51; there's a continuity, and you know what you're getting. When you make the movie, which is the skill of directing, you're all over the place, probably shooting the end scenes before you've shot the establishing scenes. It's like having a table laden with tomatoes and garlic and onions and stuff: you know that all the ingredients are good but will the final dish really taste like you want it to?

What did you want it to taste like, to use your analogy?

I wanted to shoot it like a Hugh Hudson British Airways advert. It should have been luxurious to look at, brilliant photography that was starting to get rougher as The Boil got stronger, and then when Bagley came back as The Boil it would go back into brilliant photography again, but we just didn't have the money to do it. A week before we were due to start shooting HandMade ripped a million out of the budget. It was a question of, 'Do you want to make the picture for this, or do you not want to make it at all?' It was budgeted at something like £2.8million and it went down to £1.8million. Of course I had to say, 'All right. Fuck it. We'll make it.'

Why did you go back to HandMade after all the problems you had on _Withnail_? Was that simply where the money was?

No, it wasn't. I had some serious problems on _Withnail_ until it was cut together and stuck up in front of audiences and everyone was laughing at it; then HandMade say, 'Oh, the comedy was never in question. We always knew it was going to be incredibly funny.' So now, with one eye closed, I'm the blue-eyed boy for a bit at HandMade: 'What else have you got,

Bruce?' And I'd always wanted to make *Advertising*. But our shooting days were cut down by twelve because of the lack of this million quid. Bristol was played by that great actor Richard Wilson, and when he walked in the door I knew he was perfect but because the film was off and on and off and on it was cast very fast without enough attention to detail. The sets suffered massively. A lot of the interiors are just dull, Bristol's office particularly. We had the view of the Thames, but we also had these brown flats and I hated them. It should have been like Saatchi and Saatchi, a huge white office with a Picasso at the end of it, but what can you do? We couldn't have it repainted because there was no money and there was no time, so we had to put up with it. *Advertising* suffered all the time from putting up with it, like those bluebirds I ended up with that I couldn't cut. They were a running theme in the script and they only appeared in one scene in the film because we couldn't afford the animation.

What were they meant to represent?

They were in there for a reason that was paid off, and I can't remember what the payoff was. They came back at the end of the film, and I'd have to look at the first working draft because when Bloomsbury published the script I took them out. That was another acting job for me, I was the Male Bird. That's probably why they were in there, so I could have a part. I was The Boil and The Bird.

The Boil, which the psychiatrist calls the bullying, aggressive, dictatorial side of Bagley, did allow you to spew a bit of bile.

The Boil of its nature is a disgusting, pus-filled thing. He's literally full of shit, Bagley.

In fact, it physically spews in the psychiatrist's office.

At the mirror, yeah. That was a nightmare to shoot. Dribbles of pus everywhere. I've got pictures of Richard wearing The Boil rig. His whole chest was fake to get these wires and hydraulic lines and all the rest of it up. You'd have ten people on the floor working all these levers, and in the middle of a take the tongue would rupture or an eyeball would fall out. If you made it now you'd do it digitally, but it was real Heath Robinson, hour after hour to try and make The Boil work.

One critic remarked that when Bagley simply seems to be going mad the satire is focused, but when The Boil actually takes over satire gives way to fantasy. In other words, a man who believes he has a talking boil on his neck is a more effective metaphor for national madness than a man who really does have one.

But we don't know whether he does or he doesn't, despite the fact that Julia tries to talk to it. You don't hear it talking back, and only Bagley can see it. He's a man going insane, although you could equally argue that he's a man going sane.

But you do see The Boil's head replacing Bagley's head in the hospital.

Only when Bagley's on his own, though. When the nurse comes in, when The Boil's taken over, she thinks it's *him* talking: 'I know all about your boil, Mr Bagley.' That's what always freaks me out about the notion of going into a psychiatric hospital. You're about to leave and they say [*quiet, reasonable voice*], 'Where are you going?' 'I'm going home.' 'No, you're not. You're going back in there.' 'No, I'm not. I'm going home.' 'Now, don't get hostile.' [*Shouting*] 'I'm not hostile!' You can't deal with it. No matter what you do it's symptomatic of your madness. It's like when you go and see a psychiatrist. If you're early that means something, if you're late that means something else, and if you're on time that means something again. You can't win in that environment. That's a running fear of mine, of being told, 'We're just going to give you something to make you relaxed.' 'I am relaxed!' 'Well, you're not relaxed, are you? You're being aggressive towards us.' 'I am not being aggressive!' And you are being aggressive.

In the same way as Withnail *drew accusations of homophobia,* Advertising *was criticised by some reviewers for being sexist, particularly with regard to Penny, the feminist vegetarian who comes in for a lot of stick from Bagley . . .*

Who's gone mad. Well, yeah, but so what? He hates her, that's all. I didn't eat meat for fifteen years. All these limp-wristed twats in Islington discussing fox-hunting: 'Isn't it cruel to hunt foxes?' I agree totally, it is cruel, but four miles from here is a factory producing thirty thousand eggs a night; chickens with their beaks cut off, their eyes pecked out, their arses fucked, living in hell. And pigs. And cattle. All living in hell. But because their hell isn't associated with horns and red jackets flying over the hill, no one gives a fuck. 'I'll drink this Chardonnay and eat my Marks & Spencer Chicken Tikka while I'm discussing the cruelty of hunting.' Anybody who's ever been in a slaughter-house would maybe think differently about fox-hunting. Not that one evil condones another, but for fuck's sake keep a sense of perspective. Sure, fox-hunting is cruel, of course it is, but it's cruel to get hold of a healthy young pig, haul it up by its back leg, slit its throat and let it bleed to death; it's cruel to destroy the last habitat for otters by sticking a road through it, like that ludicrous bypass at Newbury. Nobody could love animals more than my daughter but she goes out on the hunt because she loves the riding, and they've never caught a fox, never even seen one. In an area like this, fox-hunting is one of the few cohesive things you can do that involves the community.

The film isn't sexist towards Julia, either, who makes an important comment about sincerity in relation to the boil cream: 'If you knew that it actually worked you'd probably have no trouble selling it.'

Because she is a sincere person, and at the end of the film she escapes him. If I could make the film again, which of course I can't, I would expand on their characters more. I'd maybe make Julia proactive rather than reactive, trying to get his mind off it.

Bagley's working methods, pacing his office acting out scenarios for adverts, are a mirror image of your daily routine.

Very similar. Well, that's how I write, so that's how I wrote him writing, I suppose.

And his nightmare, like yours, is not being able to work.

He's got the block, yeah. And *The Block* has got Bradley, so here he comes again, in a sense. He's obviously a character that obsesses me; I don't know why.

It seems to me that The Boil on its own is a metaphor for Thatcher, and in its battle with Bagley is a metaphor for the struggle between old-fashioned liberal humanism and new-fangled conservative greed.

The Boil is the most greedy thing there is, and that was the absolute encapsulation of Margaret Thatcher's politics: greed. Who was that American economist who said, 'Greed is good'? When Oliver Stone made *Wall Street*, and the guy's got that speech about the acquisition of money and fuck everybody else, it was meant to elicit a realisation in the audience – again, didacticism, a big danger – but it didn't, it had the opposite effect: people thought he was right. Who was the actor who played that?

Michael Douglas.

That's right. People were cheering.

'Greed is good. Greed works.'

It does. Look at that slippery little crook Mark Thatcher. He was a failed provincial accountant when Thatcher became Prime Minister, and ended up a multi-millionaire with his rake off from Mum's arms deals. Greed worked for him. The interesting thing about The Boil is that even when it's a tiny pimple it knows it's going to win.

Although you couldn't match the look of a Hugh Hudson ad for British Airways, the final scene is reminiscent of a party political broadcast which he directed, the one with Neil Kinnock walking along the clifftop.

Very much so. But that's free, you see; you haven't got to build it. You get out there, find a decent looking hill, hope you're going to get sun, and wait for it to go down. We did, and when the sun comes along his arms and through his hands it's lovely. Again, thank God for Bob Smith. It was quite complicated shooting that because as Grant's running up the hill there were all sorts of tracks and weights and pulley systems and six guys tugging the camera to get it to counterpoint him. I don't know how they do that kind of thing, but they did it. I remember thinking that I wanted it to be Ken Russellish with that music by Holst.

'Jupiter, the Bringer of Jollity' from *The Planets*. Also known, ironically, as the tune to the hymn 'I Vow to Thee My Country'.

That's right. What I basically like to do is snatch music that I like from here, there and everywhere, and sling it on. It's very effective, that sort of music. 'If happiness means the whole world standing on a double layer of Odour-Eaters, then I, Bagley, will see that they get them.' He's brilliant in that scene, Richard. There are two big speeches in *Advertising*, one at the beginning and one at the end, and you may as well go home after his opening speech, where he talks about advertising. It's the best part of the film, I think. 'If it isn't high in something, it must be low in something else. And that is its health-giving ingredient.' You get a Snack Pot that's high in sugar but low in salt, so its health-giving ingredient is being low in salt.

The final speech in the film was at the end of the second act in the first assembly. If you read the published script, the speech is at the back as it is in the film; they didn't publish the shooting script where that sequence was in the middle. Andrew Birkin came to a screening – Andrew loves the film, actually; he likes it a lot more than I do – and said, 'You've got the end of the picture at the end of the second act. You've got nowhere left to go if you put it there. Make that the end of the movie.' He was dead right.

It was much better there. That's Bagley's statement of what he is. When Andrew said that to me, I couldn't wait to get into the cutting room next day with Alan Strachan. I said, 'We've got a radical idea coming up.' We did have to do quite a lot of fiddling to make it fit, because that horse-ride at the end of the film was originally done with his wife. We were chopping all the time to extirpate her and stay with him, and there is one wide shot where you can just see her horse's nose sticking in at the edge of frame. Films are stuffed with those kind of things, but you don't notice.

Fifteen minutes into the first full screening of *Withnail* – because even when it was finished Denis O'Brien didn't think it was funny – I had this fabulous Paul on the road to Damascus thing in my head: 'I don't care what he thinks. I know this film works.' I had the antithesis of that in *Advertising* where, much later in the film, about an hour in, I thought, 'This doesn't work.' With *Jennifer Eight* I had the feeling an hour in, 'Christ, this is a fucking good movie.' Until they fucked it. I remember reading John Cleese talking about a film the Pythons made, and everyone was laughing their heads off for the first two acts, then sixty minutes on the button they all stopped laughing for the last thirty. So the guys sit down and think, 'What are we going to do? We've got to get them laughing. We'll take this out, put this in, shuffle this around.' They shuffle the pack again and put it in front of another audience, who laugh their heads off for sixty minutes and don't laugh for the last thirty. No matter how they cut it or reassembled it or whatever they did, people stopped laughing at sixty minutes.

How did the film perform in this country?

It broke the box-office record in the cinema that it played in here, the cinema in St Martin's Lane, which is astonishing. The trash papers were fond of it. The *Star* and the *Sun* and the *Mirror* all gave it great reviews, but the broadsheets ripped it to bits. It's very bizarre to get a fabulous review for a film like that in the *Sun*. It didn't do badly here, but it certainly didn't last like *Withnail*. It came and then it went away again. It was a difficult film and it shouldn't have been made in the way it was, and I only know that having made it. We had to go too fast, there wasn't a chance to assess what was going on, and had we not lost that money I think it would have been much better. It would have been visually more satisfying. The shabbiness of *Withnail* helps the film, whereas the shabbiness in *Advertising* doesn't help it at all. Money is the absolute currency in cinema. Those big studio pictures go through dozens of screenings and editings, and a screenplay may go through six or seven drafts with the same writer or, not always for the best, different writers before it's turned into a movie.

I read that a friend of yours saw the film in New York and while some members of the audience left after ten minutes, shaking their fists at the screen, others cheered at the end, so at least it achieved its aim of provoking a reaction.

In America it really polarised the audience. I don't know about loved it, but people either liked it a lot or loathed it. We're talking about the time of Reagan, and I think young intellectuals could identify with what the film was trying to say, but the majority of the cinema-going public just didn't get it. We previewed it twice in two nights, once on Robertson Boulevard in Los Angeles to an off-the-street audience and the seats were going up like people getting off the *Titanic*, but the next night we showed it in the UCLA university cinema and they were all cheering and clapping. It was too esoteric an audience to sustain a feature film. You can't just have a bunch of pre-graduate intellectuals like a picture, you've got to have mums and dads like it as well. One of the most deathly sounds for a film-maker is the sound of a seat going up. We were treated to a lot of that on *Advertising*.

I've made two great errors. The first one was hectoring the audience in *Advertising*: 'Do you get it?' 'Yes, we do, thank you.' The second one was making the audience work for the story in *Jennifer Eight*: 'Why did she say that? Why has he gone there?' 'He's the murderer.' 'Is he? Are you sure?' The audience don't want to work, they want to sit there and either be scared or made to laugh or, sure, made to think sometimes, but not principally. If you see a movie about the potato famine in Ireland that moves you, it's moved you because it's dramatically satisfying not because you think, 'God, those fucking Brits in Ireland 160 years ago were cunts, what can we do?' That isn't the function of cinema. It can be the function of books, but not cinema. It's basically there to entertain. I really believe that now, and if I ever get the chance to make more films I will avoid those two things like the plague: making the audience work and trying to wake them up to something. Fuck it; they can stay asleep. As long as, in their dreams, they're laughing or crying.

Uncle Monty seems to sum up your current attitude to politics when he says, 'Shat on by Tories, shovelled up by Labour.'

I think so. In those days it angered me, and anger is a good motor-drive for writing. Now it depresses me, and I don't feel motivated to get off my arse and do anything about it because frankly there is nothing you can do. Which is why, with all its faults, I don't regret making *Advertising*. It was an expression of how I felt at the time. I can't imagine getting any fire up over this administration. It's as distant as we got with Margaret Thatcher. 'We're going to give the nurses more money.' But there won't actually be any more money. The nurses get an extra three per cent, or whatever, but some poor old bitch on a council estate won't get her physiotherapist that week. It's a castle built on sand, and it makes no difference how many flags you stick on it. This administration has got the chance of the century to make an impact on the lives of the people in England, but all they're interested in is looking after the same old fat cats.

That mad faggot Goring said, 'Whenever I hear the word "democracy" I reach for my revolver.' I would say the opposite of that. Whenever I hear not one word, actually, it would be two words, 'political conviction', I would like to reach for mine. Whenever you hear, 'It is my political conviction that there is no other way,' you know that they are full of shit. Hitler: 'There is no other way.' Thatcher: 'There is no other way.' Any of those people with 'no other way' must be fucking maniacs because things change. Macmillan was asked what is it that fucks up politics: 'Events, dear boy. Events.' By the middle of Thatcher's reign, her 'no other way' was leading to the virtual destruction of everything I love about England, and I'm afraid Mr Blair is falling into that same dreadful myopic trap.

Chapter Six

'Spewing at the speedometer'

Jennifer Eight

Jennifer Eight, a Hollywood thriller, seems an unlikely companion to *Withnail* and an even more unlikely contrast to *Advertising*.

Jennifer Eight was another bad career-move, and it wasn't a career-move I wanted to make, but after *Withnail* and *Advertising*, I couldn't get finance for anything, anywhere. I remember talking to the guy who was running the National Theatre at the time, and he said, 'You should be all right for low-budget movies now. You can do whatever you want,' and I said, 'As a matter of fact, I can't.' All the financing disappeared in England in the mid-eighties, concurrent with the collapse of property prices. It all went completely mad. I drive that old Aston Martin, and I'd be getting people coming up in the street saying, 'Do you want to sell that car? I'll give you £170,000.' House prices were going through the roof, then it all collapsed and everyone had the shits about 'cashflow'.

What projects did you try to set up?

I tried to get *High Rise* set up, but couldn't. That would have been great, because it's funny and it's also political. By then I'd learned the lesson that we've just talked about, and it wouldn't have dealt in any sense with politics, it would have been an analogy for the collapse of societies. The trouble is, it's very expensive. I've always wanted to do a film based on the Orwell novel *Down and Out in Paris and London*. I was talking to people about it after *Advertising* and got nowhere with it, but I spoke to this London producer the other day who said, 'If you want to do it, the money's there.' I may or may not. The chances are I won't, because more than anything I want to do my comedy at the moment. The trouble with *Down and Out* is I've got to write the fucker. *The Block* is there, and I feel like making it. It would have been the proper move, rather than doing *Jennifer Eight*, to have done another English film.

That was about 1988. Then I was at the Toronto Film Festival with *Advertising*, and I'd been trying to avoid my agent getting at me to do work. My daughter was born as we finished the dub on *Withnail* and by now, because of *Withnail* and *Advertising* being back to back, she was two. I wanted some time to be with her, because you have this overwhelming love, particularly when they're very young, watching them learn to walk and talk and everything. So I consciously hadn't worked for a year, and my agent tracked me down at Toronto and said, 'You're halfway to Los Angeles. You must have something to do.' Out of embarrassment – I had nothing at all – I said, 'As a matter of fact, I've got this fabulous idea for a thriller.' 'What is it?' 'I'll tell you when I see you.' The next day he phoned me back and said, 'You're going to go and pitch tomorrow at Universal, MGM and Paramount,' so I'm on the plane thinking, 'What the fuck can I write that's thrilling?'

By the time I landed at LAX, I'd come up with this idea called *Colour Blind*, the sort of thing Hitchcock would toss in his trash instantly. It opened with some men playing poker in a smoke-filled room. You see the ace of spades go down, and obviously it's black. Then you see the nine of clubs go down, obviously it's black. Then you see the king of hearts go down, and it's *black*. Because this guy's colour blind. Anyway, he gets this call that his brother's died in New York and left an apartment, and can he come and sort out his brother's affairs. Within a day or two his brother's girlfriend comes into his life and they get into a relationship. He's trying to find out 'How did my brother die?' and she doesn't know. Then, which is Hitchcock's Mac-Guffin, they're going somewhere and she's got this dress on and he says, 'That's a beautiful dress,' and she says, 'This was your brother's favourite colour.' But he knew his brother was colour blind, like him, and he immediately thinks, 'What's going on?'

She isn't what she's supposed to be. That was the premise for the movie.

How long was it since you'd actually pitched anything?

I hadn't pitched since *Advertising*, and first stop is Frank Price at Universal, so I'm panicking because I came up with this on the plane between the canapés and the first gin and tonic. I go in, and there's Frank Price, Wendy Margolis and some kid. I sit down and Price says, 'This is my son, who's getting into the film industry. He wants to see how a professional pitch works. Do you mind if he sits in?' And within a sentence or two I'm in the shit, because I don't believe it and consequently they don't believe it. If I'd told it to him like I just told it to you I might have pulled it off, but I bluff and blush my way through about twenty minutes and he suddenly says, 'Is that it?' I say, 'For the time being, yeah,' and he says [*American accent*], 'Bruce, I've been in this business forty-two years, and that's the worst fuckin' pitch I've ever heard.'

Now I'm out the door, now I'm back in the car, now I'm heading for MGM, sweating because I've got nothing else and my agent's told them all it's a great thriller. I get down to MGM, there's Alan Ladd Jr and a full board of nine people sitting around. I thought, Here it is. I'm about to die in public. But I've got nothing else so I pitched them this story, and halfway through the pitch I think, 'Price says it's shit, so I tell you what, I'll give it a happy ending this time.' So it's, 'They fall in love and live happily ever after and she's being blackmailed to set him up and blah, blah, blah.' And fuck me, they buy it! Now I'm completely freaked because I've just sold a year and a half of my life and it's nothing to do with me. I phoned my agent and said, 'What am I going to do? They've bought this story and I don't want anything to do with it.' He said, 'Well, what *are* you going to do?' I said, 'Give me twenty-four hours, I'll see if I can come up with something different.'

I'm walking up and down in the hotel, eating the walls, and I come up with this idea for a weird hand with scars on it and rubbed-down fingertips because the victim is blind. That's all I had. I phoned my agent very late that night and said, 'Listen, I've got a much better idea for a thriller.' He said, 'All right, go and pitch that.' I said, 'But what about MGM, the Alan Ladd thing?' He said, 'Go down there, unpitch that and pitch this.' So I go down there, unpitch that and pitch this, and they say, 'We could do both.' I said, 'I don't want to do both. I much prefer this one. All I can tell you about it at the moment is it's a love story between a decrepit old copper and this beautiful young blind girl, and the link between these two is this hand on a garbage dump.' 'We wanna do it.' Now I've got two movies I don't want to do, both out there. Later that day in the hotel, the name of which I can't remember . . .

The Sunset Marquee?

I think it was. I'm in there, and I run into Scott Rudin. [*Impersonates cultured accent and rapid delivery of Rudin*] 'Bruce, how *are* you? Let's have a drink.' If you look through *Venice* magazine, practically every movie made is produced by Scott Rudin. He's like a factory, Scott. He's the size of one, too. I have a massive admiration for him on the one hand and a detailed loathing on the other. These were the days when I got on very well with him. He's incredibly smart. That's one thing he has got: a very fast intellect. So I tell him I'm doing this thing for MGM. 'Fuck MGM. I'm down at Paramount; come and do it with us.' This was when I was still a slightly glimmering offshore light because of *Withnail* and to an extent *Advertising*. I said, 'What am I going to do, Scott? I've pitched it and they've bought it. I've unpitched it and they've bought the other one. Now I've got to go in and unpitch the other one.' Next thing, I'm at Paramount with Scott and a guy called Gary Lucchesi.

I came back to England to write it, and we were just about to sell our house in London because we wanted to move to the countryside, so we went to stay with my mother-in-law where there wasn't really anywhere for me to write. I ended up over the stables in this freezing room, icicles hanging off the end of my nose, going completely mad. They'd been on the phone every other night saying, 'Where is it?' I said, 'I can't write it because of the cold. I can't write it because my typewriter's junk.' This was the one that finally cracked them. My mother-in-law had a thyroid complaint and they had to give her radioactive iodine in the veins, and you weren't allowed to go near her for a week. Scott phones me up: 'How's the script coming along?' I said, 'Fucking awful.' He said, 'I know you've got problems.' I said, 'Yeah, but I've got a serious problem now. My mother-in-law is *radioactive*.' It was true, but he did not believe it. He said [*Impersonates Rudin*], 'I suppose she's clearing paths through the fuckin' snow, is she?' I said, 'I'm telling you the truth, Scott.' He phoned back in an hour and said, 'We've rented you Gore Vidal's house in the Hollywood hills,' which was a mansion that you imagine one of those big stars of the twenties and thirties would have lived in.

Where was Gore Vidal?

He was in Rome and he was renting his house out. It was, like, $8000 a week, paid for by Paramount. Now we're in the stretch-limo. Now we're in this enormous house with grapefruit trees down the side of an Olympic-size swimming pool and bluebirds and heat and blossoms. No more excuses not to write the story. I said, 'If I'm going to do this I need some first-hand police information.' Paramount find me this working senior homicide detective called T.J. Hageboeck, who was an absolute snooker table of a man, the absolute opposite of me. He used to call me [*American accent*], 'A long-haired fuckin' Commie.' He was my height but he used to look down his nose at me with his head tilted back as though he was ten feet tall. Bizarrely, he and I became very good friends, and I went through some serious adventures with him that maybe one day will turn up in a movie; the writer and the cop on the road seems to me quite a captivating idea.

They're like poets, in a way, these detectives. They see with a poet's eye. A poet looking out of my windows here is going to see things in a different way than I see them. Cops are like that: they see very hard. We'd be driving down Wilshire Boulevard in LA, and he'd say something to me like [*American*], 'What's that fuckin' nigger doin' in a fuckin' Cadillac? He's gotta fuckin' two-thousand-dollar suit on there. What the fuck's he doin' there in that suit and that car?' Terrible racism. This was before we became friends, so it used to make me quite uptight because I'm not into that kind of dialogue. We'd go into a bookshop and I'd be looking for something and he'd come round the corner of the aisle and say [*American*], 'Hey, look at this. A one-page book. A one-page fuckin' book.' 'What's that, T.J.?' '*The Black Hero in American History*.' I realised later it was a defence mechanism, something that he felt strong and secure with, because in fact he was a very vulnerable man, although hard as nails.

So we get in his red LAPD Ford Mustang convertible, and we drive up north to see where I might want to set this film. The first place we stopped was Bodega Bay, where they shot *The Birds*. Amazing being there. There's all these seagulls standing around watching you, still represented by the William Morris Agency. We're driving up to Marin County through Bodega Bay, and all the time this anti-black stuff is going on. We stop somewhere to have dinner and stay the night, walk into this restaurant in the hotel – and because we're on expenses we're staying in the best places and eating the best food – and the maître d' is a very elegant black guy, and T.J. starts going on about this. I can't emphasise the point too strongly: T.J. is a big guy, bullet holes, knife wounds, bull neck with a shaved head and a moustache. I said to him, 'Listen, T.J., I don't like some of them, I do like others. Exactly the same as I don't like some whites and I do like some whites. As a matter of fact, I don't know many black people, I wish I knew a few more. So can we just stow it, please?' He was quivering with rage all the way through dinner. I'd say to him, 'Do you want some more wine?' and he'd just look at me. We finish dinner, we walk into the foyer, and I say, 'We'd better get on the road early. I'll see you down here at seven-thirty.' And off he goes, nothing said.

Cut to next morning, down in the foyer. Still nothing. I'd hoped the wine would have changed his mood by the morning but it's just as acerbic and aggressive towards me. We get into this rural area, basically desert, and he pulls off the freeway, so now we're on a country road with tumbleweed going by. Still nothing. Total silence. Then we go off the country road on to a country lane in the middle of nowhere, and it's Cary Grant time in the maize field. Then we pull off into another place, and the first thing that comes into my head is, 'This looks to me like a clichéd version of Dead Man's Gulch.' There's a wrecked oak tree and a dried up river and vultures. He stops the car, and this is the first time he's spoken all morning. [*American*] 'I need a fuckin' drink.' He gets out, opens the trunk of the car and produces a bottle of Bourbon. I'm sitting in the passenger seat, really uptight, and behind, in the trunk, I hear his Beretta being cocked. I thought, 'Jesus Christ, he's going to *off* me and kick me in this ditch.' [*American*] 'Bruce Robinson?' I could imagine his perplexed expression, 'Yeah . . . I dropped him in San Fran. He wanted to fly back to LA. I don't know where the fuck he is.' I thought, 'I've got to take steps here,' and I got out of the car to talk to him, and the only thing I could think of to say was, 'Please don't kill me!' He'd already told me – and I later used this in *Penman* – that the first bullet always goes through the out-stretched hand: 'Please don't kill me!' as your hand comes off.

Which you used in the film too.

You get it in the hand first, then you get it in the tit. That's all I could think of. I get round there, he's got his Beretta in one hand and his Jack Daniels in the other, and now he's re-taken control. He says to me [*American accent*], 'I had a fuckin' stroke, you know.' 'Really, T.J.?' 'Yeah, I had a fuckin' stroke. You know why I got a stroke?' 'No.' 'Because I got uptight, that's why. I don't like to be made uptight.' And I'm there with my hand out ready to be shot at, saying, 'Hey, T.J., don't get me wrong, man. I don't like the motherfuckers either.' I give him this kind of routine. Within five minutes we're back in the car and he's driving along happy as a sandboy because he was in control again. He died of stomach cancer. I'd gone over to LA and had dinner with him and he was hale, hearty, boozing away. Then I was on holiday in France and someone called me up and said, 'T.J.'s dead.' Got him so quick. He was only fifty.

After this event with T.J. I learned a lot about being a copper. The way that if they go into a bar, he would sit so that his partner's clocking that way and he's clocking the other way so no one can come up behind his partner and no one can come up behind him. These things were all instinctive to him but to me they were like magic, and they were all in *Jennifer Eight*. I'm talking about the film to him all the time, and he starts telling me about this thing called 'lateral transfer' where old cops who've got trench fever can move from, say, a police department in Los Angeles to a small police department in Marin County or wherever. This gave me the idea for an old drunken cop in LA moving up to Eureka to be with his old friend and lead the quiet life. It's the most northern city in California. Always wreathed in fog and rain. It was perfect for me. I love rain in movies.

Now Stanley Jaffe, who's running the studio at the time, has got the script, and over breakfast at the Bel Air Hotel he says [*American*], 'What's this lateral transfer stuff?' I said, 'That's what these cops do.' He said, 'Maybe they do that in Limey, they don't do it here.' I said, 'They do. I've researched this carefully.' He's a very aggressive guy, and immediately he's like, 'I'm an American. You're telling me what happens in my country?' I said, 'In this case, I am.' Before we'd got through the grapefruit he was on his feet, napkin thrown down and out the door. That was the high point. That's when we were all friends. We're all sitting there with our mouths hanging open. He was out of order, actually, but he was the power. The last guy running the studio, David Kirkpatrick, had greenlighted the picture, and after this disastrous breakfast Jaffe un-greenlighted it. He very much redded it. I thought, 'Christ, this is it.' I go home, I tell Sophie and she says, 'Get out now. This bodes very ill.'

How long had you been working on the project at this point?

Probably three or four months. Anyway, within half an hour, the phone rings. It's Scott, who's in Tokyo for some reason, and he's already heard about the breakfast. He says, 'You've gotta go down there and lick some ass.' I said, 'Fuck that. Let him phone the head of the LAPD and ask if there's such a thing as lateral transfer. We're poised to pack up and hit the airport.' Then there's a lot of phone calls. Finally, I get this call, 'Stanley wants to see you again. He's got a lot on his plate and maybe we were all a bit edgy.' I go in there, he's got an office like a florist's – three hundred dollars worth of flowers on the desk alone – he's looking through these petunias and he says [*American accent*],

'We like you Limey film-makers, we want to work with you,' blah, blah, blah. 'Do this for me on the script.' Which I did, and they greenlight the picture.

The thing that I liked most about *Jennifer Eight* the studio blew out of the water. I wrote it with Al Pacino in mind, and he wanted to play the part, but he'd just had a crash with that film with Michelle Pfeiffer, *Frankie and Johnny*. He was momentarily out of favour with the studio and he wanted an enormous amount of money. Andy Garcia was very hot at that time, having just come off *Godfather III*, and they thought, 'Here comes an enormous star.' My argument was the whole *premise* of the picture. Everyone says to the old cop, 'You're a wrecked alcoholic who looks like something out of a jar that no one wanted to eat, and you're making this case so you can get a fuck off this blind girl.' The moment you bring in a handsome male lead like Andy Garcia with a beautiful woman like Uma Thurman the audience are going to think, 'They look pretty good together.' No one's going to say, 'You've only got her because she can't see you.' Forget whether Andy was good, bad or indifferent – as a matter of fact he was very good – but imagine how powerful this thing would have been with Al Pacino playing it rough.

In the rush of pre-production, I gather that the schedule and the locations were changed at the last minute and that you were unable to cast the female lead until a few weeks before shooting. Who was in the running for the part?

I can't remember. I really can't. I do know that Uma was rather late in the day and that she absolutely unequivocally refused to test for it. Anyway, the film went from bad to worse. I brought in David Wimbury, who they didn't want and didn't like, and they brought in their man, Howard W. Koch, who had been responsible for saving that picture *Ghost*. Koch is about 102; he got an Oscar for living, basically. So he's on the edge of the set, and he doesn't like me. I came in one morning at the beginning of the picture and I heard him saying to the camera crew [*American accent*], 'Where's Orson?' i.e. Orson Welles, meaning me. That was our relationship. It got to the point where I was directing Uma and Andy, and Koch, who was in his seventies, got on his feet and said, 'No, no. We're not gonna do it like that. We're gonna shoot a wide and two pops.' All Koch had done is point a camera at Doris Day at the side of the swimming pool then pan Rock Hudson in to sit down – pop, pop – now they're in bed – pop. That's how he directed. How do you shout at an old man? But I had to. I said, 'Get off this fucking set. Either you're directing this or I'm directing it.' So Kirkpatrick had gone, by this time Jaffe had gone, and now they bring in Lucchesi to replace Koch.

The producer who was at the original pitch meeting?

He was an executive, not a producer. By now there was another new head of studio, Brandon Tartikoff, a nice guy but soon to be fired himself. All these guys are telling me something different until I'm going completely bananas. We're travelling to Vancouver to shoot, and Gary – a very sweet man who I consider a friend of mine now – had never been at the coal face of making a picture. I'd be shooting a scene and he would say, 'OK, we got that,' which the crew hated him for because no one but the director can say what the take's like. The director can ask everyone's opinion: 'Did we get that?' to the director of photography, or 'What do you think?' to the actors. We'd be filming in this former loony bin, with only one more scene to shoot before getting out of there. Gary, because he was inexperienced, would say, 'Right. It's four in the morning. We're going to move to the other side of Vancouver to shoot the next scene.' Everyone knew that you don't do that, otherwise you've got to move 120 people across the city and then move 120 people back for tomorrow. Let's do this now, and do that when we're over the other side anyway. No, wouldn't have it. So we had to traipse twenty miles across Vancouver and shoot that scene, then all the equipment, all the trucks, had to come back the next day. The cost of that alone is probably something like $50,000.

Jennifer Eight was meant to cost $15million and it went up to about $30million: that would be like *Withnail* costing £2.4million instead of £1.2million, and there's no way I could have spent £2.4million on *Withnail*, I just couldn't. But with *Jennifer Eight*, bit by bit, 'We need another half a million, do we? OK, here it is.' Money wasn't part of the problem. And, as they say in AA, it wasn't part of the solution either. They were moaning about it all the time but spending it all the time. For example, because Andy was the star he wanted a Lear Jet standing by in Vancouver in case he got an afternoon off, so he could go back to Los Angeles and see his family. If I was Andy at that point I'd have wanted the same. Why not, if these guys are going to give it to you? But call it $20,000 a week, that's $80,000 a month – it was more than that, actually – to keep a jet sitting at the airport doing nothing. Koch had the audacity to tell the studio I was $600,000 overbudget in six weeks. And how would he know that? Because they were paying him $100,000 a week. He was the overbudget. If I hadn't had him I wouldn't have been over.

I take it that after Scott Rudin brought the film to Paramount he left you to it?

That's right. Scott's 'production' was a couple of hot lunches then his arse out the door in his Mercedes. Scott wasn't there for one frame. Now, I find it sort of amusing. Then, I used to ring him up in the middle of the night: 'Wake up, you cunt!' The one thing Scott can't bear to do is miss a phone call, so even at four in the morning during a night shoot I'd phone him in LA: 'What are you doing down there? Don't you realise what's going on up here?' For instance, I arrived to shoot the scene where the cop gets the idea about the witness being blind. It wasn't a set, it was a real street in Vancouver, and I'm discussing the night's work with Conrad Hall. I said, 'By the way, Connie, where's the rain rigs? This has got to be done in the rain.' He said, 'I don't know.' So I say to the first assistant, 'Where's the rain rigs? I want rain all night.' He says, 'I was told you'd cancelled the rain.'

It transpires that this Canadian production manager had decided it would slow us down, and the bottom line is *she* doesn't want rain that night. I went up to her and said, 'Did you cancel the rain?' She said, 'Yeah. There's enough rain in this picture.' I went ballistic. You can't have three captains on the bridge all saying something different because the crew will go into crisis and the ship gets sunk. I did have the respect of the crew and I did have the respect of the actors, but the studio didn't respect me, didn't want anything to do with what I had to say, and had empowered this woman to take that kind of absurd decision on their behalf.

The production managers were Grace Gilroy and Steve Lim, who also received credits as associate producers.

Steve Lim was a lackey of Paramount, a nice man but he had no real authority. Grace Gilroy was the Canadian production manager who told me to fuck off for my rain. It's something that permeates through the structure of any enterprise. If the headmaster isn't respected in a school, it finally works its way down to the dumbest kid. Because I wasn't respected by the production company, she was either given permission to say, 'There's no rain,' or she felt strong enough to say, 'There's no rain.' If that had happened to me on *Withnail* she'd have been fired on the spot. I don't like firing anybody, but I wanted to express my complete dissatisfaction and unhappiness with what she was telling me, and under a normal director–crew environment you'd fire someone for saying that. You'd say, 'It's not your decision. You either do what I tell you to do or you fuck off. If you haven't got me the rain, you're not the person I want to work with. You can go away and I'll get someone who will get me the rain tomorrow night. You've just cost us sixty grand.' But I wasn't in a position to do that because she was picking up from production, 'We don't think much of this cunt Robinson.' And if they don't think much of Robinson, so it will knock-on down through the line. Not through the senior crew – they were like the actors, part of the film-making process – but among some of the ancillary people, because Paramount were tolerating that attitude. Engendering it.

In Canada, people I'd never seen before would come up with their suits and mobiles – I used to call them 'The Armanis' – and start telling me how to shoot the scene. I remember saying to this guy once, 'Who are you?' 'I'm from Paramount.' 'Can you fire me?' 'No.' 'Then fuck off.' These executives would come up and say things like, 'When you're setting up a scene, how come Conrad Hall's choosing the lenses?' I said, 'Sometimes I disagree with what Connie's doing, but this is a man with two Oscars, and if he sticks on a lens and says, "What do you think of this,

Bruce?" and I think that's fine, I don't want to know what the lens is, I couldn't give a damn.' What I know is how to get performances out of these people. That's my expertise. Connie said the most brilliant thing that anybody's ever said to me about film-making. I said, 'How do you always know where to put the camera?' He said, 'That's simple. I point it at the story.' That's a brilliant way of talking about how you photograph a picture. You look at the story. But they were pissed off because Conrad was choosing lenses and not me, so we had to go through this farce where I'd look through and say, 'What is it, Connie?' [*Softly*] 'It's a thirty-five.' [*Loudly*] 'Can you put on a thirty-five, Connie?' Just pretending. It was nonsense.

Now they're going to fire him, and I said, 'You fire him and you're firing me.' Then that dies down. Two days later they fire his son, Conrad 'Win' Hall, who was camera operator. The moment Connie gets wind of this he's up to me and he says, 'They fire Win and they're firing me.' I was saying to the studio, 'Are you going to help me make this picture? If you're not, just fire *me*, will you?' But they didn't want to fire me, and I guess the reason they didn't want to was because they'd have had to pay me. If I'd left voluntarily they wouldn't have had to. I just said, 'Fine. If you're not going to fire me I'm going to try and direct this scene.' They needed a senior figure to fire that wouldn't actually interfere with the production, so they fired Wimbury, the only victim they could get at without actually losing me, I suppose. Wimbury is an experienced producer, a brilliant line-producer, and he knows a lot about film-making. Information had seeped out to us somehow that Andy had to be released from this film at a certain date because he was going to make a film with Dustin Hoffman.

Accidental Hero?

Yeah. Stephen Frears' picture. So we had to shoot Andy day and night. I couldn't afford not to have him for an afternoon. Koch had come up to Vancouver and ordered some sets to be built, and predicated on this information Wimbury wrote a letter to Koch saying, 'Don't build these sets. We're never going to use them.' Of course we didn't, but they fired Wimbury using that letter as the excuse: 'How dare he tell us what to do.' I remember going out for a night shoot in tears. I was in tears with rage, I was in tears with fatigue, I was in tears because I believe in right and wrong and what's fair and what isn't fair, and this was all unfair. They fired my first assistant director, and under the Directors Guild of America rules they're not allowed to do that. He was somebody else they thought they'd have a go at. I was standing there in the middle of the night on the phone to the DGA, and the DGA was saying, 'Tell your lighting cameraman to put his cameras back in the truck. You've got to shut this picture down.' 'How can I do that? If I miss this night's shooting that's one day less I've got with Andy Garcia. I can't shut the picture down.'

Was the script undergoing rewrites during all this?

Oh, yeah. I was up all night and working all day and up all night. It was hell on earth. I was so tired they'd come and knock on the trailer door and say, 'Ready for you on set,' and my spirit would stand up but I'd realise I was still lying down. I was completely and utterly fucked. I can't tell you the negative vibes that were alive and growing on that set. I'm a very accommodating director, I like to like the people I'm working with and know them by their first name and respect what they do and hope they respect what I do, but every day was a new nightmare. I remember once on a Sunday – because we worked six days – driving down to see the dailies in the studio and being so emotionally and physically annihilated that with no warning whatsoever I threw up all over the dashboard. I didn't know it was going to happen. I was just suddenly spewing with loathing and fatigue. Not a pleasant moment; I couldn't see the speedometer. That would be a good case to plead, wouldn't it? 'I'm sorry I was speeding, Your Honour, but I spewed on the speedometer.'

I had a major tantrum towards the end of the shoot, when we were back in LA. They'd assigned this bloke, I don't know who it was, to follow me around. I said to him, 'This is very weird, isn't it? Wherever I am, you are.' He said, 'The studio want me here in case you want anything.' I said, 'I don't, thanks. I've got an assistant.' He said, 'Well, they've asked me to stay around you.'

What it was about, of course, was the old sauce. They thought I was drinking – which I wasn't, not at this point. I got rid of this guy, then I was going for a piss between takes and as I walked past one of the assistants I heard via her headset [*American accent*], 'There he goes. Who's going with him?' I went absolutely bananas, screaming and raving and turning things over – it was on the police set – and even if a dwarf goes mad it's terrifying because you don't know what they're going to do. And after I'd gone mad and said, 'All right. Come on. Let's get on with it,' Connie came up to me and said, 'Do you know, Bruce, that's the best thing you've done on this picture so far. You should have done it week one, just to let them know that it's there.' That's how extreme it got: I was literally shadowed on and off set.

Finally – miraculously – we got a reasonable picture out of it, then dubbed it, and the person in charge of the dub said, 'We've got a great movie on our hands.' We started previewing it and we were getting very high scores and no walkouts, which is rare, because you're picking up audiences from the old shambling meths-drinker to the girl who sells flowers down the road. These screenings are important in the business, and suddenly everyone was thrilled with the movie, which was about two hours twenty. Then here come the studio with their axes to start hacking the thing about for this three-shows-a-night bollocks: 'We've got to get it down to two hours.' We did get it down to two hours, not including end-titles. Now I could barely follow the plot, the scores started going down and people began walking out. When it was all in there everyone loved the film, and when important pieces of linking information were ripped out, because from Paramount's perspective there was nothing going on, the audience lost interest. We almost got to the point of Andy making voice-over links, and when I hear voice-over I think a film's in trouble, normally. It means they don't know how to cut it. If voice-over is specifically orientated towards the picture that's fine – voice-over was always planned in *Withnail* – but if this had gone into the realm of voice-over it would have been a piece of junk. Even after the movie had been locked off we fiddled with the negative, which is a very expensive thing to do. Fucked it up, in my view.

Wouldn't your contract have required you to turn in a film of two hours or less?

I couldn't tell you. It may well have said that. Contracts are bollocks anyway. They say, 'This piece of writing must be in within six weeks,' and sometimes it's six months. You just don't know.

If you are hacking a movie about, I guess there are worse editors to be working with than Conrad Buff, who has since won an Oscar for Titanic.

He was excellent, such a sweet and gentle man, and I drove him mad. I like the editing process. It's one on one. You don't have to get up at four in the morning any more. It's like going into the office, and you can sit there with a cup of tea and a fag, or a beer and a fag, or a glass of wine and a fag – I would choose the latter – and work with this guy, and try things out, and fuck about.

Did you edit the film digitally?

I think Conrad would have done, but I'd had no experience with it and consequently I wanted to edit on film. I like film. It's like on here [*gestures to the screen connected to his electric typewriter*], you can put in a thesaurus programme, and you want a word like 'vile', so you type in 'vile', and 'horrid', 'dirty', 'nasty', or whatever, will come up. I would never use that. I would only use the book, because if I'm looking for the word 'vile' in a manual thesaurus, I'll see 'voluptuous' and think, 'What a lovely word. I must use that soon.' I love that word, 'voluptuous', and it wouldn't have come up in my head. The same is true of film: you're going through physically to find things. On digital you just type in 'Scene 4, Take 9' and up it will come. You won't see the whole gamut of what you shot. Sometimes when you're going through manually you'll say, 'What the fuck was that? I didn't know we had that.' If I do the comedy I'm going to cut it here at home, which will require digital equipment because there's no way I could run a staff. I would just have an editor come down here, get one of the barns converted, stick a couple of editing machines in there and he and I can cut the movie.

So it wasn't a case of being locked out of the editing room. You were still with the picture, as it was being cut, trying to make sense of it?

I was trying to make sense of what they wanted in the best way I could. It was my film; I'd been on this for a year and a half of my life. Directors work so hard that you need someone out there fighting these battles for you, and I didn't have that. Wimbury, God bless him, would have done had they given him the power. Producers are integral to the film-making process. Standing outside the industry you might say, 'How much is a casting director?' 'They're £2000 a week.' 'Oh well, we don't actually need a casting director.' But you do. That's why those people exist and flourish inside the industry. You must have those highly skilled people around you. By now Scott was in Canada shooting that film about chess players, *Searching for Bobby Fischer*, and he ordered all the rushes of my film to be sent up so he could make a cut. I went completely insane and said, 'If anyone's going to fuck this up, let it be me. I will try and do what you want.' So we did, and the figures dropped, and before the release they decide to fire Brandon Tartikoff. Brandon had two pictures: one was mine, the other was Steve Martin's film where he plays this preacher.

Come composer time, another guy, John Goldwyn, is heading the studio, and they force Maurice Jarre on me, who I didn't want. $750,000 plus the orchestra. Jarre turned out the worst music I've ever heard as a soundtrack, and I said, 'Listen, John. I'm going to cut you thirty-five minutes of film and cut his music into it, we can go and watch it in a screening room and you tell me whether you want to keep it.' In we troop, lights out. Twenty minutes later, lights on. He says, 'You're right. It's shit.' Now the guy I wanted from day one, Christopher Young, is left with two weeks to do the entire score without a big enough budget. He worked miracles. I'd use him again, drop of a hat. I think he's a brilliant film composer and he's not recognised as he should be. When you're putting a film together you take music from other films to give a sense of where you're going. The editor put in this piece of music, and I said, 'What the fuck is that?' He said, 'It's this guy called Christopher Young. He's not very well known.' I sent someone out to get all of his work, and I listened to it over a couple of days. I thought, 'This guy's great.' Jarre is a very distinguished composer but for some reason he didn't have a sense of this movie at all. Chris immediately had a sense of it and he did a fantastic job.

The film with Steve Martin was *Leap of Faith*, directed by Richard Pearce.

Yeah. Came out at the same time as mine.

Another commercial failure.

They didn't promote *Jennifer Eight*. They put these posters up saying '*Jennifer 8* is next', and the advertising campaign was meant to say two weeks later, '*Jennifer 8* – a new thriller' but they never bothered with the second half. People probably thought '*Jennifer 8* is next' was some kind of new soap-powder or something. Steve's film got the same treatment. They bombed both of them because they didn't want Tartikoff to have anything successful to leave on.

In any case, that tag-line '*Jennifer 8* is next', though it means something in the context of the ad campaign, doesn't actually apply to the film itself. The hand found on the dump already comes from the eighth victim in the file, 'Jennifer', so she isn't next. That and the fact that the word 'Eight' is spelled out on screen but written as a numeral in publicity are indicative of the lack of care with which the movie was handled.

It was a very bad time at the studio. It happens. That's the movie industry. Then, the weekend we opened, Coppola opens his *Dracula*, which had massive expectations and massive publicity. A bloody awful movie, I thought, but nevertheless it's like a little tug getting into the sea with *Titanic*. Everyone wanted to see *Dracula* and no one wanted to see the new soap-powder. It was a disaster from top to bottom. At the end I just thought, 'Well, if this is Hollywood, let me out.' And I haven't attempted to direct a film again until now. The biggest problem I had – and after all these years I'm not particularly blaming him any more – was I wasn't protected by Rudin. Scott isn't a hands-on producer, Scott is a brilliant deal-maker. He knows how to make a deal, take his wheelbarrow of money and walk off. That was the problem. Much as I loved Andy, I don't think he was old enough for that film. There was an article I read within the last year, a big interview with Scott Rudin in some film magazine, and they talked about *Jennifer Eight*. They said, 'Why wasn't that more of a success?' and he had a one-word answer: 'Miscast.' That was all he said. He should have added two more words, and the two more words were 'by' and 'me'. But he didn't.

It's a very fickle industry, this. If a film works – and who knows what makes a film work – it's a blink between being a disaster and being a hit. Sometimes, in the dead of night when I can't sleep, I mourn *Jennifer Eight*, thinking, 'Why did it have to end up like that?' No way was it ever going to be a classic, but it could have been a really strong movie. But what are you to do if someone is on your case like that? Every day there would be a new crisis. Lucchesi would come in and say, 'I've just finished this meeting with the studio. I don't know how you're going to do this, Bruce, but you've got to get another eight minutes out.' I'm on the bone now; where am I going to get another eight minutes? Cutting a film is rather like doing push-ups. The first five are easy, six is OK, seven is starting to get a bit difficult, and by the time you get to ten you're dying. That's what editing is like. By the time you're up to ten you're exhausted; you don't know where to go. Then you get into playing it at twenty-five frames per second instead of twenty-four to lose frames. When I saw the last cut, when it had been dubbed, I was thinking, 'God, this is good, this is good, this is good,' and then there was the first hole in the narrative. You can literally feel your heart sink.

Ironically, the film seems longer than it actually is because the second half is less riveting than the first. As the cuts get more severe the story loses its grip, which would have been sustained by the original, longer version.

Absolutely. It would have been a shorter film because people weren't losing interest. Connie was heartbroken because the last five minutes of the movie hit the deck, practically a whole reel. You see those little blips in the top right-hand corner of the screen at the reel change, and I should think it was five, six, seven minutes into one of those. You know she runs down that staircase, then crashes through the door and down the corridor? 'Say night night, dead girl.' And she turns round and it's Margie, the policeman's wife, taking revenge. What happened in the original was we see this weird cop, Taylor, putting his velcro bulletproof thing on, so she does shoot him but he ain't dead. Uma is in the gym, you see headlights in the distance and it's Berlin coming, then there's a noise and it's that door swinging. She stands up, and the camera starts turning in a contra-rhythm to her movements, goes right through 360 degrees to come back to her face, and as it comes back there's Taylor's face right next to it. Really chilling. When we showed that, there was a frisson through the audience, even though it's the old he's-dead-but-he-isn't shot. He doesn't care about himself any more but he wants her dead. Then Berlin arrives in the cavalry shot and kills him. It's a satisfying ending to the picture, because in that kind of picture you want the hero to get the bad guy. It was a fabulous shot, one of the best in the film, and we lost the whole thing trying to get the picture down to two hours.

In the release version Garcia heads up to the institute in his car but he never gets there. The hero doesn't save the day.

He does get there, obviously, in the one I shot, but we were looking for these magic fourteen minutes to get rid of. And it works. You can say nemesis is complete. 'This man killed my husband and now I'm killing him.' That's sort of satisfactory. But I'd like to have seen the film go out at its full length because there were so many nuances in there that I thought were really nice. Kathy Baker gave a terrific performance as the wife. She was really good in that scene – Andy was really good in it too – where she says, 'What are you gonna do about this?' 'I dunno, Margie,' and then he grabs her and she can't stand him touching her. That's a really nice scene.

The present ending, the final shot over which the credits run, works quite well. Garcia and Thurman walk through a field at dusk, he tells her the sky is red and she says, 'I remember red', a line I came across in your workbook for the film.

That was slapped over the top of it like Band-Aid. Andy and Uma, between takes, had wandered off down a field, and Connie said to the cameraman, 'Just knock that off. You never know, we might need it.' He's a genius, Conrad. That became the end of the film, and I shoved that dialogue over the top in voice-over: 'Is it dark yet?' 'No, but it's getting kinda red.' 'I remember red.' Which, in fact, was an alternative title for the film; *I Remember Red*, is quite a nice combination of words. And that saved the day. But if Connie hadn't turned the camera on those two I wouldn't have had that. For aficionados of what's fucked up in films, when the policemen first go and see the blind girl – and there's that wonderful way that Connie lit it, where she opens her door and the sun floods out – there's a cutaway to her in the kitchen making tea, and when she's having tea with them she's wearing a green jumper and on the cutaway she's got a bright red one. It's very funny: look out for it.

Did you get on well with Andy Garcia?

I liked him enormously. He's a very nice man. Someone told me the other day that he's quite a problematical actor to work with. I never saw that at all. All the actors were great. Andy and Uma and Lance Henriksen and the crew were on the side of the film. A lot of these guys had been working in cinema for forty-five years and they'd say, 'I'm sorry that this is going down like this,' because there was no need for it to be going down like that. The only thing that used to annoy me about Andy was he just would not learn his lines, and for me the dialogue is one of the most important elements in the film. I don't just write a line and think, 'That'll do,' I really do try very hard to get the rhythm right. I love it when someone is spot on to the comma, like Malkovich when he makes those speeches. But he's a theatre actor; he's used to getting out there on a stage and saying lines. Most actors in the States get into film via film.

They play little parts, then a bigger part and finally they get a lead. That's their training.

You were also working with some talented character actors: Kevin Conway as the police chief, Citrine, for example.

A brilliant actor.

And Graham Beckel as Taylor, the weird cop.

He's a fine actor too. He was in *L.A. Confidential* – playing a corrupt policeman, curiously. Because I wasn't so *au fait* with American actors I took the word of the casting director much more, but in Graham Beckel's case he came in, read the scene, and I said, 'You've got the part if you want it.' I'm like that: I take immediate fixes on things and hope that I'm right. Scott Rudin said we had to have Kathy Baker, and I trusted him and said, 'OK.'

How did the cast respond to being given line readings?

It gave us some problems up front. Here's an example, though the line was cut from the film. I put in the introduction to the *Withnail* screenplay that Vivian said, 'If there's a God, why are arses at the perfect height for kicking?' That was bullshit. I was stuck for a line in that introduction, so I pinched it from myself. It was actually a line from *Jennifer Eight*, but it wasn't in the film, so I thought, 'I'll stick it in here.' I never waste things. If it doesn't work in one thing I'll put it in another. *Roadie* featured this thing called the Cincinnati Carrot, which later turned up as the Camberwell Carrot in *Withnail* – and thank God it did. So, 'Why are arses at the perfect height for kicking?' Lance is saying this line, 'Why are *arses* at the perfect height for kicking?' – stressing it wrong. After a few takes, each time trying a nudge, I finally go up to him and say, 'Why are arses at the *perfect height* for kicking?' 'Perfect height' is where the line peaks. God, he did not like it. They don't like it, American screen-actors. Malkovich was perfect for me because he liked to do it off film then come on and get it in two takes. Andy liked to do it on film, so you're shooting thousands of feet before you get there. We can't make films like that in England. If I shot 15,000 feet a day nobody was complaining about it. Except me: I think it's a complete waste of film.

When you get to a certain level in this industry, the top level, people like Kubrick, who did eighty-six takes of Tom Cruise walking through a door, I think it's become absurd. Connie told me he shot this scene with Warren Beatty, and of course Mr Beatty has a monstrous amount of clout on the set. The shot was him walking through the door, crossing the room and looking in the mirror. No dialogue, no inter-reaction, and Warren Beatty shot it again and again and again. Now they're up to sixty-five takes, seventy-five; he's looking at the monitor all the time, 'No, it's not right.' Ninety-one takes, 'No, it's not what I want.' Connie finally turned off the camera and said, 'Warren, you don't need a director of photography, you need a plastic surgeon,' and walked off. I'd be the exact opposite of that. The minimum takes that I could get away with is what I like. If I get it in the first take and I know I've got it – they have that expression, 'One for Lloyds,' i.e. one for insurance – 'OK, we've got that. Print it. Now one for Lloyds.' If the one for Lloyds fucks up you've got to do another take, and even though you know you've got it you start using up a lot of film. Film stock's relatively cheap, but it's processing that costs the money, I suppose.

You'd worked with the same key technicians for two films: cinematographer, designer, editor and composer. Were you unable to use them for *Jennifer Eight* or did you think that an American project should have an American crew?

Very much so. I was blown away when the doorbell rings, and this sixty-five-year-old hippy is standing there, and it's Conrad Hall. He really is a superb cameraman. I immediately felt an affinity with him. My whole philosophy of film-making – not that I've done it much – is that it's a conspiracy. Conspire in Latin means 'to breathe with', and that's how I feel about making a film. I want everyone to be making the film, not just me telling them what to do, because these guys are all experts in their field. If something went wrong with the

177

camera, the last person on the set to know anything about it would be me. I don't know about the technical side of film-making. I know about lenses, I know roughly where the camera's got to be, but to have someone like Conrad to conspire with was magic. Without knowing it, he teaches so much. He covers a lot more than I would. He just likes being behind a camera that's going.

We were very *au fait*, Connie and I; we talked all the time. I think I said, 'No, I don't want it like that,' less than a dozen times in the whole movie. By and large, I'd let him get on with what he did, and I'd get on with what I could do. The only time we had a row was when we were shooting in that old nuthouse just outside Vancouver. Uma runs down the staircase, and I wanted a camera on a wire going with her from inside the stairwell. He really resisted doing this: 'No, that won't work. You won't get it.' We did get it, and it was a great shot, I think. This was a 200-foot-high hole in the middle of a staircase, and his son was dangling on the end of this rope, being lowered. They had to rehearse it and rehearse it to sync her running with him going down, having to be turned at the top by two technicians so he was going like a corkscrew. Very brave of him. We're just sitting there watching it on the monitor.

It's a very dark film.

And bleak. Connie was the perfect choice of cameraman. I thought the way Connie shot that garbage dump at night was phenomenal cinema. It was beautifully done. I like that moment in the film; it's almost my favourite moment. 'I think I found a hand.' Cut to the hand in the sweet-and-sour – like the sweet-and-sour in the sink in *Withnail* – and Berlin grabbing the flashlight. Ross says to him, 'What do you think?' and he says, 'I think you're here all day.' Cut to the wide shot of the dump. Everything after that is downhill, I guess, but I like that bit. After we shot that scene we ate all that food. It was brilliant Chinese food someone had got, and the hand was made of rubber, so we tossed the hand out and ate all the food.

That garbage dump actually wasn't a garbage dump, it was a set. It was built on a field, tin can up, by the designer. I couldn't believe it. When you get that wide shot at the beginning, when the car goes in and you see this steaming filthy heap, that is a garbage dump. But it's not. Everything was positioned by the designer, and it took them a week to build. They must have spent at least $100,000 on it. Had it been my decision, I'd have gone to the nearest garbage dump and shot on it, unpleasant as it may be. But one of the problems I had with the film was being in a Hollywood environment where I was a baby among the sharks. If I'd had more experience I would never have allowed that brilliant set designer to build a police station like a rock-etship to Mars.

Did you choose Richard MacDonald, or was he the studio's choice?

I chose him. I loved him immediately. He was a chronic old boozer but he had a lot more kudos than I did. Here was a man who'd designed some of the biggest pictures ever, and if I hadn't been so freaked by everything and everybody when I was doing it I'd have said to him, 'I want it much less high-tech.' He knew he was dying of cancer, and I think he wanted to say, 'Here is my police station.' I wanted it windowless and underground, and that's what he did, and he did something brilliant, but it wasn't right for the context. Connie hated that set. They used to argue all the time, those two, and they'd both come to me. I liked them both, and they'd both say, 'Which is it Bruce?' I came down on the side of MacDonald once, because he was right, and Connie was really pissed off with me. But I should have stamped on that set at the beginning. My intention was to shoot that police station on location; find a building and dress it to look like a country cop shop. It should have been shabby little offices.

Berlin and Helena make an interesting couple. For example, you may have lost the age gap because of the casting, but she still thinks he's in his fifties.

She doesn't seem to mind. What she needs in her life that she hasn't got is any kind of love at all. She takes it, as will anyone, from who they can. He should have been called Juan, shouldn't he? Andy would hardly have a name like Berlin. I should have changed it to something more Hispanic. There's plenty of Hispanic cops in the LAPD.

And whereas he's moody, intent on his job, and has bad dreams about God, she finds time for music and poetry and seems to have some sort of faith.

Because she says, 'Don't you pray?' It's a key scene, isn't it? That scene came from a dream, and it's the only time that's ever happened to me. God was in the dream, and someone said to him, 'Don't you listen to people's prayers?' and he replied, 'Not often. They're junk mail.' Inside this dream I remember thinking, 'I love that line. I've got to wake up to write that down' – because you never remember lines like that. Sometimes I have really great plot ideas in dreams and think, 'Thank God I've got that plot. That's fantastic. I'll work that out in the morning.' You never remember it. The famous one is that writer who had the greatest story in his dream, forced himself awake to write the story down, went back to sleep absolutely contented, woke up in the morning and picked up what he'd written down, and what he'd written was 'boy meets girl'. But that line genuinely was in a dream. And I guess it's not far off the truth. Prayers are junk mail to God, because if he listened to them we wouldn't be in the middle of Chechnya and all the rest of this shit.

Thurman has one of the film's best scenes. Garcia, in the restaurant, is telling her that cynical anecdote about God, and rather than cut between them while he's speaking, or focus entirely on him, you choose to focus entirely on her. And since her eyes can't convey much emotion she has to react to what he's saying with the rest of her face. It's quite a challenge for an actor.

She's marvellous in that scene. The whole process of being blind, especially for young people, is so terrible. Uma must have done quite a bit of research herself, because I'd read a lot and met a lot of blind people. It was a committed film. We didn't set out to say, 'Fuck it. So what? If you're blind you fall over.' Everyone was very committed, and indeed by two thirds through the picture everyone thought we were making a really good movie. Which, in a sense, we were.

Berlin is a romantic, obsessive, chain-smoking, recovering alcoholic . . .

Yes but no. Because I'm not a recovering alcoholic. I wish I was. All my characters are me. They have to be. I write about myself. If I'm a detective in Los Angeles in that situation, going off to fall in love with a blind girl, it's how would I handle that. That's part of my way of writing. Most things I write are like that.

He's as much a victim as any of your other lead characters.

A total victim, yeah. She's obviously a victim because she's blind. His pal, played by Lance Henriksen, is a victim. The wife is a victim. They're all victims. I write about victims all the time, which is probably how I perceive the human condition: in one way or another we're victimised from a very early age.

The first draft script opens with an atmospheric sequence where Berlin attends an AA meeting in a church, then follows him across the Golden Gate Bridge as he drives north from Los Angeles. What happened to all that?

That hit the fan before it even was born. I don't think I'd have got away with it with Andy, which is maybe why we didn't shoot it. Pacino is a recovered alcoholic – his career collapsed for years because of booze – so he'd have known about that. Pacino saying that opening speech would have been great, a great way to open a movie. I'm sad that we did lose that whole alcoholic angle. That dreadful Christmas Eve when it all goes very wrong, Ross is there and he has a cigarette and he says, 'One a year. Christmas,' which is the catalyst for Berlin to say, 'I'll have a drink. One drink,' and you can't have one drink if you're an alcoholic. It would have been much more potent had we had the opening speech. The alcoholics in the audience would all be saying, 'Don't take that drink, man!' The potency of that line, 'Were you drinking that night?' got lost. 'To keep out the cold?'

We all know, and Malkovich knows, that the guy's an alcoholic.

How does it open now? Oh, I know. It opens in a forest with that lovely music by Chris Young. We shot tons before that. We did shoot a boat coming under the Golden Gate Bridge, a helicopter shot, and my arsehole puckers up at the thought of it. You have the camera hanging underneath the helicopter in this steadicam rig, and the camera operator with remote controls looking through the video screen at what he's shooting. I was standing with Connie on the headland, shouting, 'I want you lower, go in as low as you can,' and the helicopter pilot couldn't hear me because of the rotor blades. He was shouting, 'What?' and I said, 'Oh, fuck it, I'll come round,' and as I moved away Connie grabbed my shoulder. I yelled, 'What's the matter?' and he said, 'For fuck's sake don't move!' He'd worked with a director who'd done the same thing: walked round the back of a helicopter into the rotor blade and ended up as a pile of ham on the floor. I shiver to this day when I think I was going to run round. You can't see the rotor; all you can see is the tail. I could have been converted into a heap of oomska on the side of San Francisco Bay.

You've talked about the influence T.J. had on the procedural aspects of the film, but did he help you get a handle on the character of Berlin?

No, I don't think T.J. had any impact at all on Berlin. The only impact he had on the development of character was I wrote the Malkovich part out of spending hours talking to T.J. about how you interrogate people. The whole thrust of the interrogator is to make you lose it in some way. The moment you lose your temper with one of those guys, you've lost, because they know how to own you. Those scenes would have been the best in the film if they hadn't fucked my cut. Tartikoff sent me a note saying, 'These are the best rushes I've ever seen.' I was really proud of Malkovich. There was a scene where he picked up the phone and said to his assistant, 'Can you bring me an ashtray?' and he put the phone down and just looked at Andy for ninety seconds of locked-off camera. Taking control. People seeing it in rough cut said, 'It's horrifying!' Of course, that's ninety seconds dead screen to the studio. To me, with nothing except them looking at each other, it was one of the most dramatic moments of the whole picture.

It was hard, not so much for me as for Conrad, to keep the camera locked-off. I don't think the camera should have an ego. There are directors, like Scorsese, who almost make the camera a participant in the film. To me, the camera is there as a privileged observer. It's lucky to see this story being told. I mean, a director is a camera, isn't he? We are all intrinsically directors. You're directing now and so am I, in the way you're looking at me and the way I'm looking at you.

Conrad Hall, interviewed for a piece on the film in *American Cinematographer*, said it taught him that you shouldn't have too much story to tell.

Well, I think that's a pretty good rule. I also think, don't have too many pages. You can reckon a page of screenplay is about a minute of screen time, so if you write a 140-page script you've got a two-hour, twenty-minute film on your hands, which is too long. I always try and write now to about 120, because by the time you've edited it, 110, that's about right for a movie. The thing about 'Don't have too much story to tell' is I think you can tell as much story as you like providing you don't have to cut the story. You can't play *Hamlet* and say, 'I have of late, wherefore I know not, lost all my mirth.' Cut! You know what I mean? You can't do it.

I think the narrative holes only start to become really evident when you reach the interrogation-room scenes, which contain some abrupt jumps in continuity. The plot spirals out of control at the point where Berlin figures out who the killer is and why. It becomes confusing and unsatisfactory . . .

And expositional. Far too expositional. Yeah, you're right. I have to accept responsibility as the writer and director for what went wrong. I can't say, 'It was their fault, their fault, their fault.' Clearly it was my fault because my name's on the film, and I should have been more skilful in the way I constructed that third act. Probably the way to navigate that – and I considered doing it when I was working the film out – is to let the audience know from the word go that Taylor is the killer rather than hold back the revelation for Berlin to discover. Then you don't need any plot. Maybe if I'd let the audience in early they'd have stayed with it, because rather than trying to work with Berlin they're saying, 'Come on! Haven't you got it?' It's virtually the same picture, just a different way of doing it. I've seen thrillers done that way and they're great. It's choices, choices. I wanted the feeling that something was going to happen, and I kept the something happening too late in the picture. The rest is drama between the people. That was my choice, and I think my choice was a mistake.

It's like I said, you need to make a film before you can make a film. Where we also got it wrong was the police station should have been much shabbier and the blind institute much sunnier. They paint blind places in very bright colours, because some people who are partially sighted can just about get the doorknobs together and see people against a brilliant background. It's trying to balance one thing against another in terms of cost and time. I would never want to make the film again, but if I could, I'd shoot it in black-and-white using hand-held cameras, faces moving in and out of the frame, and I don't care where they come in and where they go out. Connie would have been a genius in black-and-white, only it would have put another eight million on the budget. It's incredibly expensive, black-and-white. It takes twice the time to light, for one thing. I could have made *Jennifer Eight*, looked at it and said, 'Now I know what's wrong with this,' then gone to Stanley Jaffe and said, 'I tell you what, Stanley, let's make it again.' [*American accent*] 'OK, Bruce. That's a fuckin' good idea. What do you want?' 'Another forty million.' 'Sure, man.'

Mike Figgis went through a very similar experience to yours, at virtually the same time, with his film *Mr Jones*, and he's apparently been given a chance to put together a director's cut of the movie for DVD. If you were asked to do the same for *Jennifer Eight* what would your response be?

'No.' I wouldn't go anywhere near it.

Even allowing for the fact that you didn't like the final cut of the film, you must have been disappointed that Paramount consigned it straight to video. Do you think there was something personal in the fact that Britain was the only major territory in which the film didn't get a theatrical release?

I think there may have been. It certainly got a theatrical release in France. Koch is an icon at Paramount, and I don't think insulting him like I did went down at all well. Originally, after the screening where we were getting these magnificent results, they were going to have a première for it in England. There was a guy from Paramount UK at the screening and he was saying, 'We'll get this out in March and put on a big show.' They were all so up on it. I mean, they needn't have got Lady Di into Leicester Square for it, but they could have stuck it on in the Odeon Hammersmith and given it a week or two and see what happened. I was extremely disappointed. *Jennifer Eight* is such a gang of remorse. The two worst things that have happened in my career are *Fat Man* and *Jennifer Eight*. There are subsidiary niggling horrors like *Return to Paradise* and *In Dreams*, but I wrote both of them as a working writer.

It's done very well on video, though. It gets very positive word of mouth.

I know. It's remarkable. One of the perks in this business, particularly as I wrote and directed it, is you get video residuals. Even now it's still pulling in healthy residuals, so people are hiring it. Maybe it'll work better on TV than on a big screen. Some films do work better on television. I don't think it's my genre. It's not a genre I'd like to work in again. When I was in Toronto and my agent said, 'You must have something,' I don't know why the word 'thriller' came out of my mouth. Everyone was making police thrillers and serial killer pictures, and that's probably why I said it. If only I'd said, 'I tell you what, Rand, I've got a great comedy,' I'd have gone down with a pitch and they'd have said, 'What's the comedy about, then?' 'It's about a guy who finds himself in a situation where he's a brain surgeon by mistake.' That's all I'd have needed to say. They'd have said,

'Great.' I could have written something like that. But imagine going into Universal Pictures and they say, 'What's your comedy about, Bruce?' 'Well, it's about two out-of-work actors who go on holiday in the countryside and then they come back.' 'Wow! We can't wait to finance that.'

Jennifer Eight was your third film, a major studio production, yet you don't take a proprietary credit: 'A Bruce Robinson Film' or 'A Film by Bruce Robinson'. Were you unable to put your name above the title, or unwilling?

Unwilling. Totally unwilling. Always will be. It would completely repudiate my notion of the conspiracy. It can't be 'A Film by Bruce Robinson'. I just think it's stupid, frankly. I don't know what it means. That *auteur* thing was invented by the French in the sixties, and it's caught on. Everyone does it now, and so few deserve it. The people who really can say 'A Film by' are the people who don't need to. Woody Allen doesn't take a proprietory credit. Of course it's 'A Film by Woody Allen'.

If you had a choice between making a film on a low budget or a high budget, which would you prefer now?

The one that gave me most control. That's the name of the game as a director. You must be in control. There's only one voice of authority on a film set, and that's the director. He's the guy who has to make the decisions. If he's a twat he won't listen to anybody. If he's intelligent he'll take on all the different points of view and then make the decision. The trouble is, on *Jennifer Eight* I was being second-guessed all the time. I would make my decision and the decision would get unmade somewhere else, and then the row would start. There is a lot of interest in *The Block*, but one of the reasons it's wound up but difficult to let go is because I'm asking a lot. If I'm going to direct another movie I must take as many precautions as possible against what I know can go wrong. I must have cast approval. If I want Al Pacino and he doesn't want to do it then I can't have Al Pacino, but if he says 'Yes' I want to be able to say, 'I'm having him.' And, within limits, I want final cut. If I come in between 88 and

110 minutes, it'll be as I want it. If I come in at 121, sure, you've got a voice.

These kind of things are hard to get. Very few directors will get final cut, the star directors: Scorsese, and obviously Spielberg, because there's no higher authority than him. It's a hierarchical system. Those guys with the beards and the shades and the baseball caps are the kind who can handle Hollywood; guys who have done years in television before they start directing movies and know everybody and have massive authority. Imagine Spielberg asking his production manager, 'Where's my rain?' and her saying, 'You've got too much rain in this picture, Mr Spielberg.' There'd be a streak of fire as she was leaving the set. I was out of my depth making a Hollywood picture, I don't deny it. If I'd had a quarter of that money in England I could have made a movie, but it was running away from me all the time. It got made almost by default, and in the end that may have been the cancer cell that destroyed it. From the moment it was invented in that hotel room in Hollywood, *Jennifer Eight* wasn't healthy.

Chapter Seven

'A producer in the grave'

Return to Paradise and *In Dreams*

Return to Paradise **was eventually directed by Joseph Ruben for Polygram, but originally you were going to direct it for Disney, is that right?**

That's right. I was in a hole in the business because of *Jennifer Eight* – I was a leper for about six months – and I was in a hole in my life because I didn't want to do anything. Then a French producer called Alain Bernheim and the American producer Danny Arnold came to me with it and sent me the original film. It was a small French film, black-and-white, about fifty minutes long, and I was intrigued by the idea.

According to my research, the original version of *Force Majeure* **was in colour and eighty-five minutes long.**

Really? I thought it was about fifty. The one I saw was definitely in black-and-white, but it was probably just a video transfer, a cheap print. It was good; a bloody good idea. Jeffrey Katzenberg was with Disney at the time, and I remember saying to my agent, 'There's no way I could do this without going in to see Jeffrey, because this doesn't sound anything like the kind of picture that Disney would do.' So I go in and see Jeffrey. [*American accent*] 'Hey, buddy. How ya doin'?' 'I'm very interested in this idea. I'd like to be involved. What would my involvement entail?' 'We wanna make this like a European picture. Do whatever you wanna do.' So I did what I wanted and wrote this script. Did you like it?

Yes, I did. Most of what's good in the film, and it's not a bad film by any means, is due to the remnants of your script.

I liked it. And I liked it in the sense that it was for me to direct, and I know exactly what I would have wanted from it. Did you ever see a wonderful French film called *Incident at Owl Creek*? It won the Palme d'Or at Cannes though it was only eight minutes long. I don't know who made it and what happened to it. It's about a guy in the American Civil War who's taken on to a bridge in this beautiful wood on a wonderful summer's day, and they're going to hang him. They put the noose round his neck, kick him off, down he goes to be hanged, and the rope breaks! He hits the water and swims underneath it and escapes. At the end of the movie he's running towards his wife and child, they go into slightly slow motion, he's embracing his wife and child, and – whack! – he's hung.

That's what I wanted to do with *Force Majeure*, to make you think that this was happening when in fact it wasn't happening at all, it was all a fantasy. We realise that all this is going through Sheriff's mind before being hanged; what he would have done had this coin gone the other way, what would have happened had he been the one who'd gone back. When the guy's in the cell at the end, he says, 'I've got to toss the coin. There's no choices here. The coin's gonna be tossed,' and – whack! – we realise that the spinning coin at the start didn't come down heads, it came down tails, and that was the reality. I liked that. So predicated on Jeffrey saying, 'Do what you wanna do, Bruce. We want it to be a European film. We want it to be a cheap film . . .'

Cheap in this case being . . . ?

$15million, but they didn't follow through with that. Anyway, I deliver the screenplay, then Jeffrey falls out with Disney – he's off and he's sueing them for $100million, or whatever – and I wouldn't do what Danny Arnold wanted me to do. He was saying, 'If you don't do this, we'll fire you,' and I said, 'You can't fire me, I'm a partner on this,' and mid-argument he dropped dead. He had a heart attack, poor fucker. He was sixty-odd. Now I've got a producer in the grave affecting this picture. He's literally producing from his tomb, because everything he said before his death pertained after his death, and I wouldn't do what the dead guy wanted. Despite the fact that my agent had negotiated a contractual turnaround shared between me and Danny Arnold – and if he's dead he hasn't got the turnaround, it belongs to me – there were all sorts of terrible legal threats from Polygram and I just let it go. And then they fucked it up.

In other words, you found yourself in a similar position as you'd been in with Jennifer Eight, except at that point you chose to pursue it and in this instance you heeded the warning bells and walked away.

Well, had I not done *Jennifer Eight*, maybe I would have tried to accommodate what they wanted to stay on the picture. I'm a real walker now. Thirty years I've been writing screenplays, and I've learned now when the time has come to say, 'No. Sorry. Enough.' I can see the horror spread out like jam in front of me and I just don't want to go through it, thank you. Too old for that. If you want to pay me to do what you want even though I disagree with you, all right, but don't expect me to bring an artistic commitment. But if you'll conspire with me I'll work on the thing for as long as it takes, providing you don't say at the end of that, 'Thank you very much, Bruce, what's Wesley's phone number?' It's out of order.

Did you read Wesley Strick's draft of the script?

No.

What did they want you to do?

They wanted to take out that whole notion of the coin and fate. When the guy tosses the coin at the front of the film, if it had gone this way he'd have stayed and if it had gone the other way he'd have left, so the whole movie is about the fact that Sheriff didn't leave and was arrested. I think they were foolish not to have gone down that street at least some way with me.

If you take out the coin device, presumably you have a linear narrative in which Lewis hangs rather than Sheriff?

I guess, yeah.

Which is what they shot.

Is it? I've never seen it. It's another of the movies that I've got my name on but I've never seen. It's very difficult for me to talk about *Return to Paradise* because if you hadn't told me that was what it was called I would barely know. I can only really talk about the screenplay, and the screenplay has become academic. About six people on earth have read the screenplay, of which you're one, so it's not entirely fascinating. It's not fascinating to me because I don't know what they've done with it. As soon as Jeffrey left Disney the project was sold on. It ended up with somebody else, then somebody else, and went through so many different hands, so many different stages, that before you know it it's got nothing to do with you. It's like talking about a house I lived in once that someone else has completely refurnished and redecorated. 'What do you think of the living room, Bruce?' 'I don't know, I haven't been in it.'

The thing is, people reading this, particularly anyone who wants to be a screenwriter, will be interested to see . . .

Just how awful it can get.

Well, that too. But I was thinking more of pointing up what works and what doesn't between your version and their version. *Return to Paradise* is not the film it could have been if your original script had been made.

I like that script and I wish I could have made it. It would have been interesting to see what it would have been like. It was a cheap film, why couldn't I have just done it?

Joseph Ruben adopts quite a gritty style for the film. After the golden glow of the opening sequence in Malaysia, it's grey streets and hand-held camerawork most of the way. How would you have approached it?

I guess I would have done what he's done. The most beautiful picture postcard places with the worst horror on earth going on in terms of these characters. I do see elements of New York as hell on earth. I would have pushed that quite hard. The first time I ever saw a dead body was when I was researching *The Killing Fields* in northern Thailand. You think, 'My God, this is unbelievable, there's a body in a ditch,' but if you walk around Brooklyn or Harlem you see junkies and trash everywhere. We all sit there, eating our popcorn and Häagen-Dazs, thinking, 'Aren't these foreign places terrible?' Well, the reality is, rather like when the IRA were active a few years ago and all those American stars wouldn't come to England, you are a hundred times more likely to get shot in the face in Los Angeles than you are in Belfast. It's our perceptions that are fucked.

Did you actually go to Malaysia, or were you able to draw on your research for *The Killing Fields*?

No, I didn't, because I was smelling the same streets. I really didn't need to go. I do like to go normally if I'm writing a film. I like to go down a coal mine, horrifying as it is, and I like to go into the jungle, horrifying as that is. Anywhere south of Rome horrifies me, frankly, but I have to go there. If I'm doing something set in New Mexico, like *Fat Man*, I have to go there. It's worth 500 books, going there.

A couple of the reviews suggested that, via *Force Majeure*, the film is based on a true story. Did you ever hear that?

I think it is sort of a true story, yeah, and there are a lot of stories like that. They hanged an Australian woman and her son who were smuggling smack – I think it was smack – out of Malaysia. But you're a bloody fool, aren't you? You'd have to be a mental deficient to do it. They *will* hang you. You go through airports in Thailand and there's skull-and-crossbones signs saying, 'Smuggling narcotics in or out of this country results in the death

193

penalty.' I don't approve of it any more than I approve of this country's drug laws, jailing the sick. I think it's a terrible outrage to put someone to death for drugs, but that's how they do it. That's what's so great about the initial concept of *Force Majeure*. In my script, Sheriff says, 'I wouldn't go through that border with a fucking aspirin.' It is *force majeure*, an act of God. That's what makes it a powerful drama.

The film has an appropriate semi-documentary approach. But once the moral dilemma has been presented it starts to drag. There's a long middle act in a grey New York in which Sheriff and Beth argue about whether he will go back to Malaysia, with occasional cuts to Lewis in an equally grey Penang prison. But in your version there's more variety to that section, which includes scenes such as Sheriff impulsively robbing a Korean grocery store at gunpoint.

That was their most hated scene, and I wouldn't cut it. That's where the rot set in, on that scene. I think it's a great scene, where he robs someone and then gives them the money back.

Well, Beth — or Jane in your version — gives the money back. He's taking it, and she's giving it back out of her own pocket. She has the money because she pawned her wedding ring to pay Sheriff to go back to Malaysia. He in turn needs the money to support his young daughter while he's in jail over there.

Is the daughter still in it?

No, she isn't.

We were talking about victims. There's no greater victim than Sheriff, which is why if I'd seen the film I'd really mourn the loss of his little girl who's got nothing but him. Almost everything I've written is victim-orientated. *Return to Paradise* is not what I wrote, but it's a story that I was attracted to about a victim. *In Dreams* is the victim; *Fat Man*, the victim; *The Killing Fields*, the victim; *Penman*, the victim; *Advertising*, the victim. It's a running theme in my work, even though I'm not totally conscious of it. When someone says, 'Do you want to write this?' my subliminal radar says, 'Is there a victim in it?' Withnail is a victim. The only person that justifies his existence is the 'I' character and the 'I' character has gone on, grown up. *The Block* is about a victim. I tell that story again and again.

In America, the title *Force Majeure* turned into *Uncontrollable Circumstances*. In your script, and in the film to a lesser extent, there's a parallel between the uncontrollable circumstances of the death penalty faced by Lewis and the uncontrollable circumstances of the love affair between Sheriff and Jane.

It's very hard for me to look at it. You look at it from the critic's point of view. It's like when we talk, we talk, and whatever we say, we say, and then somebody else can say, 'Having listened to Bruce Robinson for an hour, obviously he is obsessed with . . .' whatever, whatever, whatever. But you never know that yourself. All I try to do is write a dramatic movie. I wasn't thinking about love and death. I can't remember what I was thinking about when I wrote it. I suppose I was thinking about injustice. In political terms, and in film terms, whether it's their version or my version, you're sitting there in Thousand Oaks, California, and the Malaysians are obviously the baddies. 'They're going to hang this guy. It's the most terrible thing!' But the Malaysians don't apply the death penalty with anything like the ferocity of the United States. There's nowhere else in the so-called enlightened world that has the death penalty.

That point is made in your version, but not in theirs.

Is it? I can't remember. But it's true. The Yanks execute more people than the Iranians. The more the merrier. It's very difficult for the United States to take a moral stance on the death penalty. In Malaysia, taking or supplying drugs is a capital offence, and maybe for their society they consider it such. It's all about the economy, the death penalty. The Malaysians in their economy don't want a bunch of junkies everywhere. America's economy needs those junkies, in a sense, and can tolerate them.

Unlike your script, the film has a courtroom scene in the final act, which includes a speech by a Malaysian judge about how his country doesn't understand the American attitude to drugs.

In my version, as I remember, all three boys go to their parents with this dilemma. Sheriff goes to his dad, who works in a laundry. The middle boy, who was an actor in my version, Tony, goes to his dad, who's a priest. And, of course, Lewis goes to his mother with his dilemma, i.e. 'I don't want to die.' What the Malaysian judge says in the release version, I believe was said by Sheriff's dad in my version, and the only line I can remember is, 'I don't give a fuck if they take him out the back and beat him to death with a shovel.' [*American accent*] 'We got the shit of the world on our streets, we got muggings, we got murders, we got . . .'

Strick seems to have taken that . . .

And given it to a judge. Now, the judge is meaningless to me in dramatic terms, whereas the father, one on one with the principal character, has a lot of meaning. So I immediately don't like what he's done with it. I would never do that. Make it personal, because all the best screenwriting is about the person, sucking you in and trying to make you feel what you might feel if you were in this situation. When he goes and talks about faith to his preacher father, that's great. If it's an abstract preacher brought in to talk about the death penalty, it doesn't mean a thing.

The parents were cut. Sheriff goes to see his dad, who works in a garage, just once and Tony doesn't go to see his parents at all. Probably that was in an effort to bring Sheriff further into the foreground, but it means that there's less variation of character or location in the long middle act. Bringing the parents in expands the moral dilemma beyond Sheriff and Beth, or rather Jane.

I think so. I think I watched ten minutes on a dubbing cut, with all the numbers and slashes on it. It was horrible; I couldn't bear it. In the ten minutes I saw, Lewis was in Penang actually associating with drug dealers and buying drugs. Terrible mistake. The whole point of the film is that the drugs were just there, and he's not a bad guy, he's not a drug dealer. That was the studio freaking out, saying, 'How can we hang someone at the end unless he's a bad guy, unless he's got the elements of being a drug dealer?' They were just *there*, they had dope, and my dope, your dope and his dope is cumulatively enough to make it a hanging offence for one individual. That's what makes it a potent drama.

In fact, Lewis doesn't buy any drugs, and he doesn't because they're offering him rhino horn aphrodisiac, which expands on his ecological stance. But more importantly it's a way of establishing that the Malaysians are loud and violent. The added scene is actually quite xenophobic.

Yeah, they're horrible. They become horrible people. I remember I'd got hold of a lot of footage about Malaysian jails – they're really tough places to be; you don't want to be in there – and Danny Arnold's idea is this: Sheriff goes back with Lewis to serve his sentence, and this guard comes over to Lewis in a threatening way, and Sheriff puts one on his chin and lays him out. That is like [*American accent*], 'He lands on Mars and just breathes that fresh air, boy!' In reality, if you did that to a guard in a Malaysian jail you'd be flogged nearly to death. But it's that American thing, it's like John Wayne. 'Put John Wayne in prison in Penang and see what would happen. Man, he'd take it to pieces!'

Another review of Return to Paradise pointed out that it's hard to feel sympathy for a group of guys who see Malaysia as a seaside resort of easy sex and cheap drugs, the sort of attitude which is helping to corrupt the culture of the Far East. I think that criticism also applies to your script.

And to about fifty-six million Westerners every year. All this 'Paradise Island' shit. We fuck the world up. And it doesn't only apply to the Far East. Renaissance cities completely destroyed by eat a little, drink a little, see a little Yanks – and Brits and Japs. It's quite appalling. [*American accent*] 'Who designed that, then?' I don't fuckin' know. Where do you get your hamburgers?' And where *do* you get them? In the Venice branch of

McDonalds, that's where. It's a nightmare. It should be stopped. We need to scrap ninety-five per cent of airplanes. Stop them. Stop all this madness. Everything's fucked and full of hamburgers. Thailand is an ancient, beautiful, albeit very conservative culture, totally screwed up by the Vietnam war. Virtually every girl and boy there is a prostitute for rich Yanks, Brits and Japs.

Return to Paradise is very reminiscent of The Killing Fields, tackling friendship, loyalty, guilt, responsibility and a moral dilemma. Presumably if you'd directed the project it would have been an opportunity to tell a similar story, albeit with a downbeat ending, keeping the humour which was cut out of the earlier film.

Yeah. Because that's quite funny in parts, that script. There are things in there that made me laugh when I was writing them, and that is my criteria of what is funny: something that makes me laugh over the typewriter.

The reunion of Sheriff and Lewis, in either version, reminded me of the final scene in The Killing Fields, except that in this case there is guilt on both sides: Sheriff feels guilty because he almost didn't go back and Lewis feels guilty because if the shoe had been on the other foot he wouldn't have.

Doesn't he say in my version, 'I wouldn't have gone back'?

Yes, he does. But in your version Lewis seems very calm and collected, and in their version the two years in prison have obviously taken their toll. He talks a lot about God, which may have been extrapolated from the scene in your draft between Tony and his father the priest.

I think in my script Lewis does talk about God a lot, doesn't he? I remember writing something about the other prisoners: 'We've got a guy down there who shaves his head because God told him to, and we've got another one who grows his hair because God told him to.'

Several of the reviews also mentioned *Midnight Express*, produced by Puttnam and directed by your friend Alan Parker, a similar film in many ways. Was that an influence on the script?

No, not at all. It never crossed my mind until you just said it. When I sit down to write a script, I'll never think of another movie as a starting point. I'll think of what the character may be, and then think what can propel this character through this story. Should he be a market gardener, should he be a photographer, should he be a ballet dancer, should he be whatever he is. In my version Tony's an actor, and it's curious, going back to the chicken thing, that he's mimicking a chicken in the drama class. So there's my chicken again. I don't consciously think, 'Where am I going to get my chicken in?' like Hitchcock thought, 'Where am I going to get *me* in?' but for some reason a chicken has to come in. Sophie pointed that out to me. I almost said, 'I've done one without a chicken.'

Strick hasn't slung out your script by any means. For instance, Sheriff is illiterate in your version, which prompts a scene in the film with Beth where he tells her he wasn't keen on reading at school but now he's trying to educate himself.

I was just trying to think where that would have come from. Doesn't he encourage his daughter to learn? That's probably where that came from.

He also says he's going to learn to read in jail so he can write to her.

Again, it's like giving it to the judge to say rather than the personal thing of the father. To me, if he says to his daughter, 'I'll learn to read and write so I can write to you,' that's heart-rending, and the other version isn't. Most films, I have to say, I find really quite depressing: formula things with the same kind of actors and the same kind of dialogue, the same love scenes with the same actresses doing them. I do find it very narrow. It's like cars. In the thirties, cars were designed by designers; now they're designed by computers, so they all look the same. They feed in the requirements of what this particular car needs to do – i.e. it needs to carry four people and do thirty-eight miles to the gallon – and that's how films are made. 'What are the requirements 199 of this film?' 'Well, it needs to satisfy 800 arses on seats and we want them to laugh a little and we want them to cry a little.' That's what it's got to do. This is why there are so many cases of 'Man overboard!' – people who go to Hollywood and think, 'I can do this slightly differently.' You cannot fight it. You either go with it and say, 'Yes, Danny,' or you don't. You don't go into a studio expecting anything other than that, because that's what it is.

Jane is one of the most well-rounded female characters in your work to date. Allowing for the fact that many of your scripts haven't been made, and those that have didn't follow the order in which they were written, there are still more men in your scripts than women. Do you find male characters easier to write?

God, I don't know. I really don't know how to answer that. I remember going years and years ago for a pitch-audition for Jane Fonda, and there was this committee of brutal feminists who said to me, 'Do you know how to write a woman's part?' Of course you can. If you write, you write. I can write a woman's part, a girl's part, a man's part, a boy's part and a dog's part if required. I never think when I'm writing, 'Holy mackerel, a woman! How am I going to write a woman?'

It's not that. It's whether you feel your voice as a writer is more a male voice.

I think it is. I think I am more of a writer of men than a writer who writes women.

In one interview, responding to a question about the absence of women in your work to that date, you said that you'd written one script with no men in at all. Do you know what that would be?

I was probably bullshitting to make the interviewer feel like a twat. I've never written a script for all women.

However, to segue neatly, the lead character of In Dreams . . .

There's a potent woman's part in *Germinal*, the girl Catherine. The lead character in *The Block* is a woman, she's got a lot more than the man; although there is a line in the script that says, 'No women. He doesn't want any women,' which I only remember because you just brought the point up. But let's allow the segue to survive.

OK. The lead character of *In Dreams* . . .

Is a woman, yeah.

Claire Brickman in your script, Claire Cooper in the film.

What a breakthrough that was! [*Earnest voice*] 'Hey, I just had this fabulous idea. Let's call her Cooper instead of Brickman.' 'Wow, Neil, you must have been up all fucking night for that!'

When you were discussing *In Dreams* – when I first met you and the recently completed script was called *Blue Vision* – you described it as . . .

Repulsion meets *Don't Look Now*.

Right. Which in retrospect surprises me, because I've never heard you talk about anything else you've written in that way.

Does that sound like Hollywood to you?

Yes, it does.

Because Spielberg said it, that's why. Even if you don't want to be a gun for hire, if Hitchcock, Chaplin or Spielberg phones you up and says, 'Write a film for me,' you say, 'Of course, Alfred. Of course, Charlie,' and, 'Of course, Steven.' Because these are icons, aren't they? Spielberg's going to be a legend in the same way Hitchcock is. No disrespect to Neil Jordan, who's a very fine film-maker, but if he'd phoned me and said, 'Write this,' I'd have said, 'No.' I'd rather do my own stuff.

There are strong similarities between *In Dreams* and *Jennifer Eight*. Both films are psychological thrillers in which people are slow to

believe that a woman is in jeopardy from a serial killer motivated by events in his childhood. The main difference is that second sight replaces lack of sight.

What are you, perceptive? That must have been what attracted me to the story somehow.

This script was your first foray into the supernatural, where there are events happening on the page and on the screen which are completely inexplicable. Did you try and keep the story rooted in some sort of reality, or were you able to indulge your imagination more than usual?

I'm incredibly sceptical of things that go bump in the night, of ghosts, poltergeists and all the rest. I would go out of my way to try and rationalise the possibility of something shifting in the attic at three in the morning. It must be to do with the central heating system rather than to do with the proverbial geist. We had one in this house. We had two exorcisms because we got to the point where I could no longer explain it away. I think that was the area *Blue Vision* was working in, and I do believe there are people who have phenomenal insights into inexplicable things.

So the haunting here coincided with writing the script?

Yeah, it did. Strangely.

Did you research the subject and the locations?

Where was it set in the film?

New England.

I knew that area. I read a shit load of books on clairvoyancy; talking to the dead and that kind of junk. For example, you saw a massive rise in things like spiritualism after the First World War. People couldn't come to terms with the fact that half the young men of England had been killed, so here come the spiritualists to put people in touch with this legion of dead. 'Can you hear me,

Bill?' 'Sure I can.' 'What can you tell me?' 'Well, I can tell you you're a fucking idiot.' The menace of spiritualism was at its height in the twenties. It flourished again in the sixties, although in a rather distorted way, after the Vietnam war.

What exactly was your brief from Spielberg?

He originally wanted a psychological drama of extreme darkness, not a thriller but what *The Shining* should have been if it had been right, very much into relationship of characters. It turned into a kind of repulsive horror film that no one would want to watch, least of all me. I just don't know why Neil did that. It was such a confused film. We don't know what's going on, why it's going on and how the fuck you get out of the cinema. That was the most important part of it for me: where's the nearest exit?

Did you know it was technically an adaptation?

I never knew about that until I finished the script. Then someone told me, 'By the way, you've adapted this from a book.' 'Oh, really? I've never heard of it.'

Why was the original script called *Blue Vision*?

Some police departments – not in major cities like Los Angeles, but in certain rural places – have Blue Vision departments. When the detectives run out of any way to solve this crime they go to the Blue Vision people, who are usually coppers but are always psychics, and they give them all the evidence, and these people try psychically to see some way back into the case.

That's a great idea for a movie. Somebody could still go out and make that.

Well, that was Spielberg's idea. I was probably instrumental in talking him out of it, because I remember saying at the first meeting, 'I've just done *Jennifer Eight*. I want nothing whatsoever to do with the police.' The producer, Walter Parkes, said,

203

'What would you do, then?' so I pitched the idea back in a different way, and that was the beginning of the rot.

It took you about a year to write, didn't it?

It was a while. It wasn't a quick one. It was terribly difficult. The great challenge – and whether I pulled it off or not is moot, because the film was never made like I wanted it to be – was to write a film about a paedophile and not show a child in jeopardy. That's the essential thing. It's a very sensitive area: I'm a parent, and probably forty per cent of the cinema-going public are parents, and none of us really wants to be entertained by seeing a dead child. The first thing that Neil does is have this kid killed.

Not on screen, though.

Not on screen, but she comes out of the water. You see that poor little murdered kid coming up and you just think, 'Fuck this. Why do I want to pay five quid to see this?' I don't want to see a child in jeopardy as a piece of entertainment. You've only got to pick up the newspaper and see Grozny or any other horrible place in the world where nightmares are going on.

In a recent interview with *Empire*, Jordan admits that the problem with the film was killing a child in the first twenty minutes.

He actually admits that now, does he?

It depends on how you look at it. A child is killed within the first twenty pages of your script, so he could be saying that your version was wrong as well.

The whole point was that the little girl *wasn't* killed by the serial killer, and therefore the authorities could think, 'This woman's suffering such grief from the death of her daughter that she's having visions about other daughters.' If her daughter is killed by the killer, anything she says about her visions of the killer have a kind of validity; if her daughter *isn't* killed by the killer, then she becomes like a madwoman. If there was a strength in it,

204

that's where the strength was. It was a terrible plot mistake that Neil made.

Was the notion of a serial killer who's killing children part of the brief given to you by Spielberg?

I think that was intrinsic in it, yeah.

So, given your antipathy to showing a child in jeopardy, did you ever consider turning down the commission?

Not really. If the phone rang tonight and it was Spielberg saying, 'Bruce, I've got this thing I wanna do,' like I say, I think I'd do it because it's him. It's either that or get a footnote in cinema history as the man who turned down Spielberg. 'What's the idea then, Steven?' [*American accent*] 'Well, this thing comes from outer space, an extra-terrestrial, an ugly rubbery kind of thing.' 'What does it do?' 'Well, it gets kids to ride bicycles.' 'Really? OK, I'll write that.' There are very few people in this industry that I feel you can't turn down. For example, I couldn't have turned down Kazan, who's a director I admire enormously irrespective of his abysmal politics. If Kazan phoned up, or Scorsese, and said, 'Would you write this for me?' I'm going to write it, or do my best to, no matter what.

When you delivered the script to Spielberg, did he like it?

He seemed to. I went through a misguided period of thinking he was going to direct it.

Why didn't he?

It was very heavy, and something in his head, or someone like his wife, may have said, 'Look, Steve, you're the man who does *E.T.* Do you really want to do a film about a child-killer? Your public may be very unhappy about you doing a subject like this.' It doesn't immediately lend itself to mainstream cinema, and that was the great problem of writing the bloody thing.

After he bailed out, was there ever any possibility that you were in the frame to direct the film, and would you have liked to be?

No way would I have wanted to direct it. The possibility wasn't there, and even if it had been I wouldn't have wanted to. Not my kind of thing.

Did the producers show you Jordan's rewrite before it was filmed?

Yeah.

What were your comments?

My comments were basically what they would be now if I could be bothered to rake them out of my memory.

Presumably they didn't listen?

I wasn't consulted at all. Neil never called me once. That's the way, I'm afraid, with a lot of directors: 'Fuck that. I'm going to do it like this.'

How did you come to see In Dreams, since you haven't seen either Fat Man or Return to Paradise?

Stephen Woolley, Neil's producer, phoned me up and said, 'Come and have a look at it.' He screened it in this enormous cinema, part of the brand new Warner complex in Bristol, and it felt like 36,000 seats because I was the only person there. I went out afterwards to have the proverbial Chinese with Stephen, and I was racking my brains to find something nice to say about it. It was an extraordinarily ugly film. Apart from anything else, it had become hideously ugly. It was a terrible film, wasn't it?

The opening in the reservoir is incredibly eerie, and for about twenty minutes the film almost works, but when the dreams start coming it begins to fall apart. You wrote a two-hour or 120-page

screenplay, and the film is just over ninety minutes long, frantically encompassing the present, the past and the future.

It was a complete and utter mess from top to bottom. I thought *Jennifer Eight* was a low point, but Christ almighty, this hit the floor and dug. I didn't intend to make *Jennifer Eight* anything other than a good movie, and I'm sure that Neil didn't intend to make that anything other than a good movie, but it really didn't know what it was. I thought it was a revolting film. A well-made revolting film. Suddenly we're into all sorts of horrible horror scenes that were never in my head when I wrote it. The only horror scene I wrote was the husband being eaten by the dog, which is pretty horrible.

That and the scene where Dr Silverman gets a pair of scissors in his neck, which actually wasn't in the film. That part was played by Stephen Rea, who acted alongside you in *Still Crazy* after appearing in *In Dreams*.

That's right, he did. The psychiatrist in my version of it was a much older man, certainly not Stephen. I remember him talking about *In Dreams* and saying he had high hopes for it. There were things in it that were all right – the technical stuff was terrific – but mostly it was all over the place. In that scene where she's loading apples into the sink for no good reason, with the camera jerking backwards and forwards, I just thought, 'What the hell is going on? Have I missed something here?'

The scene is in your draft of the script, which must be draft two.

But the apples have a *resonance* in that draft that they don't have in the film. In my story she comes into the kitchen, becomes more and more nauseous from something, goes into the larder and finds cooking apples which she's got to get rid of and doesn't even know why. The way that Neil shot it, they might as well have been apricots or boiled eggs. She turns round, and suddenly the table is laden with apples, and who brought them there? I don't know.

You've got the same problem with the cider press where the serial killer lives, which is meant to be disused but is filled with . . .

Fresh apples, yeah.

Which had to have been picked. Now, you could argue that the film is following dream logic, but it's still meant to be grounded in some sort of notional reality.

Where did they all come from, these apples? Now, what I wanted was an overgrown Grimms' fairytale orchard with apples growing. And what the fuck was Robert Downey Jr, a very fine actor, doing dressed as a nurse cutting people's throats? I didn't know what any of that rushing around was about.

Again, this was in your script.

No, it wasn't. In my first draft the mother and the girl end up in a shed in the orchard all chained together by the killer, and he's going to kill them. There are no policemen, no helicopters, no snipers, no nothing. In the second draft I was asked to put the helicopters and the police and the snipers in.

Claire is put through a terrible ordeal. She loses her daughter, her husband, her liberty and, in the film, her life. Do you think the script, via Jordan's rewrite, inflicted more suffering on her than audiences were prepared to accept?

I don't know. I think there was no intention when Neil shot the film to bring in the coda of the fist through the mirror, he haunted her and now she's haunting him. I think they put that in because audiences thought, 'Why have we sat here for two hours to see this woman ritually pecked to death by the film-maker?' I hated that, because when she comes back to haunt him she's as bad as he is.

Another hitch is that Claire, like the Jack Nicholson character in The Shining, starts on the verge of hysteria and has nowhere to go but complete insanity.

I know. It's like the old Jack Warner thing: 'Start with the earthquake and work up to the climax.' I'm afraid that's what happened with this.

The critics compared it to *Blue Velvet*, *The Eyes of Laura Mars*, *The Innocents*, *A Nightmare on Elm Street*, *The Night of the Hunter*, *Psycho*, *The Shining* and *The Silence of the Lambs*, not to mention the Holy Bible, the Brothers Grimm, Greek tragedy and Bruno Bettelheim.

I would agree with all that except Bruno Bettelheim, because I've never heard of him.

He's a Freudian writer, concentrating on fairytales.

Oh, is he? It becomes academic to even analyse something so awful. It's like, 'What kind of brown is this shit?' You know what I mean? 'Would this shit be better light-brown? If it was softer, do you think, or more crisp?' Shit is shit. It unequivocally sustained a shafting, didn't it? I never read a review.

These comparisons were not in its favour. Most reviewers thought that it was a half-digested mish-mash of . . .

Bullshit. Yeah, very strange. A weird thing to have happened. I really believe it was nothing to do with me, and nothing to do with Neil. It played for about four days in the States and then folded, because once his family had seen it no one else went. I genuinely can hardly bear to talk about this thing. I can talk about nearly everything that I've ever done, including things that will never be seen, but this, to me, is just a piece of chewing gum stuck to my shoe. But the upside was I got paid and I got to meet Spielberg.

And yet, Claire is an illustrator like Sophie; the killer is called Vivian Thompson, which is an amalgam of Vivian MacKerrell and Eric Thompson; and there's the recurring rhyme 'My daddy was a dollar', which refers to the dollar which your real father gave to your mother. It's almost as if you started writing the script as a paycheque gig and personal stuff kept falling into it.

Well, it does. The dollar is in *Penman* as well: 'Took the dollar and drilled the luck right out of it.' My mother gave me this dollar when I was twenty-one and never told me where it had come from, and it was something that her lover had given her in the war as a memento. The only thing on earth I've got that my real father has touched is this dollar, and consequently it has some resonance in my thinking and does come up quite a lot. The coin in *Force Majeure* was probably one of the reasons that I said, 'I'm not going to fuck with this,' because it's terribly important to me. Had my silver dollar, which I guess came down tails, come down heads, then maybe my eighty-two-year-old father would be sitting in the other room now smoking a cigar. I don't know.

An article in *Creative Screenwriting*, and two-thirds of the broadsheet reviews, don't mention your contribution to the script at all, and only one critic suggests your work was rewritten by Jordan. Which is more irritating, not receiving any credit or being regarded as a full collaborator in the finished product?

Being regarded as a collaborator. Definitely. I don't want anything to do with this thing, and I bet you Neil doesn't either. It was just one of those horrible errors that you make. Neil's a bloody good film-maker, but everyone can fuck it up and that was a fuck up. All the other things that we've talked about – indeed, the majority of most people's work that you could talk about – have some saving graces. Much as I dislike *Return to Paradise* – I assume I dislike it – I'm sure there are saving graces in there. If I'd seen it I could say, 'Well, at least that works, and that's a good idea.' *Jennifer Eight* is a masterpiece compared to this. *In Dreams* is absolutely unadulterated brown. Out of all the things I've ever been associated with, I hate that film most. I'm sure that Neil has completely exorcised that movie from his head, and if he hasn't he should. I think Neil and I should go to the same funeral of this picture and just say goodbye to it gracefully and put a big fucking slab on top of it. Anyway, he's vindicated himself with his next picture. I hear it's excellent.

In fact, it's easy to tell that you didn't have anything to do with Jordan, Strick or Joffé simply because of the way the credit appears on screen: '&' indicates collaboration whereas 'and' means that the writers worked separately.

Anyone who knows my work knows what I can do as a screenwriter, and quite frankly you can't see what I can do in those films, I don't think. Vincent Canby, the late *New York Times* film critic, wrote when he saw *Fat Man*, 'I can't believe this is the work of the guy who wrote *Withnail & I* and *The Killing Fields*.' That was one of the few liferafts I had, and the reason he couldn't believe it was because he was right, it wasn't my work. I'm sure Roland is a better director than I could ever be, because he's into stuff that I don't know about, but I'm a better writer than he could ever be, so why couldn't we collaborate?

Jordan, Strick and Joffé probably regarded your scripts in much the same way as you regarded the original film of *Force Majeure*, as the basis for their film.

The difference between *Force Majeure* and what I'd written is that this was a small, totally unknown foreign film, and no one in the business can say I'm an unknown commodity as a writer. I mean, for fuck's sake, I was nominated for an Oscar for *The Killing Fields*, so it's not like I don't know what I'm doing. Anyway, *Jennifer Eight* was a fuck up, then *Return to Paradise* was a fuck up, then *In Dreams* was a fuck up. My career as a writer has been a string of American disappointment and I really should have learned my lesson by now. If you're going to do something for the studios don't become emotionally involved, because the chances are you're going to get fucked. And that's rule number three: prepare for a good fucking. Unless, like I'm saying about *The Block*, you can control the thing. If it's a masterpiece, me and my cast and crew will grin as we take the praise, and if it's a complete disaster: 'Sorry, Bruce. It's your fault.' That's how I want it to be. Thank God I've got a plinth to stand on in this sea of angst, which is *Penman*.

Chapter Eight

'A completely disfunctional family'

The Peculiar Memories of Thomas Penman

When did you first consider writing the novel?

It's been suppurating away for half my adult life or more. I started it in 1976, but most of the protagonists were still alive then and their very existence militated against me writing it. As soon as they all croaked, except for my mother, it was easier. It's quite an aggressive book towards my family.

What steeled you to sit down and try again?

I'd made enough off *In Dreams* not to worry about money for a while, but I became incredibly depressed about the work being turned into this nonsense, and Sophie said, 'If that's what's making you unhappy, do something about it.' 'What can I do?' 'Well, you've been moaning about this novel since I've known you. Now you've got money in the bank you could write it.' My agent and lawyers and all the rest were really antipathetic towards me doing that book, because obviously they weren't getting anything out of it. They just thought, 'Oh God, we won't see him for eighteen months,' and they were right.

It's ironic that you lifted yourself out of a depression by tackling something which could have been very depressing to write.

Yeah, but it made me laugh. One of the few up-sides of being a writer is that you can take astonishingly depressing situations and make them funny. *Penman* is like that to me, a horrible time in my life – and my childhood was horrible – but funny, too. 213

That was my intention: to extirpate all that vileness but at the same time make people laugh at it, which is my favourite kind of comedy. Chaplin offers us laughter or tears, and I think I'd rather laugh, even if it's a nightmare.

Thomas is fourteen years old at the start of the novel. Why did you choose to begin his story at that particular age?

The 'magic moments' of my childhood were the violence of my stepfather, the death of my grandfather, and the awakening of what I call 'the poison of puberty', becoming aware of girls and falling in love. That's why I set it at about fourteen. It's the end of childhood and the beginning of adulthood. As a matter of fact, my grandfather died when I was eleven, not fourteen. I kept him alive for a bit for the purposes of the novel.

You've described *Withnail* as being about twenty-five per cent autobiographical. What would *Penman* be?

Well, I would say that *Withnail* is a lot more than twenty-five per cent. I would say that *Withnail* is about seven out of ten and *Penman* is probably eight out of ten. It's very much autobiographical. Virtually everything in the book happened at one time or another in my life, but didn't necessarily happen in the sequence presented. *Penman* is almost an autobiography, really, given the constrictions of writing about a person's life and all the baggage that those characters bring with them that has to be dealt with. It's like any other piece of writing. Things that happen in *Withnail* over a period of two weeks happened over a period of four years, and things that happen in *Penman* over a period of two years happened over a period of ten years.

Most of the protagonists are named for their progenitors: Thomas's stepfather Rob, mother Mabs, grandfather Walter, grandmother Ethel and sister Bel.

Not my sister's name. Certain names were changed to protect the innocent.

Mabs has an affair with a GI during the war, Rob finds out when he returns and that's when the horror begins. The reader learns this through the clairvoyant, Madame Olanda, but I believe you learned it from your grandmother in 1976.

Something like that, yeah. When she was dying. My mother absolutely, irrevocably and fundamentally refused to discuss this with me. Then, last Christmas, she said, 'He wasn't your father. I've had this secret for all these years.' Was it a secret this man wasn't my father? No, anyone could have told you that years ago. But she finally admitted it. A great load off her shoulders, I suppose. When I finished the novel she phoned me up and said, 'I'm going to buy your book today to burn it,' because even then she wouldn't accept what had happened. She told me that after the war she met her husband, my stepfather, at the railway station and they shook hands. Can you imagine coming back from the war and shaking hands with your wife? Quite extraordinary. But I couldn't carry that, as I think she was prepared to do, to the grave with me. If you won't tell me the truth, don't criticise me for writing *my* truth. If I don't know who my father is, what my past is, and why I am who I am, I'm going to have to invent it because that's what I do. If you don't like what I'm saying, tell me something different.

Similarly, the novel begins with Thomas shitting himself, which draws on something a psychiatrist said to you at one point, and you give that line to the grandfather.

That's right. The psychiatrist that I've seen for twenty-five years told me about that syndrome. He told me things that were incredibly apposite, as far as I was concerned, about the child. You can see now, although I'm not a greedy person, I'm very acquisitive. I like books around me, I like pictures around me. It was the same when I was a kid. In Freudian terms it's called 'archiving'. If you haven't got a background or a family life that is emotionally satisfactory to you, you archive. I took it to an extreme in the novel, but my bedroom was like an antique shop and the rest of the house wasn't, because I was making an archive for myself that would give me some security as a kid to say, 'This is where I exist. This is where I can function.' My grandmother would always say, 'What, more books?' At the weekend I would go out on my bicycle, and I'd have two-and-six pocket money and I'd buy books with it. They were the set-dressings of my childhood, books, and they became very precious things, although I suppose they've all gone over the years. But now, is this the same thing? Is this a more sophisticated version of that? They're almost like a defensive wall, aren't they?

They're all the way round the room.

They would be if I could get them in, like a defensive wall in my life. The shit thing was a regular occurrence when I was a kid. For example, my son's six and no way would he shit himself, but I used to shit myself up to the age of about ten. According to Freud, shit is one of the first communicatory and reward functions that a child has. If you shit when your parents want you to, they pat you on the head. If you don't shit in that way, you can punish them. You can say, 'I don't feel I'm being loved, therefore I'm going to shit myself, and I'm going to keep shitting myself, and you're going to have to clean it up.' Because I wasn't being told I was a good boy I shat inappropriately, and I used that in the novel. Obviously I turned the volume up a bit, I wasn't shitting myself when I was fourteen, but as a little boy I did, basically saying, 'You don't love me.' The whole book's about animosity, and if Hunter Thompson hadn't used the title I would have loved to have had *Fear and Loathing in Thanet*, because that's what it was. Did you have a happy childhood, or relatively happy?

Yes, I did. Very comfortable.

I can't say we were uncomfortable. We were well-fed and well-clothed, but there was this underlying stratum of hatred that everybody had for everybody in my family. I don't know if I say this in the book – I don't think I do – but the only time my stepfather ever touched me was when he was hitting me. That's all I remember from my childhood. Even in relationships which aren't the height of passion, sometimes you see your mum or dad say, 'Give me a cuddle.' I never saw that in my life. I never saw him kiss her once, never saw him do her a kindness. For most of my childhood my parents slept in different rooms. When you're a child it doesn't really impact on you; you think this is the norm, this is what people do. But of course they don't; normally parents sleep in the same bedroom, indeed in the same bed. It was a completely disfunctional family. Steve Woolley says in the documentary that it was almost like the Addams Family. It wasn't 'almost', it was. It's quite normal for families to be so disfunctional that they fall to bits, but normally the bits fly off in their own orbit. What happened with my family was that for one reason or another they stayed together.

There was an implosion rather than an explosion.

That's right. They imploded. That thing about her going off and divorcing Rob then coming back and cooking him dinner was one of the most brutally ridiculous things that's ever happened in my life. I couldn't believe it. 'How was the divorce?' 'Oh, it was all right. What do you want for dinner?' That's absolutely true. Neither my sister nor I could believe that had happened. The worst thing is that my mother had no contact with him other than rage, so she would find ways to enrage him. You'd be sitting there having a perfectly normal lunch and she'd say, 'Did you see' – in the *Telegraph* or the *Express*, which were their principal organs of communication – 'that some students have freaked out at the LSE?' She'd bring this up to be the catalyst for him to be enraged, because without his rage she had no contact at all. I tried to make that come through in the book, the fact that anger was their currency and the only way she could deal with him was to get him inflamed – a very easy thing to do.

I used two pieces in the book. One was where he says, 'Hang Mykarios. String up the Micks,' and the other was the Cuban Missile Crisis: 'The Americans haven't got the guts to do anything.' He was like that every day, a cyclone of rage coming into the house. Whatever he'd seen, the knuckles would go white, the rage would put colour in his head and he'd start. The only thing my stepfather had that I don't allow him in the book was a fabulous sense of humour, although I think he's written as a comic character in the sense of his absurdity and extremism. There's that line 'I'll never cry because of you and never laugh because of you,' and that's what I felt about him. He was quite a nob – he went to school at Rugby – but he had this northern-nightclub humour. The jokes were always anti-black, anti-Japanese, anti-whoever. He hated everything and everybody, including himself, I suppose. At Sunday lunch, particularly when I was older and I'd have friends round, everyone was laughing at his repartee, and I never laughed, not once, no matter what he said. Even if everyone else was pissing themselves I'd sit there like one of those presidents carved out of the rock. I wouldn't react to him, ever.

Rob also says something which you describe as the worst thing anybody had ever said to Thomas: 'Shut up, you're just a loud-mouthed lying little cunt.'

Well, what a terrible thing to say to a kid. I think I was about fifteen when he said that to me. In the book the word 'lying' is an addition. In truth he said, 'Shut up, you're just a loud-mouthed little cunt.' I can't think of a worse thing to say to a young boy going through puberty. The only thing worse than that was actual physical violence. In fact, I'd much rather have got a smack round the chops than have that said to me. Even to this day – and it was forty years ago or whatever – it stings me. That's not normal social intercourse for a family. If we interpret what he meant by 'loud-mouthed', it was 'Shut up, you're just an intelligent little cunt,' because the one thing he couldn't handle was the fact that I was intelligent.

I feel more sympathy towards my stepfather, now he's long dead and I'm a lot older, than I've ever been able to feel before, and I wish I could say to him, 'I understand now why you were such a fucking *oberleutnant*.' If I found out tonight that my little boy wasn't my little boy but was a bit of lipstick and a shag round the back of the Odeon, I wouldn't love him less. I would love him differently, but I couldn't possibly take this fantastic creature and say one day 'I'm manically in love with you' and the next day punch him in the face, because what's it got to do with him? Unfortunately, my stepfather wasn't like that, and he punished my mother by hurting me. That's not hyperbole. I remember her shouting, 'Stop it! Stop it! You'll kill him!' when he was beating me. That scene where he chases Thomas into the sea with a riding crop happened. I don't think I could have invented that.

Thomas's defence against Rob is to pile saucepans behind his bedroom door, keeping a power-drill handy so he can attack his stepfather and a hacksaw in case of power cuts. That kind of paranoia . . .

That's true. That isn't an invention. I think the saw is an invention, and the drill is probably an invention, but the piling of saucepans and things that would clatter in the dead of night if anyone came into my bedroom is not invention. I was that paranoid of what he may or may not do. My plan literally was that if saucepans clatter, jump out the window. There was a period where I genuinely thought he might come through the place and off the lot of us. He was like a knuckle. His whole personality was like a fucking knuckle. I thought he might lose it one night, get arseholed on whiskey and think, 'Why don't I off the lot of them just for the fucking laugh of it?' Or if not the lot of them, at least me. That was a genuine concern of mine, which is a terrible thing. It would be a terrible indictment of me as a parent if my child went to bed tonight with something even remotely like that crossing his mind: 'Maybe my dad will come in and smoke me.' But he wasn't a parent. He didn't give a damn about being a parent.

One of the things he got me into as a child was guns. When I was twelve or thirteen I was obsessed with guns. Retrospectively, I realise why. Why do we have witches and giants in fairytales? Well, the witch is the mum and the giant is the dad. Why did I want a gun? Because he was a very potent and aggressive man, and a gun is an equaliser. He had a pistol by the side of his bed. It wasn't a Beretta, it was a Ruger automatic pistol, but Beretta is more sinister-sounding. My stepfather had the muscle, had the thighs, had the neck, had the running, had the rowing, had the rugby, and I assume having guns as a child was not only saying 'I can be strong like you' but also that I can protect myself. So I wanted guns as a child, and I got them. He bought them for me. I guess it was one of the few ways he could relate to me, one of the few ways he could get through to me, to give me an automatic rifle.

The relationship between Thomas and Walter, his tenderness towards the boy, their communication through morse code and so on, is perhaps the emotional heart of the novel. What memories do you have of your grandfather?

Morse code was an invention for the book. What it did was represent a kind of a communication that there was between myself and my grandfather. It's like we talked together without needing words. My stepfather, who was never there for me as a kid, was replaced by my grandfather. My grandfather was an excellent carpenter. He used to take me to the model shop and buy wood, and make me bridges for model railways. He genuinely gave me an affection that I never had out of my stepfather, so I felt very warm towards him. I remember going out with him in the Wolsey as a little boy, and he would take Christmas boxes to various poor people in Broadstairs. Long after he died I spoke to a cousin of mine, Laurie Marshall, who's a High Court judge now, and he said to me, 'Your grandfather was a real left-winger.' Of course, I didn't know that as a kid. It's like someone saying, 'He's a Jew.' It doesn't mean anything. Anyway, Laurie said he was a real old leftie, and I thought, 'I shared quite a lot with you.'

He was an incredibly weird guy, though. As it says in the book [*Cockney accent*], 'He went weird after the wawer, the First World Wawer.' He was completely obsessed with sex, a pornographer *par excellence*. He did have two filing cabinets stuffed with fabulous pornography, the sort of thing which would now be construed as art because it's got some years on it, and they burned the lot when he died. If only I had it now. Not for prurience but for the great souvenir. Amazing hand-coloured photographs of dirty activities. It was heavyweight stuff. I don't know whether my grandfather did or did not fuck some girl in France that he was in love with for the rest of his life, but the fact that he had that relationship with Adele in the book – and she's called Adele because of me doing that Truffaut film – suited my purposes, and then to repeat that for Thomas.

A couple of chapters are called 'The Sins of the Forefathers', parts one and two, which points up this repetition of events.

The same thing that happens to the grandfather happens to the boy, they both lose the love of their lives, which I thought was an interesting thing to have a go at. That's invented. What isn't invented is the grandfather being hit at Passchendaele. He told me that's what happened.

The First World War scenes are stunning. Walter gets half his head blown off, and survives firstly because maggots eat the gangrene and secondly because the Germans stuff the brains back in. Is there an element of hyperbole there?

Not much. Not much at all. The new thing now is medicinal maggots to clean wounds, and that was a story which was often reiterated by my grandfather, He wasn't a liar, he was a very moral guy in many ways, in spite of the pornography. I believe that to be the truth. Of course, he may have added a few frills, and now forty years later as a writer I may have added a few frills, but that's basically what happened to him. He was mortally wounded, he was dying, and he was out there, he reckoned, for ten or twelve days. It's the most powerful part of the book, the best part of the book, I think: Walter in the First World War and Thomas playing at war on the beach, murdering crabs with depth charges. I was very pleased with the way that came out. It was so hard to write; I did it again and again and again.

The battlefield sequence also parallels the war of attrition which is happening between the members of this family.

Very much. There's certainly a kind of love between Ethel and Walter. Reciprocated by Walter? I'm not sure. Is it love or duty that Mabs has for Walter? I'm not sure. I don't think you could say there is even a fragmentary shadow of love between Rob and Mabs. There's nothing. It's a cold war more than anything, an environmental decay that they both got themselves into. God knows why they sustained it.

There's also a parallel between Thomas shitting himself and Mabs

overfeeding the dogs so they shit themselves, which is his way of communicating with her and her way of communicating with Rob.

That's right. And that, too, is all true. The dogs did start shitting themselves all over the house. I used that in the book so the grandfather could explain the relevance of shit, via the dogs, so the boy comes to realise that the dogs are shitting themselves because she isn't loved and maybe he's shitting himself because he isn't loved. The catalyst of which is Olanda, probably the most accurately described character in the book. I hardly invented anything in respect of her. I'll never forget that fight Rob had with her in the yard, where she threw a rock through the windshield of the Wolsey. I was fourteen or fifteen when that happened, and here he is fighting this fortune-teller at dawn. It's pretty far out. You couldn't invent that. That had to have happened, otherwise you'd never have it in a book. I don't know how you'd film that, actually, because part of what makes that sequence funny is one's own imaginative take.

Although the novel doesn't have a plot as such, one of the narrative strands concerns Thomas's obsession with locating the key to Walter's filing cabinet and finding out what's in there, and in the process coming across letters from Madame Olanda to Walter.

That was made up. Her relationship with my grandfather certainly existed, to what end I know not. The scene where Thomas goes to see her in that hut full of steam was made up too, although she did have a hut on the seafront at Broadstairs which did fascinate me as a kid. There used to be a penny arcade, and she was next door. The celebrity who visited Thanet, I remember, was that guy Jack Warner.

Dixon of Dock Green.

Yeah. He was the celebrity in the window. She was very weird. She hated my stepfather and my stepfather hated her, but she was always quite charming to me. About two weeks after she stuck the rock through the windshield she wrote me a letter. I wish I'd kept it, it would have been interesting. It was quite a long letter. She said, 'You're going to be incredibly famous at what you do,' and then she said, 'Fame in many ways.' I'm still waiting for the 'incredibly' and the 'many ways', but I've got a little bit of recognition as a writer.

You appeared in a few things as an actor. Now you're known as a screenwriter, a director and a novelist. She might not have been too far off.

Well, I've done something. But it's weird she should have said that. When she died – this was a long time ago – she was found rolling in some gutter in Broadstairs with about £3500 on her, which was an enormous amount of money in those days. You could buy a house for that.

Who inspired Thomas's girlfriend, Gwendolin?

Her real name was Jennifer, and she was my first girlfriend. There was no sexual connection between us, but I remember lying on her parents' sofa once when her parents were out, and I was saying, 'Oh, Jenny! Oh, Jenny!' among other inventive foreplay, and suddenly she said to me, 'Do you want to touch me up?' A huge shock. 'How could you possibly think such a dreadful thing, you hussy?' Of course, all I wanted in the world was to do that.

Thomas's friendship with Maurice Potts is important to him too.

Yeah. He wasn't a vicar's son, but he was probably the most corrupt person I've ever met. I was, like, fourteen, fifteen, and he was my best friend. He taught me the art of masturbation and all of that. He was a really corrupt little boy, as we both were in our different ways. There was another guy at school who had this wonderful name, Maurice Gubb, and my friend Dick Potts and Maurice Gubb became Maurice Potts. Those people, Maurice Gubb, Dick Gollick, were my contemporaries at school, so they all came up in my head. I can't remember any of their faces, all I can remember is those names. There was a girl there called Fanny Shackles.

Very Dickensian.

Fanny Shackles is out of a minor Dickens novel, isn't it? There are parts of *Penman* that I think even Dickens would have been pleased with, but obviously I'm not comparing my writing to his; I think he's a giant. *David Copperfield* started out as an autobiography and then he turned it into a novel, precisely what happened with *Penman*. He was enraged at his treatment as a child. He couldn't understand why a sensitive and intelligent kid was sent to a blacking factory. Hence, you get *David Copperfield*, you get *Oliver Twist*, you get *Great Expectations*. They're all the same theme, of the little boy who wins. He does it again and again and again.

Given your obvious sympathy for and apparent empathy with children, why did you write the novel in the third person rather than the first person?

As a matter of fact, the other reason I couldn't make it work when I started to write it in the seventies was because I wrote it in the first person. If you write, 'I had a great stool hanging out of my arse' it wouldn't be funny, because there's something dreadful about talking about shitting yourself. It took me twenty years of writing education to realise it has to be done in the third person. *Withnail* is in the first person, and nothing happens without the 'I' character being there. I break the rule once or twice, maybe, like right at the end of the movie where Danny the Dealer says, 'I recommend you smoke some more grass,' and Marwood says, 'No way,' and fucks off. I purposefully made it into the third person there because the relationship was breaking.

I will not forget Page 49 of *Penman*. I nearly abandoned the book. Over a period of two weeks I couldn't write Page 49. You always get one page in a script, or a book I suppose, where you can't do it. No matter which way you approach it, you just do not know how to do it. Andrew Birkin, if a Page 49 comes up, just says, 'Fuck it. This is when . . .' and writes Page 50. I can't do that. I can't go on unless I've done it. One of the most difficult parts of *Penman* was where he goes and puts pennies on the old man's eyes and he's not dead yet. Now, in the context of the book, it washes over you and hopefully just seems amusing, but I really sweated over whether I was going to do that scene. Finally Sophie said, 'Do it,' so I did. It's like Hemingway said: 'Never end your day's work without knowing what your next day's work is going to be.'

Do you think you'd have been a writer if your childhood hadn't been so awful?

I don't know. If I hadn't had that childhood I think I would have been an actor, playing some minor role in a provincial play. That's what my fate would have been. If you show an inclination for something when you're twelve, thirteen, fourteen, fifteen, that's probably what you're going to end up doing. I clearly had an inclination for drama, and by the time I was sixteen I thought, 'I'm fuck all use at anything else; maybe I should be an actor.' So that was the road I went down. If I'd gone to grammar school or public school, because I was receptive to literature I might have circum-navigated the whole acting experience and perhaps gone to university to do English and been in the university dramatic society like those *Beyond the Fringe* guys, Alan Bennett and Peter Cook, etc. Retrospectively, I like the fact that I went to a secondary modern and didn't get exams and university and all the rest, because drama school was a good three years' worth, although it didn't work too well for me. I was too young, I suppose.

It's ridiculous to take children of ten and a half and make judgements that will affect them for the rest of their lives. How do you know what kind of intellectual capacity a child has at ten and a half, or what psychological disturbance may be fucking them about, or whatever? You just don't know. 'You were able to work out how long the bath takes to fill, you must be a grammar school boy. You don't know how long the bath takes to fill, you must be secondary modern.' In my view, you could say to those same two boys, 'You know how the bath fills and you don't, but let's hear you both describe a flower and see who can get closer to what a flower is,' which to me is a much more important test, not of intelligence but of being alive. I think it was awful that they did that to kids in those days, because a lot of kids in my year who were marked down as milk-float drivers were clearly intelligent, and I don't know why they ended up there any more than why I ended up there.

David Copperfield is important to Thomas in the same way that *Oliver Twist* was to you. I believe that you read the novel when you were in bed with asthma at the age of thirteen or fourteen and it was a turning point for you.

The lights went on, yeah. One of the masters, who taught English and drama, gave it to me, and it really was a revelation. It was around the same time, at about twelve or thirteen, that I first got my arse on a stage in the school drama society.

Herbert Pocket in a stage version of *Great Expectations*, for example.

That's right. I went to the Charles Dickens School, where there was this bust of him with a plug of chewing gum up its nostril. They always have those sort of schools in England, particularly secondary moderns: the John Keats School or the Florence Nightingale School. We were saturated with Dickens in Broadstairs. He comes up a lot in my novel. Dickens' house, *Bleak House*, actually *is* in Broadstairs. I started getting obsessed with Dickensiana as well as his books, and I've got all sorts of stuff to do with him.

You started reading, you started acting and you also started writing – using a typewriter belonging to your grandfather.

A very old black Olivetti. I remember the first play I wrote – the first two plays I wrote – when I was still at school. Then I had a little Brother portable, then I had an Olivetti electric, then I got the IBM golfball which was my favourite typewriter. The old metal golfball types were smashing typewriters, then they became totally obsolete – you could still get the parts but nobody knew how to mend them – so about fifteen years ago I moved on to this machine, also obsolete but still built under licence in Kentucky. I like paper. While I'm typing I like to be able to grab a pen or a pencil and write in the margin. If I'm writing a piece of dialogue I might whip the paper out of the machine and look at it and think, 'I love that line; I love that line; that doesn't play; this is horseshit; what would it be like if I put that there?'

Why didn't you write any more plays later?

I was always in films. Had I been acting in plays I probably would have started writing plays, but because my first professional experience was with screenplays I started to write them. The first play I wrote was about a man who had murdered his brother for his money, and one night he's sitting alone in evening dress in his study in his house on the Norfolk Broads and the brother comes back as a spectre to haunt him, and he ends up dying in exactly the same way that his brother died. I can't remember what it was called, it's in the attic somewhere. I wrote that when I was about fourteen. The second one was about a guy who was going to be hanged the next morning, a Derek Bentley type, and his relationship with his two warders, and one of them was friendly towards him and the other was torturing him, making what's left of his life more miserable than it should have been. The play was about the death penalty. That was when I was about fourteen or fifteen. Victimology, isn't it? It's about victims.

I think the first thing you wrote was A Book of Inventions and Experiments.

Christ, where did you hear about that? Yeah, I've always been interested in explosives and pyrotechnics and that kind of stuff, like the fireworks in *Penman*. Thomas does what I was doing, and if you go into my workshop now there's a cupboard in there stuffed with potassium chlorate, hydrochloric acid, all the things I used to use as a child. Why I've still got my hands and eyesight I don't know, because as a kid I did make a lot of bombs. If my boy was into that I wouldn't allow it. I built this bomb when I was thirteen or fourteen and blew up the hut that the cricket team used at school. I shoved the explosives in – electrically detonated nitroglycerine – and I thought I was just going to blow a hole in it. The fucking thing was in the air. I used to design all sorts of bits and pieces, and still do. I invented this system for tyres on a road using the same technique as a gramophone record, needles hitting grooves and making sounds, so as the tyres went over it the road would talk to you and you'd hear, 'Slow down!' It's perfectly feasible to do that. You could have advertising coming through the tyres. Everywhere you drove you'd be hearing voices.

Thomas also writes, as his surname suggests; poems rather than plays.

Indeed, there's a poem in the novel where he says, 'You tell me of the ecstasy of our love's complexity,' and that was a poem I wrote when I was about fourteen. I found it in a box in an old notebook and I thought, 'I'll have that!' There was another one I wrote, about Christmas, that was actually a good poem, I think, where he talks about Auntie somebody driving the ghost of a sprout deep into the dog-rotten upholstery. My Dylan Thomas phase. 'The ghost of a sprout' is a good euphemism for a fart. I wouldn't be dissatisfied with that line if I came up with it now.

You're obviously not dissatisfied with the novel as a whole, either.

Withnail and *Penman* are the only things I feel I've totally controlled as an artist, and I'm happy with those because they're mine. I really believe that's my stuff. *Advertising* is my stuff too, but I would have liked more money for it. *Jennifer Eight* stuck me down a street I didn't want to be in but didn't know how to walk out of, and as soon as I wrote *Penman* I got out of that street. I thought, 'This is all right. I'm a fucking writer. Now I feel I could direct something again.' I've exorcised the past by putting a big brick wall between *Jennifer Eight* and the future, and that's *Penman*. It was one of the best moves I've ever made. I can't tell you how fulfilling it is to go into a bookstore and see people picking it up and paying for it. It's great.

If you didn't have to support your current lifestyle do you think you'd be happier as a novelist than a film-maker?

No, I'm essentially a dramatist. If I can do something best, what I can do best is dialogue. Novels very often aren't about dialogue, they're about internal thoughts. I feel most comfortable when I've got a run of people talking to each other. So I would always have ended up, and will end up, as a screenwriter. When I'm writing, because I am basically a screenwriter, I would tend to see it as a visual train of thought.

Conversely, when you were working on the novel were you thinking ahead to a possible film adaptation? For instance, we were discussing the juxtaposition of Thomas blowing up crabs and Walter on the battlefield.

I do see it like that. I do see scenes. *Penman* almost drifts into screenplay from time to time, and that's one of the scenes where it does. If you actually drew lines there and put scene numbers on it, you're virtually reading a screenplay: 'Scene 96, woodland in Ypres, they load the gun. Scene 97, the boys on the beach. Scene 98, the shell goes off. Scene 99, a massive explosion, the boys are running. Scene 100, Walter hit.' There was a bloke who wrote in one of the papers criticising *Penman* who brought that up: 'It's a screenwriter's novel, not a writer's novel.'

Isn't that sort of comment beside the point? Lots of novels are cinematic and lots of films are novelistic.

Well, you're either a writer or a writer. All those famous novelists who went into the studios in the thirties, Hemingway and Faulkner and Wodehouse, didn't give a fuck about films. They were writers. My interest is in the word all the time. Curiously, the thing that really turned me on to cinema was Charlie Chaplin's *The Gold Rush*, which hasn't got any words in it. I went to see it when I was twelve, and it's still the funniest film I've ever seen. There are myriad references to it in *Withnail*, and I wasn't aware I was doing it, but I can see now that they're there.

So if you were to pick the two biggest influences on your work as a writer and director, it would be Dickens and Chaplin?

They're both massive influences on me. Dickens wrote forty-four books, and these aren't novelettes, these are a kilo a piece. If I'm not working I feel guilty, and he must have had that in bucket-loads. He was only fifty-nine when he died, and he basically worked himself to death. He must have been writing all day every day. I sometimes come in here of a winter's night when there's a gale blowing, and pull out a book I've read a hundred times – *A Christmas Carol*; the first two hundred pages of *David Copperfield*; the first three chapters of *Bleak House*; the first chapter of *A Tale of Two Cities*. I've read them so many times I can almost quote them, but they're so emotive. For me, they're the apogee of what writing is.

Do you feel writing the novel has helped you personally as well as artistically?

Helped in what sense?

In the sense of catharsis, getting all this stuff out of your system.

No, not at all. It's that Hemingway cliché: 'What do you need to be a successful writer?' Actually, knock out the adjective there. 'What do you need to be a writer? An unhappy childhood.' I definitely had an unhappy childhood, there's no question of it, a very unhappy childhood, so I fulfil the criteria that Hemingway set up admirably, and it is one of those things that makes me go back again and again and again to the typewriter, I suppose, to try and find a solution to it. And I can't. Because there is no solution to your past. Freud called it 'the unfinished business of childhood'. It is my unfinished business and I don't know how to get rid of it. How can I? How can I get rid of that past? It's the thing I hate most but it's the thing that motivates me most to be a writer, to put myself in the situation of Dith Pran, of Thomas Penman, of whoever. That's what I do. Everything I write's about me, in that sense. I can act, but it was never anything I could excel at. Writing is something that I have to excel at, because it's the war against that. There's no way, touch wood, I'm ever going to turn in a piece of crap writing, because I can't. I'm playing tennis with my childhood, if you like, and I'm going to win every fucking stroke now.

Which is presumably why, firstly, you feel guilty when you're not writing, and secondly, you treat your own children in quite the opposite way?

That's very weird, isn't it? If your father is violent to you you're likely to be violent to your children. The absolute antithesis is the case with me: I'd rather cut my throat than hit my kids, anyone's kids. Once, when Lily was about four, she was being so impossible to both me and Sophie that I did slap her on the back of the leg and say, 'Stop it!' And she did stop it. But I still feel guilty about it. I think it's a terrible thing to do, to hurt a child. I take a very aggressive attitude towards people who hurt kids. Rob says in the book, 'I'm the boy to hang Mykarios.' Well, I would never have hung Mykarios, but if someone was absolutely categorically proved to have killed a child, I am the boy. I could go in there and shoot the cunt. It wouldn't bother me. It wouldn't bother me to shoot someone like Ian Brady. I don't think it would give me bad dreams to kill someone like him. Twenty years ago I would never have said that or thought that, but I do now.

In the last five years I've revised my point of view about a lot of things. The death penalty, for example. I don't believe it should be available to courts *ad hoc*, but anyone who purposely, with malice aforethought, sets out to murder a child forfeits their right to life as far as I'm concerned. That's quite conservative. On the other hand, the intellectual side of the radio in my head cuts in and says, 'Wait a minute. Why did he do it? Maybe they've got problems you don't understand.' But I allow my emotion to overrule my intellect in terms of anything to do with hurt children. I can't stand it. I support a few charities, but Save the Children, because of the word 'Children', is probably the most important to me. Save the Bruce Robinson – is that what I'm really up to? What is it that gets me sitting in this room at seven in the morning to work? It is guilt, I guess. And where does the guilt come from? The guilt comes from anger. And where does the anger come from? The anger comes from the fact that he told me, 'You're a useless cunt.'

Although it was conceived first, *Withnail* could almost be a sequel to *Penman*, the second part of an autobiographical trilogy.

And now I need to do one about this period in my life. It was the transition from being a child to being a very young adult in *Penman*, then a young adult into a relative grown-up in *Withnail*, and now it should be the transition from a relative grown-up into middle-age and what impact that has on you – and it does have a profound impact. I haven't got a narrative, that's the problem.

To coincide with the novel, Bloomsbury published one of your short stories, *Paranoia in the Launderette*.

People send me letters about *Paranoia in the Launderette*, saying, 'I was on the bus and I felt embarrassed because I was laughing all the way into work.' That's the greatest compliment anyone can pay to me as a writer. It's that classic thing with the two masks: one's crying and one's laughing. I need people laughing off the page. *Paranoia in the Launderette* is almost like my diary: I *am* paranoid. I don't consider myself a mad paranoid, but I do consider myself someone who finds a lot of situations difficult that most people find easy. I'll see things in them that I don't like. Which is why I try to avoid watching television, because it's a polutant, and being on television, because I can't bear being recognised. I'm paranoid if someone looks at me and thinks they know me. They don't say, 'That's Bruce Robinson over there,' they think, 'I know that guy from somewhere,' and they look at you with quizzical eyes. It freaks me out. That's part and parcel of why we're down here in the countryside, to escape all that.

Perhaps you'd be recognised more often if *Still Crazy*, the film which you acted in after finishing *Penman*, had been a big success.

It wasn't a bad British picture. I thought it was going to do some business and it didn't. The reason it didn't was because young audiences don't want to see old men playing rock and roll, they want to see Blur and Oasis playing rock and roll.

Were you flattered to be approached?

I suppose in a way one's flattered that someone out there still thinks of you in terms of a potential performer. It was a kind of amateur flattery because I thought, 'If I say no they're just going to get some other bastard anyway.' But when it came up I'd been sitting in here for sixteen months doing *Penman*, and Sophie said, 'For God's sake, get out of this room.' So I got out of this room. I liked the director, Brian Gibson, and I thought, 'At least it's two or three weeks away from the typewriter.' That's the reason I did it. Sophie was instrumental in getting me to write the novel, and Sophie was instrumental in getting me out of this room when I had.

It was a very canny piece of casting, though.

There's plenty of excellent fifty-year-old actors, but this character Brian Lovell hadn't been seen for years, and I fulfilled that side of it admirably because I hadn't been. I hadn't acted for over twenty years.

Brian Gibson said in an interview that the film's about the indignity of getting old and being given a chance to feel empowered again. Was that something you related to in the script?

No, I never had an opinion on it. I came in, stood there like a good bloke, did what I was told and went home. I don't know if there was a 'message' in the film. I had no interest in that side of it at all. It was quite a simple gig and they were very nice to me. The only time I've ever been able to act with a camera stuck at me was in *Still Crazy*, because I didn't give a damn whether I was good, bad or indifferent in it. Brian was over a barrel because firstly he wasn't paying me – I did it for Save the Children – and secondly I wasn't interested in being criticised. I said to him, 'If I'm rubbish don't start giving me a bollocking. You can fire me with impunity and I won't go home crying,' and he bought that rule. It was quite enjoyable.

What preparation did you do for the role?

Just learned the lines and got out there. They paid for the guitar

233

lessons, and a teacher came round every other day to teach me this riff. By the end I could play it, not very well, but at least it looks right in the film. If you look at the fingers they are correct, but I can't play a bloody note.

What was it like working from a script by Dick Clement and Ian La Frenais?

I was originally offered the film to direct about a year before they made it, and I wrote Dick and Ian quite an acerbic letter about the script. Originally this character had taken holy orders, and you ended up with the nuns and the priests rocking, for Christ's sake! But they're very talented blokes, Dick and Ian, they know a lot about what they do. They don't write the kind of comedy I like so much. They write joke comedy and I'm not into that. But I did my best to say the dialogue; I didn't change anything. That would have been like coming in and threatening the project, saying, 'I want the dialogue different' and 'Why are you putting the camera over there, Brian?' I completely acquiesced.

In fact, your scenes in *Still Crazy* are not joke-orientated. You get that lovely quiet scene in the garden, and it's scenes like that which work best in the film.

You're right. I was lucky, because I got the best song, 'The Flame Still Burns'. It was quite a thrill, because when we shot that scene they had 500 extras at the front and they were told I was a star like David Bowie, so on every take I'd come out and they'd all scream and rave. You think, 'Fuck! I wouldn't mind being a rock star!'

Having written a rock-and-roll film, *Roadie*, did it give you pause being offered *Still Crazy* as director and actor, in the sense of wishing yours had been made?

No, I never think like that. I can't think like that. Fuck it. I do it, if it doesn't happen I'll do something different. Except for *The Block*, I never hold on to hopes of past work.

Chapter Nine

'Fuck Jesus, give me Shakespeare'

From Hollywood to Herefordshire

Among your recent projects was an educational film for the Millennium Dome. Given your dislike of the Dome, why did you agree to write it?

Because it was Puttnam, and if he asks you've got to do it. As I understand it, they had something which wasn't working. Puttnam phoned me up and said, 'We've got this twelve-minute film, we've been through six writers and it's all a nightmare.' So I ended up doing it – for Save the Children again – and Tesco's are financing it. I got this idea like *Jack and the Beanstalk*: a magic seed which grows into this Tree of Knowledge, and anyone who gets the seed can fulfil what they want.

Was this for the Learning Zone?

Yeah. I haven't seen it, but what happens is you walk into this school corridor with a vaulted roof on the way to the cinema, and you hear recorded school sounds as you're waiting to go in. Then you walk into the cinema, and projected on the screen is the corridor that you've just come out of, and running down that corridor is a little girl who's late. Then a real girl bursts through the back doors and runs past the audience and reappears through a door which is now projected on the screen. Her teacher calls her at the end of the day and makes her hold her hand out, and she thinks she's going to get the cane because she was taking the piss, but instead the teacher puts a seed into her hand. She's intrigued by this seed and realises it's important, and she tries to look it up on her brother's computer but he's busy playing games, so she puts it in a special box in her bedroom and overnight it starts growing through the roof of her house. The audience see this, then they're invited to walk into an orchard full of these magic trees, and you go up and touch the fruit, and have some kind of educational experience via the inter-active computers. That's all it was, an allegorical thing.

You've also written a children's book, due to be published later this year.

The story is called *The Obvious Elephant*. Sophie's had five or six books published and she was scratching around for an idea, and I came up with this simple tale for three-, four-, five-year-olds. It's about an elephant that pitches up, and no one's ever seen an elephant before. They think it's a railway train and give it some coal. They think it's a refuse collector and make it suck up garbage. They think it's a fire engine and try to put fires out with it. There's a little boy there who knows what it is but no one will listen to him, and they finally work out that it's just an elephant. It's basically a vehicle for Sophie's illustrations.

Not being believed seems to be a recurring theme in your work. Bagley isn't, Berlin isn't, even this little boy isn't.

I've never thought about it like that. I've only ever thought about my work from the perspective of the victim. But it's true. It's Kafkaesque, isn't it? Kafka constantly dealt with being in an environment where you feel completely sane and everyone else is insane. I think that comes directly out of one's experience of being a kid: my parents wouldn't believe I was bright. My sister got the advantages, 'A' Levels and all of that, and I went to a secondary modern. That's like not being believed: 'I'm not stupid' 'Yes, you are.'

Madness is another favourite subject. The madness of Cambodia, of The Bomb, of Withnail, of Bagley, and so on.

That must say something about me, but I don't really know what it is. There are things, of course, that are the furniture of our ives, things that keep coming back time and time again. For example, in *In Dreams* – although it wasn't in the film – the psychiatrist talks to her about *Hamlet*. In *Penman*, Charles Dickens is the writer. In *The Block*, Dylan Thomas is very much the writer. That constantly reoccurs in my work, what I love and what I like. I can't avoid it; it's the chicken syndrome. Those are the things, I guess, that are bubbling in my pot. Every time there's another story I stick the ladle in, pull out a whole gang of stuff, and it's likely to be chickens, dollars, madness and spew, plus victimisation, injustice and hopefully comedy. That's my potful. That's about what I've got.

Is there an element of autobiography in the character of author Bradley Boys in your rewrite of *The Block*?

He's another part of that maniac side of me, I suppose. Totally paranoid. And blocked. But I just know he's going to be funny if I can find the right actor and someone to finance it. *The Block* isn't about anything except laughs, but if the film is made there'll be somebody saying, 'This film is clearly about the invasion of the British psyche by American culture and the fact that we are hopelessly chained by . . .' You know, they'll always find something in it that isn't in it. *The Block* isn't setting out to be didactic in any way. This girl should be utterly charming, smart but dopey, in a little story that should be done as cheaply as possible.

You originally considered Richard E. Grant for the part of Bradley, didn't you, along the lines of a follow-up to *Withnail and Advertising*?

The Block was originally set in England with an English writer, and it kept asking for an American. Then I did quite a lot of work on it, throwing things away and putting new things in, and he most definitely developed into an American. Because the lead girl is English pretending to be an American, you can't have an Englishman pretending to be an American as well, so Richard couldn't do it. Maybe one day we will do something together again, I don't know. Maybe he'll write something that we could do. He is writing a screenplay, and has been for about two years,

I think. I imagine he could write a very good script, Richard.
liked his film diaries, I thought they clipped along and were
interesting. It just occurs to me: you don't think, do you, that
The Block is a reiteration of *Advertising*?

In *Advertising*, Bagley is pretty much the whole show, whereas in
The Block, Bradley enters thirty pages after the female lead Mint.
Bradley, unlike Bagley, therefore has a foil for his madness.

Yeah, it's her story, not his. She's the lead, isn't she? Plus the
block isn't the essence of the narrative. In *Advertising* the fact
that he can't do it is the essence of what the picture's about, and
in *The Block* the fact that he can't do it is the essence of what
her picture's about. She has Withnailesque qualities. She is the
shit around which the universe revolves. She cares about
nothing but herself, and Bradley cares about nothing but
himself, and the curiosity is they liberate each other and allow
each other to grow up. At the end they become different people
and what those Americans call the 'character curve' is fulfilled
in that story. They both go somewhere in their lives at the end of
it.

One of the reasons I'm delayed on *The Block* was because
within a month of the script being out there, Fine Line said
'We're going to make this film and we don't want it going
anywhere else.' So we sat on our hands for seven months, then
I went for a meeting with them, and this young chick out of
New York with a degree in dick-oiling starts talking about
character curves. I laughed in her face. I said, 'I'm sorry,
don't know what that means.' I did, of course, and it was
patently clear, because there was a table full of these character
curvers, that I was talking my way out of working with this
company.

Do you ever get the block?

I'm probably in one now, which is why I don't dare try and
write anything, because I may put a piece of paper in and realise
I'm blocked. As it stands, I haven't got to put my toe in the
238 water, so I don't know whether it's hot or cold. Yeah, I have

had the block, and it's a seriously unpleasant place to be. Subjectively, suffering them, the blocks that I've had are utterly gruesome. Objectively, if you look in the mirror at how you behave, they're funny. Bradley cleaning the oven at three in the morning with that awful shit-eating smile is funny to me. I remember years ago, Sophie having tea with somebody when I was blocked, and the person she was with didn't know me but knew I was a writer. So they're having tea, and I'm lying on the carpet between them, weeping, and they're passing biscuits and couldn't be less interested. 'What's the matter with him?' 'Oh, he's got the block.' But that's what it's like. It's a nightmare feeling, and the worst part of having the block is you don't know when you're going to become unblocked. It's that thing people say when they go mad on LSD: 'I thought I was never going to come down.' You don't know. You might be cleaning the oven forever.

Does it only happen between projects or has it struck in the middle of one?

The block when you're actually doing it? Oh, don't. Just don't. That's too horrendous to even think about.

Budding Prospects, an adaptation of the novel by T. Coraghessan Boyle which you script-doctored for Columbia Pictures and *The Full Monty* director Peter Cattaneo, also seems to be delayed.

I was talking to Cattaneo a few weeks ago and he was saying, 'We need more laughs at the back end of the film.' I don't dispute that, but if you read a line like, 'He's going to come down and see us next week and sort us out' and the reply is 'Fuck off!' unless you read it with the correct voice in your head, it isn't funny. For me, some of the funniest lines in *The Block* are lines that people wouldn't even notice as being funny. I think that's one of the problems Columbia have got with *Budding Prospects*: it's a comedy but it hasn't got any jokes. What they'll probably do, if they go forward with it, is hire somebody who's good at the one-liners.

I never write jokes. That's why it's difficult to write the kind of comedy I like. The first joke I've ever written is in *Budding Prospects*. I nearly cut it, but I liked it so much I kept it in. It's quite abstruse. You've got a very rich man, Vogelsang, in this astonishingly opulent house, and this other guy Gesh, a scrap-metal dealer covered with muscles and tatoos. Vogelsang offers him wine, and Gesh says, 'Not for me. I don't drink wine. Reminds me of alleys. I got people drinking wine around my yard.' Vogelsang says, 'Are they on Lafite?' and Gesh says, 'No, on their asses.' I had to keep that.

Following the double whammy of Return to Paradise and In Dreams, you swore blind that you'd never accept another commission.

That's right. And I won't. I'm not going to write for anybody any more except myself. What's the point? I'd rather do the same job for a fifth of the grief on a rewrite, which is what this is. This is the only time in my life that I've done it. Why did I do it now? I did it for a plethora of reasons. I liked Cattaneo when I met him, I liked the senior executive on the project, a guy called William Horberg who I've known for years, and I liked the thought of getting paid a lot of money for six weeks. Both of those projects were completely ruined by what they did to them, but if they fuck this up what do I care? I haven't got any emotional commitment. So I did it.

Having had your own screenplays rewritten, how do you feel about changing another writer's work?

I don't know who these boys were who wrote this. When you read it, you know it's a couple of young guys. They haven't quite learned the craft, the dozens of rules that you teach yourself. It's been my intention in the last two or three years to write a book about how you write a screenplay. I gave two lectures at the Royal College of Art, and I was thinking, 'It's taken me thirty years to learn what I'm giving these guys for nothing. What am I telling them for?' There are certain inviolate rules of screenwriting, and it might be an interesting book to put together. Not all this character curve horseshit. There is no such thing as a character curve. There is a character and there is a curve; I don't know where they join each other. A guy starts the film hating blacks and by the end he's shagging a black girl; there's his character curve. Well, thank you very much. Have I really spent all my adult life learning that?

There are a lot of screenwriting books available, but most of them have been written by people who have never had a screenplay produced.

Probably not. They're also like reading a manual for an electric lawnmower. They're not getting into the meat of it. For good or ill, I write scripts in a different way to most people. I take as much trouble over the descriptive side of them as I take over the dialogue side. If the script is a comedy I want you to be laughing through the stage directions as well. The same pertains to something like *Jennifer Eight*. I don't think it's a good idea to say, 'Interior. Blind Institute. Night. The building echoes and is full of darkness.' You need more than that. In screenwriting at its worst you'll see stage directions like 'Alice walks into medium close-up. Bobby looks up, peeling an apple', followed by interminable drivel and the much-needed advice from the writer, 'This is a funny scene.' I call that gin-and-tonic writing. 'Like a drink?' 'Yes, please.' 'What would you like?' 'Gin and tonic.' 'Ice?' 'Yes, please.' 'Lemon?' 'Yes, please.' People fill pages with that kind of nonsense. Awful things like 'We see' or 'We track slowly in'. 'We' don't 'see' anything. 'We' are the reader. It's incumbent on the writer to make the reader see what you want them to see, so rather than say, 'We move into extreme close-up on Rupert's eyes', I'd say, 'Rupert's pupils narrow' and you know you're in extreme close-up on his eyes.

That can be a good technique to adopt if your work is realised by other people. I remember an interview with director Jon Amiel about *The Singing Detective*, and he said that Dennis Potter never used camera directions but from the way it was written you always knew . . .

Where the camera should be. That's right. I'd never mention the camera unless I was going very fast and I had to shorthand things. I also think information in a screenplay should be released as the audience get that information. He's a very fine writer, but I once read a script by Melvyn Bragg and it started with something like 'Wide shot of a lake with a motorcycle moving around it. There are two men on the motorcycle. The man in front is a thirty-five-year-old professor of mathematics.' Now you tell me how, if you see two people riding around on a motorbike, you can know that one of them is a professor of mathematics. We don't know that yet. We will know that later in the story, and that's the proper place to introduce it. 'He's a professor of mathematics, he has two children and he lives in Leominster.' 'Oh, really? Fascinating.' A new character comes into the story, we've got to be introduced to him, and people actually write, 'Frank, this is Bert and this is John.' But the audience already has that information, so there are techniques that you use not to reiterate those introductions, even though this character doesn't know these two, Bert and John.

You also work hard to achieve a naturalistic feeling on the page.

I always try, yeah. You could look at *Withnail* and think that Richard Grant came up with all that, which isn't a bad thing for the film, but he didn't. Every line was written down by me a year before I even met Richard. There's a wonderful rhythm in people's natural conversation that the screenwriter is obliged to find in an artificial way. Go into a pub and listen to a couple of old wankers having a chat with each other: they never mis-stress anything, a line or a word, their timing is always perfect. It's one of the facilities of being a human being that we stress absolutely correctly. Now then, if you wrote down what I've said in the last minute and gave it to someone who wasn't an actor, they'd fuck it up, stress it completely incorrectly. Which is what being a great actor is. Really good actors can look at Shakespeare and know how to say it. It's weird that we can all do it naturally, but if you ask someone to do it artificially they can't, because they're not actors.

I really think audiences love good dialogue. Brilliant photography costs a lot more than crap photography, whereas good dialogue doesn't cost any more than bad dialogue, so even a cheap film can have great dialogue in it. It's not that common, I don't think, in cinema. There are some American television writers who write fabulous comedic dialogue, really good stuff, but it's not very often that I come out of a film and think, 'That was great writing.' The writing in *Shakespeare in Love* was good; I didn't think it was fab, but it was good. Normally it's just [*American accent*], 'Come on, Boss, let's make him dead.' That kind of dialogue. 'You fuck with him, you're fuckin' with me.' You get a lot of that. If you go to the theatre, where dialogue obviously tends to be much higher quality than it is in the cinema, and you get someone who knows their job, it's magic listening to it. I love it.

I notice that you jot down a lot of dialogue in your workbooks, which you keep by your side as you're writing the script.

It's forever there, yeah. If there's an idea, it goes in there. If there's something I read in the newspaper that's apposite, it goes in there. They become like a guardian angel, because when you're thinking, 'I don't know where I am, I don't know what I'm doing,' you can look at them. I've got dozens of little notebooks, and every time I get an idea I put it in there, even though I don't know what it might mean. I know that one day I might need it. That's the hardest thing in this caper, to get the idea. The reason that I bought *The Block* back from Paramount after all those years is it's a good idea. There's 2500 books in this room, and you could pull virtually any one of them out and there's maybe a movie in there, but they're not an idea. If you've got boy meets girl, boy falls in love with girl, parents of boy and girl adore each other, and they live happily ever after, you haven't got a story. What you need is boy meets girl, boy's parents hate girl's parents; then you've got *Romeo and Juliet*.

This lady was after me in Los Angeles because she'd acquired the rights to a biog of Castro. So we sat down for lunch and I said, 'What is it, then?' 'Well,' she says 'In 1959, Castro invaded Cuba and overthrew Batista.' I said, 'Yeah, I know that. What's the story?' 'Well, Castro managed to run guns in, and then he got the

Russians on his side and the Americans were very upset, and then there was the Bay of Pigs.' 'Yeah, yeah. I know all that. What's the story?' 'Well, they put Batista in jail, and then Hitler was in power and Winston Churchill decided to bomb Germany and the German army crossed the Rhine.' You know, none of that's the *story*. What *is* a story is that while Castro is running the guns, some boy who's madly in love is on the side of Castro, and the girl he's in love with is the daughter of Batista. Then you've got a *Romeo and Juliet* situation on your hands.

Somebody tells you about the Battle of the Bulge. Well, great, thanks. What's the story? That isn't a story, that's just something that happened. There's a film about the Second World War. Hitler's got a secretary, and the secretary falls in love with the bloke who wants to kill Hitler. Then you've got a story. Don't keep telling me Castro did this and did that and did the other. What's the story? In screenwriting terms, you can write a scene in a script, 'The German army crosses the Rhine.' I mean, is that twelve million dollars' worth of film, or is it a general saying [*German accent*], '*Oberleutnant*, ve vere here on ze map, und now ve are here, across ze Rhine.' Ten-dollar scene. I get a lot of that, people sending me a book about something and I can't see the story. What's it about? The greatest artist that's ever lived, in my view, never mind the greatest writer, is Shakespeare. He writes a play about racism, with that consummate genius that he brought to all his great plays, and he deals with the personalities. It's triangular. It's Othello, Desdemona and Iago. It's just three people yakking.

Shakespeare is obviously another of your passions. Did you discover him at the same time you discovered Dickens?

No, I didn't read Shakespeare until I was in my twenties. Thank God, because it didn't get destroyed for me at school. The thing about going to a secondary modern is that they think you're cerebrally inelegant, to put it at its mildest, and consequently they wouldn't hit you with that kind of stuff. Now, there are parts of *Hamlet* and *King Lear* that I can't read because I cry. I really do. It's the most beautiful art on earth, and as ordinary writers we're lucky if we can get a sniff between his toes. Shakespeare, to me, is a greater miracle than Jesus Christ. All the people that I've ever admired historically are as dwarves compared to this guy. Fuck Jesus, give me Shakespeare. That's what you should call this book.

I might have trouble getting it past Bloomsbury.

Well, it could be a chapter heading. But you know what I mean? I don't think anyone's even in the same league as that bastard. I don't understand it. I can't believe that anyone is capable of knowing so much and expressing it with such inimitable beauty. I've got a lot of books about Shakespeare. He would literally have actors come up to him and say, 'This isn't quite working, Will, "Shall I be alive or shall I be dead".' And he'd say, 'All right, say, "To be or not to be".' That, from what we know, is how this fucker worked. He just wrote it, like Mozart – who I do not enjoy, incidentally – because it was a God-given gift.

Have you considered filming Shakespeare?

I'd love to do *The Tempest*, but I'm not a visually orientated director. I'm interested in dialogue, and you've got the best dialogue ever written in that. In the late eighteenth, early nineteenth century, painters like Fuseli and Dadd did drawings of Titania and Ariel, and to make a movie of *The Tempest* looking like a Richard Dadd painting would be fabulous. It's interesting, *The Tempest*. That last line of Prospero: 'Now my charms are all o'erthrown, and what strength I have's mine own.' Then he breaks his staff on his leg, and Shakespeare never really wrote another word. Very weird, is it not?

Taking into account *In Dreams*, *Jennifer Eight* and *The Acid Vampire*, and bearing in mind your extensive research on Jack the Ripper, you also seem to be fascinated by serial killers.

I haven't got a fascination with serial killers *per se*. I'm not interested in their murders; I'm interested in their mindset. Taking Haigh and The Ripper as examples, they would be normal blokes you could have a pie and chips with. Haigh, had he not got so over-confident, never would have been caught. The Ripper never was caught. That's the side of them that interests me. I'm not interested in madmen. I mean, anyone who did to prostitutes what The Ripper did is ostensibly insane, but only that facet of him. One of the reasons the police never got on to The Ripper at the time they were looking for him is all this British pomp and circumstance. They could not and would not believe that a gentleman, an Englishman, could do a thing like this. It had to be either a foreigner or a Jew: 'This is an animal doing this.' But of course it wasn't an animal. Look at Haigh: neat white shirt, drove an Alvis, took his hat off to the ladies. This is who Jack the Ripper was. He was someone massively disturbed in one department of his head, but perfectly capable of going about his business with the rest of it. He was a 'pillar of society.'

The biggest point of interest about The Ripper is that it definitely happened. There was a person, whatever his name was, who did those things. Lots of murderers have never been caught, but it was a combination of that type of crime – which was relatively unusual but not as uncommon as we are told it was – and the beginning of the mass media: three primary London evening newspapers, twenty daily papers, the telegraph, and telephones just about extant. All those things collided with these events and the papers went to town on it. One of the assistant Aldermen of London was invited to see Mary Kelly's mutilated body on the morning of the Lord Mayor's investiture, and he says it was almost impossible to describe the thrill in the city at what was going on with Jack the Ripper. There were journalists dressed as prostitutes hoping to be accosted so they could nab him. The whole notion of the murder story in popular fiction was very fresh, and here was a real live one. This was 1888, the year of *Jekyll and Hyde* and less than twenty years after *The Mystery of Edwin Drood*.

And contemporary with Arthur Conan Doyle. It's no coincidence that films and literature have sometimes depicted Sherlock Holmes on the trail of Jack the Ripper.

Well, exactly. And Dodgson – Lewis Carroll – he's been a contender. Dr Barnardo has been a contender. 'Who was in the East End at the time?' 'Dr Barnardo.' 'Well, he must have done it, then.' The number of contenders is phenomenal. There are all these theories of the Queen's grandson, the Duke of Clarence; the Queen's doctor, Gull; and so it goes on. If all the contenders for Jack the Ripper had been in the East End at the same time, they'd have been bumping into each other up the alleyways: 'Who are you?' 'I'm Jack the Ripper.' 'No, you're not, you cunt. I am.' There would have been about thirty-five Jacks out there on any given night. And that's the other thing that fascinates me about The Ripper: how did he murder those five women right there on the streets, with the bodies cut down where they lay except for the last one who was sliced up indoors?

Whenever it is portrayed in the media, it's usually a top hat, a cloak lined with cerise silk, a blade in the doctor's bag and the swirling fog, but it wasn't like that at all. Yes, it was a honeycomb of byways, but it wasn't quiet footsteps on the cobbles. The East End, particularly Middlesex Street which is now Petticoat Lane, was the epicentre of the London foodmarkets, with Spitalfields and Smithfield not far away. The whole East End was bustling twenty-four hours a day, seething with cops, pubs always open, the underground railway going in just as it does today, thousands of people out on the streets with nowhere to live, hundreds of prostitutes all over the place. A lot of public-spirited people with hypocritical attitudes towards sex had forced the city police to shut down a lot of the brothels, and consequently all these old hags were stuck out there as perfect targets.

What's the likely outcome of your proposed Ripper film for Columbia in the light of the rival version, *From Hell*?

Judging by the rest of this book, fuck all. I think it'll go down the proverbial toilet. As you said yesterday, if it's brilliant I can't win and if it's shit I can't win. No one's going to put up with two Jack the Ripper pictures, especially when one of them is a star vehicle with Johnny Depp. [*Hands me a pair of comic books*] This is what it's based on.

It looks rather lurid.

It probably rather is. I like Johnny Depp, I think he's a smashing film star, but what he's doing in that I don't know. Any movie can have a slasher scene in it, and The Ripper did murder these women with escalating brutality, but that isn't what's interesting about him at all. Nevertheless, it's fucked up mine. I suppose my particular interest in The Ripper can no longer be from a cinema point of view, but I know I'm going to write something.

Fiction or non-fiction?

I wouldn't write fiction about it. It would definitely be real, as real as I could get it. I'd write it with the same intensity as *The Killing Fields*. But he's a character now, isn't he, embodied in myth? Jack the Ripper, Donald Duck, Sylvester Stallone and his tits. He's part of that.

In striving for that kind of intensity, have you ever been influenced by the work of other screenwriters?

I like William Goldman's work a lot, I think he's a fabulous screenwriter. But if I look to people who have influenced me as writers, they wouldn't be screenwriters, they would be novelists and poets. The thing I learned from reading people like Burroughs and Miller and Orwell is being able to say the most with the least words. Some people use words like 'solipsistic' when you can say 'self', or 'nugatory' when you can say 'slight'. It may be thought that the use of bizarre words is indicative of being a writer, and it's not. If you're starting out, reading other people's screenplays is a good way to learn screenwriting, to see how it's done, and then get ready for at least ten years of sitting there on your own scratching your arse in front of a typewriter or a computer or whatever, and writing. And when you can't write it any more, write it again. That's the only advice I would give to anyone trying to be a writer. If you want to be a concert pianist you've got to be prepared to sit there for eight hours a day practising, and even then you might not make it. You've got to pay your dues in this business, unless you're extraordinarily lucky and happen to get a million-pound advance for your first book. There are writers out there with two dozen books under their belt who are lucky to get five grand.

I get lots of young guys – not very often women – sending me scripts. Don't send them to me, just keep writing. It's no good sending them to me. I can't read them, I wouldn't have a minute to do my own work. I'm pleased to say that in all those bad years I had as a writer I never once sent my work off to another writer I didn't know. It's that thing where your girlfriend says, 'What have you done with the script?' 'Oh, Harold Pinter's reading it.' But that doesn't mean a thing, because frankly Harold Pinter isn't reading it, it's sitting on a pile somewhere and he's wondering how to get it back without being too insulting or offensive. What you're doing is trying to leapfrog the agony of years and years of writing. It's a complete waste of time. Even if I read something and I thought it was Byron, there's nothing I can do with it because I'm not a producer and I'm not an agent. The only thing I could do is say, 'I've read your script and I think it's more than promising, now go out and buy *The Writer's Handbook* and try and get yourself an agent.' Because they're in the business of reading scripts and trying to sell them to people, and I'm not. I find it hard enough to get my own work in the place I want it. They're under this misconception that all I've got to do is sit here over a wet weekend, knock something out, send it off and someone cuts me a cheque for five hundred thousand bucks. Sadly it isn't like that.

It's naïvety, I suppose. They have no idea how awful it is to be a screenwriter. Somehow they think it's glamorous, but it isn't. It can be a soul-destroying prospect, writing for cinema. You talk to any screenwriter, they'll tell you the same thing. All those silly jokes about the dumb starlet who slept with the writer to get ahead are very much on the money. Writers are dirt in this business. No one would dream of coming along and saying, 'We're going to make *The Rose Tattoo* by Tennessee Williams. Let's have a go at some of this dialogue.' Or Chekhov or Shakespeare or anyone. What happened in cinema was they didn't need writers. When the girl was tied to the railway line and the express train was coming, anyone could work out, 'What do we need here? "Help!" Put it up on a card.' It wasn't until the talkies came in that they thought, 'We need someone to come up with words that these people can say.' On early talkies the writer gets a credit somewhere between the boom operator and the make-up man. That's permeated through the public understanding of what screenwriting is: 'Oh, it's just screenwriting, it's not proper writing. Proper writing is novels or poems or plays.' And here's the tragedy. Fred Astaire said, 'If the work shows, you're not working hard enough.' Making a screenplay look like anyone could do it makes everyone think anyone could do it. But it's the most important facet of film-making: no-one works without the writer. I believe we've now reached third position in the credits: director, producer, writer.

There was a change not too long ago. It's now about fifty-fifty. Sometimes it's director, producer, writer. But equally often you see director, writer, producer. The writer has moved up to second place.

Well, quite right too. But the writer, because we were unwanted in this industry, is still treated like shit. No-one would dream of taking a painter, not even a third-rate Picasso, and saying, 'Oh, I see you've got blue trees in the background here. I think we'll make those green.' With a writer, they take unbelievable licence. 'We want to make *Budding Prospects*. OK, let's wheel these guys in to do a draft. Didn't work. All right, let's get that bloke Robinson, he can do a draft.' First class, stretch-limos from the airport, blah, blah, blah. As soon as you've delivered you're *persona non grata*, because now they're going off to do it and they don't need you. Everyone else working in the film is hands-on for that day; the writer's done all his work. If the writer was on the set, like a boom operator or a make-up man, it wouldn't be that easy to screw up the writer's work. Which is why I'd like to do another book, or why I wouldn't mind staying in screenwriting providing I can have a go at directing my own stuff. And if I fuck up, all right I fucked up, but at least the words that I write get said.

Puttnam will listen to you as a writer, but most of them won't, a case in point being *Return to Paradise*. They said, 'We want it like this.' I said, 'I can't do it like that. It won't work. It won't work for me because I'm supposed to be directing it.' 'Well, fuck you. You're fired.' There was no discussing it. That, as I've said to you until I'm blue in the face and you're green in the ears with listening to it, is the reason I wrote the novel: to be in charge of the words again. I couldn't stand putting in all that effort and never having anything out there that I could say, 'That's mine and I believe in it. With all its faults, that's what I wanted to say.' I'm setting myself up in a difficult situation with *The Block*, because I don't want to compromise. Of course, there are compromises all the time if you're taking money off somebody, they've got to have a voice, but I don't want to do it in a way that isn't satisfactory to me as a creative artist. You know that joke, 'How many studio executives does it take to change a lightbulb?'

No.

Oh, well. 'How many executives does it take to change a lightbulb?' Answer is, 'Does it have to be a lightbulb?' That's a Hollywood cliché but it's a truthful cliché. These people know very little about writing, so they go out and hire somebody who does know something about it. As soon as you've done it, behold! One of several little Shakespeares! You sometimes sit in these production meetings and someone has a brainwave, and this brainwave – they call them 'bullet points' – probably occured to you four months ago and you rejected it for this, that and the other reason. I've said it often and I'll say it again, because it's a very important thing to know if you want to be a screenwriter: when you accept the commission, they haven't got an idea in hell how to make it work. As soon as you've written it, they all know everything there is to know about drama and character.

With several towering exceptions, half of Hollywood middle-management is virtually redundant. Before anyone can make any decisions the readers get the script, and they're usually frustrated writers; and if it gets through them it goes to the executives, who have got their Porsches to run; and then the 'Can't he be a she?' dialogue starts. I've been there and back so many times listening to this kind of junk. Trying to get the money for *Withnail*, people were saying [*American accent*], 'Sure, we'll finance it, but it's got to be set in San Francisco.' Then you get, 'Hey! Wouldn't it be a good idea if the dealer was a girl? We haven't got any girls in this. How about Danny being

Daniella? Or Withnail. What if Withnail's a woman?' All this sort of stuff goes on. Twenty-six years old and they get a job in the film industry, and within ten minutes they're an executive. They think, 'Fuck me, I'd better say something otherwise they'll think I'm just a piece of furniture.'

I remember being in a meeting with Spielberg where exactly that was going on. There's him, his two producers and me sitting at the granite table, with an outer aura of Armanis and phones. Spielberg's talking about something, and one of the Armanis will say [*American*], 'Hey, Steven, wouldn't it be a good idea if . . . ?' 'No, it wouldn't!' He knows exactly what they're going to say, because the idea is going to be a he-and-a-she idea, and then he gets back into the discussion. It's constant, and half of them do it to justify their salaries. They'll come up with absurd notions that they haven't thought through just to keep the gas going into the Porsche. Even before you come to shoot the movie some of these guys get hold of the script, and it's like a blacksmith opening up the back of a wristwatch. A brief look inside and he says, 'This wheel is going like crazy, but these two big guys with the teeth aren't even moving. Fuck them, then, they can come out.' Watch stops. That's how screenplays are treated all the time. A good screenwriter doesn't put anything in a script that's not wanted on the voyage; it's all there for a reason. *In Dreams* is a perfect example, and maybe Neil should have shown more caution. 'I'm going to take this out, turn it round, and put it back in.' The story stops dead in its tracks.

Robert Towne spent two years writing *Greystoke*, then a very good friend of mine, Hugh Hudson, came along and had the back end of the film completely rewritten. An error, in my view. Guys who write these scripts, and I include myself, know something more than people who don't; we must do, otherwise those people would write scripts. They get scenes and they don't know why the scene is sad or they don't know why the scene is funny, so they either write it themselves or they cut it, very often to the detriment of the piece. Towne has written some fabulous movies, so why isn't there more respect for him? I don't understand it. Supposing you hired Pierce Brosnan to make a movie and then you said. 'By the way, Pierce, for Scenes 36 through 73 we've hired Jack Nicholson.' That's what happens if you're a writer. It is a species of prostitution, screenwriting. You get paid so much money it's like being a classy tart. They say, 'We want you in high heels and an oxygen mask,' and you say, 'OK, you're paying me a grand a night, I'll wear what you like.' If you write a novel or a play there isn't a huge amount of money up front, there's only money if you're a success, whereas a successful screenwriter gets paid a shit load of dough whatever. It's prostitution. And you can't whine if you're a prostitute, can you? Especially if you're an old and ugly one.

This is why so many screenwriters move into directing.

Or in my case try and be a novelist: to get some satisfaction out of the words. It is incredibly hard work, but there is something very fulfilling about directing a film. My problem was after *Jennifer Eight* I never wanted to do it again. Even out of that I was offered things to direct, and I wouldn't do them; I just couldn't bear the thought of it. And now I do want to do it, get out on the floor and work with other people, it's proving difficult because of raising the finance. I don't want Dustin Hoffman in *The Block*, genius actor though he is, but Hoffman or an equivalent will get you a movie made. They always say a good script is a script that someone like, what's her name . . . ? *Silence of the Lambs.*

Jodie Foster.

Yeah. [*American accent*] 'Jodie wants to do it, it's a good script. She passes, it's a bad script.' That goes on all the time in Hollywood. Who can 'open' the movie. You look at a lot of big successful pictures and you think, 'Why?' It's the stars, particularly in the States. Not always, there are massive exceptions to the rule, but if you've got Jodie Foster in a picture people go and see it. You will do a great opening weekend because of her, then it's down to the flick. It may fall off and disappear down the toilet a week later, but she can open the picture. They care desperately about that. Like any other artiste in this business, I'm antipathetic to the suits and phones, but these guys have stumped up millions of dollars, and that's a lot of money.

They want to make it back, and their chances of making it back are remote. That's why it's oil and water, this constant conflict between them and the film-makers.

American cinema, of course, is totally different to our version. Over here there is still some pretension towards art because we haven't got the money. If English cinema had massive injections of cash, bollocks to the art. It's a word one can shelter behind. Out there it really is a money-making industry like General Motors. Compared to them we're Skoda. Spielberg, with his enormous talent, is always moving on, and the flops immediately get slung overboard. By the time the flop's flopped, he's already made two more pictures. You don't remember Spielberg for *The Color Purple*, you remember him for *E.T.* You don't remember him for *1941*, you remember him for *Close Encounters*. Chaplin made some appallingly bad films, but he was always making another one. Neil Jordan does the same thing. *In Dreams* didn't hurt Neil because he was already making another picture. If I have a badly received film that's a kick in the knackers for a few years.

There's a mantra in Hollywood, isn't there? It's not the movie you're making now that's important . . .

It's the one you're doing one after it. If you keep making movies you're going to make good ones, bad ones and indifferent ones, like every other director. Because I've only made three films, I've made one that I think's very good, one that isn't bad and one that's got lots of faults in it.

That's where directing other people's scripts comes into its own.

Yeah, because there's some other cunt sitting next to an ashtray, in fact dozens of cunts sitting next to dozens of ashtrays, all over LA – all over the world, if you like. They come in and you say, 'Don't like this, don't like this, don't like this. Piss off and do it again.' You can do that in a day, then it's another six months for the writer to interpret this stuff, then you pick and choose what you want to do and you do it. If I had a mind to do that kind of thing, not to mention the clout, while I was shooting *The Block*

I'd have people working on The Ripper. Meanwhile, while they're working on that, I'm setting up *Penman*. In a period of three years there's three pictures going to come out, and you only need to hit big with one and the others can go and die where they like. If you want to look for it, and then write it, and then direct it, it's two and a half times as long. If I'm going to do The Ripper I've got to write the thing first. A director can make a film a year because all they've got to do is eat the dinner. I've got to kill the pig, and that's a big difference. That's one of the reasons I haven't got a big body of work. If I was a director I'd probably have quite a few films under my belt now.

We've talked about Chaplin, but you're also a great admirer of Hitchcock.

The two directors who have given me particular enjoyment are him and Chaplin. The first time I went to LA, I went with Puttnam and we stayed in the Wilshire Hotel in the middle of Beverly Hills. The first morning, I come down looking for somewhere to get breakfast, and there, where the cars come in and go out, is a black Roller, and it's Hitchcock sitting in the back like a caricature of himself. I swear this is true. Alfred fucking Hitchcock was the first person I saw in Los Angeles. I thought, 'My God, this must bode well for something.' He knew how to do something, didn't he, Hitchcock? How the fuck did he know how to do it? He made so many innovative and brilliant movies. *Psycho* I put in my top five. Did you know that until the composer Bernard Herrman was brought on to that picture they were going to re-cut it for television and make it a fifty-minute show? Hitchcock was tramping around in despair at the back of the theatre because he thought it was the worst movie he'd ever made, unwatchable trash, and I think it's far and away his greatest picture. Some of those directors are quite fabulous. Who directed *Serpico*?

Sidney Lumet.

He uses the obverse technique of most directors. If we were going to cut into this room from nowhere, you'd probably start with a drink going up to my mouth and widen to you. He puts the camera over there on a wide lens. Weird, but beautiful. Ken Loach is an amazingly talented director, and he doesn't get on roofs and shout about it, he just makes his movies. Sometimes a lot of people go, sometimes no one goes. It doesn't phase him either way, it seems to me. We had a movement teacher at Central called Litz Pisk who used to suck Bertolt Brecht off in the thirties, and she would say, 'Darling, what you need is the second simplicity.' Do you remember that film about the spy, Guy Burgess? Alan Bates was in it.

An Englishman Abroad?

Yeah. Lovely simple picture. Now, who directed that?

John Schlesinger.

Well, there you are. There's an example of the second simplicity. That's what you need. For example, it is pointless someone like me saying, 'I'm going to direct a film, and I'm going to have a chase sequence that will end in a car crash,' because I can't do it as well as it's been done, so I'm not even going to bother. What I can do, hopefully, is say, 'I'm going to have a scene that's going to make people laugh.' Simple, but very difficult, if you can pull it off it's fab. I couldn't possibly shoot a scene like that one in *Bullitt*, the Steve McQueen picture. It's brilliant. It's the car chase to end all car chases. After that, why bother?

When you're writing, do you prefer to get your head down and get it done or do you share the work in progress with friends and colleagues?

You can't. That's one of the great horrors of writing. I can nearly share some of it with Sophie. Sometimes I'll read her a passage and say, 'Do you think this works?' I guess one of the difficulties of being married to a writer is that what I do is a kind of perversion, something you do on your own. I creep off, I shut the door, and I go through my perversion, looking into a place where my wife and children can't come. They can't go where I want to go. Which is why I use red wine. Alcohol is a solvent, it attacks your brain, but it also attacks the inhibition that may try and stop you going where you want to go. If I have a bottle of wine I can gatecrash certain areas that I can't get into without it, and I actually hate wine for that. I use it as a tool. I come in here sometimes at eight in the morning and within ten minutes I'll have knocked back a bottle of Rioja, so by half-past eight I'm ostensibly oiled. I'm not so drunk I'm going to fall over; I'm drunk in a place I want to be to hear the voices coming in. And some days they don't, of course. But some days they do, they come in so fast that I write like a fiend for an hour and then wig out. Even go back to bed. Then I'll come in here again at ten o'clock when I'm kind of straight and look at this crap and think, 'There's a line that I can use,' and maybe spend another two or three sober days interpreting that first drunken hour of hearing these fuckers coming in. But I'm getting too old to use that technique now, I really am, because what's beginning to develop is I come in here at ten-past one and nod out. I won't hear the voices, and I say to Sophie, 'I can't write this character. I can't hear him. I've got to be able to hear him.' You wait and you wait and you wait, saying, 'Please, please,' and then maybe you just get a whisper of him or maybe he starts to shout.

It's almost akin to schizophrenia. If they pay you, you're a screenwriter. If they don't pay you, you're a nut. I saw someone ranting and raving last time I was in London, in Regent's Park, and everyone was saying, 'That person's a maniac,' and I thought, 'Maybe they're a screenwriter.' I'm in the business of hearing voices, and most people who hear voices are given Largactil or locked up. I'll tell you what the difference is. The schizophrenic has no choice: they *hate* hearing the voices. I'm the antithesis of that: I *want* to hear them. I'm struggling to hear them, and the schizophrenic is struggling not to. That's why I'm not mad and they are. You get away with a lot if you're a writer. If I wasn't a writer and I was sitting here saying, 'Alistair, I can't hear the voices, I can't hear the voices,' you'd be in the kitchen in twenty-six seconds saying, 'He's in there saying he can't hear the voices. What are the voices? What voices does he want?' Because I'm a writer I can legitimately say, 'I can't hear them.' It's in the suburbs of hysteria, writing. I honestly think, hand on heart, that if I wasn't a writer I would be on heavyweight sedation. I spend my life in this room, and the only good thing in here is the view outside. I don't like being in here all day every day of my working life, I find it very lonely.

You told one interviewer that there are three stages in a writer's career: at first you're turning out rubbish because you've not learned the craft, then you've learned it and what you're turning out is good, and finally what you're turning out is without joy because you've become bored. This was ten years ago, and you said that you'd already reached stage three, so where do you think you are now?

Probably fucked. That's the awful paradox. I get offered an enormous amount of stuff to do, but I haven't automatically got the rage, if you like, to necessarily do it. It would be nice to write something again as simple as *Withnail*, but it doesn't get easier as you get more experienced, it gets harder, because that springtime has gone. Famous writers like Hemingway talk about that at length. I'm in the winter of writing, I suppose, or the late autumn. I'm fifty-four, and at fifty-four I'm not as intellectually agile as I was at thirty-four. My writing routine, for example, at that period where I was really prolific, was ridiculous. Start very early, bash through, and by noon I'd have done five hours' work; five in the afternoon I'd have done ten hours; nine in the evening I'd have done fifteen.

I can't do that now. My body just can't tolerate that kind of punishment. I was writing every day, seven days a week, because I was driven by guilt. I don't feel such a compunction to do it any more. I'm a middle-aged man, I've got a wife and children and other responsibilities. My wife has always been incredibly supportive of me as a writer, but twenty years ago I wouldn't have my little bloke – who I absolutely adore – banging on the door saying, 'What are you doing, Dad?' 'I'm writing.' 'Well, I'm coming in.' And in he comes, and what can I say? 'I want to do pirates. I want to do football.' And you have to do it, because you love him. It comes as a big shock, being fifty, because fifty is a serious grown-up age. The next large one is sixty, and that's getting on. I remember hearing that

Welsh actor on the radio the other day. You know, Hannibal Lecter?

Anthony Hopkins.

Yeah. He was saying, 'I feel like I've wasted my life.' He's had a terrific career, but once you get beyond fifty that black confetti is getting closer every year. Seventy-four is about it, isn't it? So twenty more Christmas trees and I'm history. I might live longer, I might not live that long, but you get to the point where you start thinking, 'Is this it? Is this what my life has been?' Lots of people my age have made a dozen movies or written a dozen books. I haven't done anything like that, and that's worrying. Thirty-odd screenplays is a fuck of a lot by the stretch of anybody's imagination, and yet I genuinely feel like I've done nothing, that I'm going to wake up one day, tomorrow or the day after, and think, 'It starts now.' But this isn't a rehearsal; this is my life. If half the stuff that I've written had been made I'd probably feel more content, but to have major scripts like *Germinal* and *High Rise* languishing forever is very depressing. I keep them out of vanity, I suppose, to say, 'This is what I've done,' and when I croak, my kids can say, 'This is what he did.'

One of the reasons screenwriting pays so well, of course, is to compensate for seeing your work stuck on a shelf.

Sure. I know screenwriters in Hollywood who haven't had a film made in ten years, and they're still dining in Spago with a red Roller outside because of development deals. It's the problem of Parkinson's Law. If you earn money you spend money, and then you need to earn more money to sustain what you've spent it on. We could flog all this off, go and live in a cottage by the sea and probably survive for the rest of our lives. Which is why I want to orientate myself more towards directing and novels. I've got fifteen more good working years to do two or three movies or two or three books. I'd feel good about that. Then, I guess, I could say, 'Fuck it. I'll go out and sit in the orchard and read Dostoyevsky.' Normally I don't get enough

259

time to do that because by the end of the day I'm just exhausted.

One of the big down-sides about living here is that nothing ever happens. The sun's out or it isn't, that's about what happens. I think that's very bad for a writer, in a way. For example, *Withnail* and *Penman*; neither of those two experiences in my life are anything to do with writing, but all the time you are accumulating information that you will write about. Had Mickey and I not made that trip to the countryside *Withnail* would never have existed, and had I not had a maniac for a father *Penman* would never have existed. *Advertising* is the same. If I hadn't gone through that period of insane antipathy to Mrs Thatcher's administration I wouldn't have written that. But sitting here for five years, what am I going to write about? Diapers and menopause and who the vicar's shagging? I couldn't give a fuck who the vicar's shagging. I don't even know if there *is* a vicar. I'll have to turn into Laurie Lee and write about badgers, or something.

Because of the children, there's a routine. They've got to get up, they've got to get dressed, they've got to have their breakfast, they've got to be on the school bus, they've got to be met off the school bus, and so it goes. If I was Fay Weldon I'd probably find something to write about in that, but I don't find the countryside stimulating at all, it's just animals and shit. No restaurants, no art galleries, no cinemas – I don't care that there's no theatres because I don't like the theatre much. Having said that, once the idea or the story is in place you couldn't have a better place to be. It's Catch-22: it's a fabulous place to write once you've got something to write about. That's always the difficulty: what do you write about? If I make *The Block* I definitely won't have any alcohol this year, which is good – it's good for you not to drink all the time – but at the same time, I use alcohol to drown boredom. I'm not actually a bored bloke, because despite what I said earlier I love to read and can read ten books a week and enjoy them, but nevertheless there is something magnificently tedious about living in the middle of the countryside.

Why don't you like the theatre?

There is an uneasiness about being there and being able to touch the actors, a silliness about theatre that film has somehow managed to navigate to one side. If you see Dustin Hoffman in a street in New York playing a cop, he is in a street in New York and he is dressed like a cop and he is a cop. But if you saw an English actor playing a cop on stage at the Aldwych, there would be something dopey about it, I don't quite know what. I can buy the notion of a black man murdering Desdemona on film, but when I see it on stage I just know that half an hour later they're going to be down the boozer having a fag. It's always brilliant pantomime, even at its best.

If you saw something like *The Killing Fields* on stage it could not have the impact of a movie. You're always on the same lens in a theatre, about a 50mm, which is the audience's eye. That lens never changes, no matter what the intensity of the production, and sometimes you need a 150mm. Sometimes you don't want to see the other character, you just want to see Othello's face as he's choking this woman he loves. You're not interested in the curtains, you're interested in the veins on his temples. Film has a reality for me that theatre doesn't. Having said that, the thing that I love about theatre when it's working is listening to fabulous words. There are some things I've seen in the theatre, certain Shakespeare, certain Eugene O'Neill, a bit of Arthur Miller here and there, when I've come out on a high. But I don't think stage acting gets anywhere near Gene Hackman doing something fantastic on screen.

A journalist once asked how you'd react to yourself if you were an outsider, and you replied that you'd probably frighten yourself.

Maybe at the time the question was asked, in the ranting phase, the answer was apposite, but I don't think I would now. I don't know what I'd think of myself now. I think that people who like *Withnail* and *Penman*, if they want to be writers, see me as something they would like to be: 'God, that's a good career.' I don't, I see it as a failed career. That's genuinely how I see my career. *Withnail* and *Penman* seem like very good things to have

261

written, but there's not enough of them. One of my reservations about doing your book, or Sibley's documentary, is that I've got such a tiny body of work compared to most people who do these kind of things. I kept saying, 'But Adrian, I haven't done enough to justify putting an hour's film on television,' and his answer was, 'To the people I'm making this film for, you have.'

He's right. *Withnail & I* and *The Killing Fields* are both in the BFI Top 100 British films and *The Peculiar Memories of Thomas Penman* was very well received. That's major contributions to three disciplines: director, screenwriter, novelist.

Well, three things is better than two things, and two is better than one. I'd rather have two or three things that I'm very pleased with than a dozen things that I don't really care about. Laurie Lee, a famous writer, only wrote four books in his entire career.

I only know *Cider With Rosie*.

That's his *Withnail*. I get offered every *Withnail* film I could want to write. There's a guy now in America talking about Pink Floyd: 'Can you write a film about Syd Barrett?' After *The Killing Fields* I got offered every war story there was. After *Withnail* I've been offered every druggy story. Everyone who wants to make a film about people taking drugs asks, 'Is Bruce Robinson about?' But I've done it. I've written that story. P.G. Wodehouse, God bless him, wrote variations of the same novel for fifty years. I have no interest in doing that. A lot of writers have done that. Somerset Maugham, kind of. Burroughs certainly did. *The Naked Lunch*, for my money, is the greatest novel of the last century, a towering piece of literature, but in comparison the rest of his work was a pile of fabulous junk.

Do you get tired of being labelled as some sort of bad boy?

That does get wearing. You know me well enough now to see that I'm not really like that at all. I'm a very responsible bloke. I feel concerned about many things going on in the world that I happen to live on in the time that I happen to live in.

262

Rather than puffing grass, swilling booze and ranting at everything that moves?

I can't say that I haven't been like that in my life, because I have. I did a radio phone-in thing for this station in Sydney, Australia, and they were most disconcerted that I was antipathetic towards drugs. They thought, because of *Withnail*, that I was going to be championing drug-taking, which I'm not. As a matter of fact, I don't entirely approve of it, even though I've taken a potent drug all my life – alcohol.

Because you're actually a bloke who lives in a rambling farmhouse surrounded by trees, flowers, animals, kids and a wife?

Well, that is basically it. And books. If you look over the hedge into my life you probably think, 'What's he got to moan about?' and I've got very little to moan about. I'm relatively well-off, I've got a beautiful family, home, pool and car. That book I bought today was a hundred quid, and it doesn't bother me to spend £100 on one crummy old book. Would you say that I'm lucky? I suppose you would.

I think most people looking over the hedge, even if they knew about the ups and downs of your career, would say you were.

Well, yeah. But when I work, I work incredibly hard. I really do. And part of working hard, as I said, is to make it look like I haven't worked on it at all. When you read a really good piece of prose you think, 'You bastard. How can you write like that?' I know bloody well that the bloke has suffered to get it like that, that it may have taken him two weeks to write, but I read it in two minutes and think [*grits teeth*], 'How can he do it?' And how he does it is with monstrous effort. When you watch a conductor you think, 'Jesus Christ, look at that guy. Any fucker could do that.' But in fact what you're watching is the result of weeks of rehearsal with the orchestra. Same thing when you go to a specialist if you've got something wrong with you. 'What was the doctor like?' 'Oh, he was marvellous.' 'Did he diagnose what was wrong?' 'Yes, he was very good. But do you know, he

263

charged me 150 quid for twenty minutes.' Well, you're not paying £150 for twenty minutes, you're paying for forty years of learning how to do the twenty minutes. I think it's exactly the same with writing. When you pay for a paperback, you're paying for years of learning how to do it, unless the writer is very lucky and can do it without all that work. Some writers can. I'm not one of them.

Andrew Birkin says in the documentary that what makes your writing unique is the fusion of pain and humour. Do you think that's true?

I would hope. That's a hard arena to work in, I think. Like that thing I told you about Viv with his throat sewn up, pouring whiskey through a funnel straight into his stomach. I loved the bastard, God rest his soul, and that's one of the most tragic things I've ever seen, but I've got to use that for a character because it makes me laugh. I really don't know why comedy's so important to me as a writer, but it is. I want to get a laugh out of the atomic bomb, even. The best kind of comedy, I think, is about truths, telling a truth about something in a way that makes you laugh. Growing up through the radio age you had Ray Galton and Alan Simpson's brilliant dialogue for Tony Hancock. Lines like 'I thought my mother was a bad cook but at least her gravy used to move about' are indelible in my mind. Almost jokes, but not. I thought they were brilliant, those two, with him; a trio of utter geniuses. Withnail and Hancock share that same pompousness, that total sense of self-worth, and they constantly lose their dignity, being slighted by the plebs that they run into.

I've sometimes thought in the dead of night, 'Look at your life, Bruce, rip out the writing, and with all these boiling frustrations and opinions what would you be?' I'd be in trouble, wouldn't I? Or I'd be in jail. Because what would I do with it? If I felt like I felt at the period of my antipathy towards Mrs Thatcher and I didn't have the facility to write the rage out, I'd have been a member of some absurd workers' revolutionary party, yelling my head off. My greatest fear is not being able to write. I'd be dead. I might carry on living, eating boiled eggs and Weetabix, but I'd be a dead man. It's the greatest anxiety in my life and I've got it even now. While we're talking there's a part of my brain that's focused on what I'm going to write. Every time I start a new project I hold my nose and jump in and just hope I'll be able to do it. But who says that you can?

By the way, there's a question I've been meaning to ask since we started: why is there a large hole in the cover of your IBM?

Because I hit it with a poker. It wouldn't do what I wanted. It's terribly frustrating when you can't hear it or you can't do it. I just got hold of something and I whacked it . . .

Credits

Writer/Director

Withnail & I
HandMade Films, GB, 1986, 108 mins WRITER/DIRECTOR Bruce Robinson PRODUCER Paul Heller, in association with Lawrence Kirstein EXECUTIVE PRODUCERS George Harrison, Denis O'Brien CO-PRODUCER David Wimbury DIRECTOR OF PHOTOGRAPHY Peter Hannan PRODUCTION DESIGNER Michael Pickwoad FILM EDITOR Alan Strachan COSTUME DESIGNER Andrea Galler ORIGINAL MUSIC David Dundas, Rick Wentworth PRINCIPAL CAST Richard E. Grant (Withnail), Paul McGann (. . . & I), Richard Griffiths (Monty), Ralph Brown (Danny), Michael Elphick (Jake), Daragh O'Malley (Irishman), Michael Wardle (Isaac Parkin), Una Brandon-Jones (Mrs Parkin), Noel Johnson (General), Irene Sutcliffe (Waitress), Llewellyn Rees (Tea-Shop Proprietor), Robert Oates (Policeman 1), Anthony Wise (Policeman 2), Eddie Tagoe (Presuming Ed)

How to Get Ahead in Advertising
HandMade Films, GB, 1989, 95 mins WRITER/DIRECTOR Bruce Robinson PRODUCER David Wimbury EXECUTIVE PRODUCERS George Harrison, Denis O'Brien CO-PRODUCER Ray Cooper DIRECTOR OF PHOTOGRAPHY Peter Hannan PRODUCTION DESIGNER Michael Pickwoad FILM EDITOR Alan Strachan COSTUME DESIGNER Andrea Galler ORIGINAL MUSIC David Dundas, Rick Wentworth PRINCIPAL CAST Richard E. Grant (Bagley),

Rachel Ward (Julia), Richard Wilson (Bristol), Jacqueline Tong (Penny Wheelstock), John Shrapnel (Psychiatrist), Susan Wooldridge (Monica), Mick Ford (Richard), Pip Torrens (Jonathan), Tony Slattery (Basil), Pauline Melville (Mrs Wallace), Roddy Maude-Roxy (Dr Gatty), Sean Bean (Larry Frisk)

Jennifer Eight

Paramount Pictures, US, 1992, 127 mins WRITER/DIRECTOR Bruce Robinson PRODUCERS Gary Lucchesi, David Wimbury EXECUTIVE PRODUCER Scott Rudin DIRECTOR OF PHOTOGRAPHY Conrad L. Hall PRODUCTION DESIGNER Richard MacDonald FILM EDITOR Conrad Buff COSTUME DESIGNER Judy Ruskin ORIGINAL MUSIC Christopher Young PRINCIPAL CAST Andy Garcia (John Berlin), Lance Henriksen (Freddy Ross), Uma Thurman (Helena), Graham Beckel (John Taylor), Kathy Baker (Margie Ross), Kevin Conway (Citrine), John Malkovich (St Anne), Perry Lang (Travis), Nicholas Love (Bisley), Michael O'Neill (Serato), Paul Bates (Venables), Bob Gunton (Goodridge), Lenny Von Dohlen (Blattis)

Screenwriter

The Killing Fields

Goldcrest/International Film Investors/Enigma, GB, 1984, 141 mins DIRECTOR Roland Joffé PRODUCER David Puttnam SCREENPLAY Bruce Robinson ASSOCIATE PRODUCER Iain Smith DIRECTOR OF PHOTOGRAPHY Chris Menges PRODUCTION DESIGNER Roy Walker FILM EDITOR Jim Clark COSTUME DESIGNER Judy Moorcroft ORIGINAL MUSIC Mike Oldfield PRINCIPAL CAST Sam Waterston (Sydney Schanberg), Dr Haing S. Ngor (Dith Pran), John Malkovich (Al Rockoff), Julian Sands (Jon Swain), Craig T. Nelson (Military Attaché), Spalding Gray (US Consul), Bill Paterson (Dr MacEntire), Athol Fugard (Dr Sundesval), Graham Kennedy (Dougal)

Fat Man and Little Boy

Paramount Pictures, US, 1989, 127 mins DIRECTOR Roland Joffé PRODUCER Tony Garnett SCREENPLAY Bruce Robinson, Roland Joffé, story by Bruce Robinson EXECUTIVE PRODUCER John

Calley DIRECTOR OF PHOTOGRAPHY Vilmos Zsigmond PRODUC-
TION DESIGNER Gregg Fonseca FILM EDITOR Françoise Bonnot
COSTUME DESIGNER Nick Ede ORIGINAL MUSIC Ennio Morri-
cone PRINCIPAL CAST Paul Newman (General Leslie R. Groves),
Dwight Schultz (J. Robert Oppenheimer), Bonnie Bedelia (Kitty
Oppenheimer), John Cusack (Michael Merriman), Laura Dern
(Kathleen Robinson), Ron Frazier (Peer de Silva), John C.
McGinley (Richard Schoenfield), Natasha Richardson (Jean
Tatlock), Ron Vawter (Jamie Latrobe)

Return to Paradise
Polygram Filmed Entertainment/Propaganda Films/Tetragram,
US, 1998, 112 mins DIRECTOR Joseph Ruben PRODUCERS Alain
Bernheim, Steve Golin SCREENPLAY Wesley Strick, Bruce Ro-
binson, based on the motion picture *Force Majeure* written by P.
Jolivet and O. Schatzky, directed by Pierre Jolivet EXECUTIVE
PRODUCERS David Arnold, Ezra Swerdlow ASSOCIATE PRODU-
CER Dannel Arnold CO-PRODUCERS Michael E. Steele, Charles
Wang DIRECTOR OF PHOTOGRAPHY Reynaldo Villalobos PRO-
DUCTION DESIGNER Bill Groom FILM EDITORS Andrew Mon-
dsheim, Craig McKay COSTUME DESIGNER Juliet Polcsa
ORIGINAL MUSIC Mark Mancina PRINCIPAL CAST Vince Vaughn
(Sheriff), Anne Heche (Beth), Joaquin Phoenix (Lewis), David
Conrad (Tony), Vera Farmiga (Kerrie), Nick Sandow (Ravitch),
Jada Pinkett Smith (M.J.)

In Dreams
DreamWorks Pictures, US, 1998, 99 mins DIRECTOR Neil Jor-
dan PRODUCER Stephen Woolley SCREENPLAY Bruce Robinson,
Neil Jordan, based on the novel *Doll's Eyes* by Bari Wood CO-
PRODUCER Redmond Morris DIRECTOR OF PHOTOGRAPHY Dar-
ius Khondji PRODUCTION DESIGNER Nigel Phelps FILM EDITOR
Tony Lawson COSTUME DESIGNER Jeffrey Kurland ORIGINAL
MUSIC Elliot Goldenthal PRINCIPAL CAST Annette Bening (Claire
Cooper), Aidan Quinn (Paul Cooper), Stephen Rea (Dr Silver-
man), Robert Downey Jr (Vivian Thompson), Paul Guilfoyle
(Detective Jack Kay), Dennis Boutsikaris (Dr Stevens), Katie
Sagona (Rebecca Cooper)

Published Fiction

The Peculiar Memories of Thomas Penman novel (Bloomsbury, 1998)

Paranoia in the Launderette short story (Bloomsbury, 1998)

The Obvious Elephant short story for children, illustrated by Sophie Windham (Bloomsbury, 2000)

Published Screenplays

Withnail and I and *How to Get Ahead in Advertising* (Bloomsbury, 1989)

Withnail and I with new introduction (Bloomsbury, 1995/1998)

Film Performances

Romeo and Juliet as Benvolio (Franco Zeffirelli, GB/Italy, 1968)

I Love You, I Hate You aka *Sleep is Lovely* as Colin (David Hart, GB, 1968)

The Devil's Widow aka *Tam-Lin* as Alan (Roddy McDowall, GB, 1969)

The Music Lovers as Alexei (Ken Russell, GB, 1970)

Private Road as Peter Morissey (Barney Platts-Mills, GB, 1971)

Violent Summer as Brook (Matthew Chapman, GB, 1975)

The Story of Adele H as Lt Albert Pinson (François Truffaut, France, 1975)

The Brute as Mark (Gerry O'Hara, GB, 1976)

Kleinhoff Hotel aka *The Passionate Strangers* (Carlo Lizzani, Italy/Denmark, 1977)

Still Crazy as Brian Lovell (Brian Gibson, US/GB, 1998)

Stage Performances

Early Morning in various roles (Royal Court, London, 1968)

Journey's End as Hibbert (Mermaid Theatre, London, 1972)

Film Awards

The Killing Fields
British Academy of Film and Television Arts Award (Best Adapted Screenplay, 1984)
Writers Guild of America Award (Best Adapted Screenplay, 1985)
Withnail & I
Evening Standard British Film Award (Best Screenplay, 1988)
Empire Film Award (Favourite Cult Film, 1996)

Unpublished Fiction

Normal Things novel (c. 1968)
A Kitchen Sink Drama epic poem for children, date unknown
Drama School Love Story novel, title and date unknown
Withnail & I novel (c. 1970)
Nat the Wad & Alley Soper's Cake & Jumper Shop novella (c. 1973)
How to Get Ahead in Advertising novella, original title and date unknown

Unproduced Scripts

Spleen feature film screenplay (1968)
Benny Hill Comedy feature film screenplay, title and date unknown
Private Pirates feature film screenplay, with Michael Feast (1972)
Crazee stage musical, with Michael Feast and David Dundas (1973)
The Acid Vampire feature film screenplay (1973)
Dracula – Lord of the Stars feature film screenplay (1973)
The Molecatcher television play (1973)
Nat the Wad & Alley Soper's Cake & Jumper Shop television play (1973)
Revelations feature film treatment, with Andrew Birkin (1974)
Garrett's Guitar television series (1975)
A Pin in the Nose feature film treatment, with Matthew Chap-

man (1975)

The Silver Palace feature film screenplay, story by Keith Williams (1976)

Rage feature film screenplay, with Matthew Chapman (1976)

The Moderns feature film screenplay (1977)

Roadie feature film screenplay (1978)

An Act of Love feature film screenplay (1978)

High Rise feature film screenplay, based on the novel by J.G. Ballard (1979)

Germinal feature film screenplay, based on the novel by Émile Zola (1987)

The Block feature film screenplay (1999)

Budding Prospects feature film screenplay, first draft by Steve Pink and D.V. DeVincentis, based on the novel by T. Coraghessan Boyle (1999)

Index

A NOTE ON THE EDITOR

Alistair Owen started writing for *Time Out* at the age of eighteen, and now contributes to the *Independent on Sunday*. This is his first book.

A NOTE ON THE TYPE

The text of this book is set in Linotype Sabon, named after the type founder, Jacques Sabon. It was designed by Jan Tschichold and jointly developed by Linotype, Monotype and Stempel, in response to a need for a typeface to be available in identical form for mechanical hot metal composition and hand composition using foundry type.

Tschichold based his design for Sabon roman on a fount engraved by Garamond, and Sabon italic on a fount by Granjon. It was first used in 1966 and has proved an enduring modern classic.